Theologies of the Gospel in Context

The Promise of Homiletical Theology

Volume 3

Theologies of the Gospel in Context

——— The Crux of Homiletical Theology ———

The Promise of Homiletical Theology

Volume 3

Edited by
DAVID SCHNASA JACOBSEN

CASCADE *Books* • Eugene, Oregon

THEOLOGIES OF THE GOSPEL IN CONTEXT
The Crux of Homiletical Theology

The Promise of Homiletical Theology 3

Copyright © 2017 Wipf and Stock Publishers. All rights reserved. Except for brief quotations in critical publications or reviews, no part of this book may be reproduced in any manner without prior written permission from the publisher. Write: Permissions, Wipf and Stock Publishers, 199 W. 8th Ave., Suite 3, Eugene, OR 97401.

Cascade Books
An Imprint of Wipf and Stock Publishers
199 W. 8th Ave., Suite 3
Eugene, OR 97401

www.wipfandstock.com

PAPERBACK ISBN: 978-1-4982-9925-1
HARDCOVER ISBN: 978-1-4982-9927-5
EBOOK ISBN: 978-1-4982-9926-8

Cataloguing-in-Publication data:

Names: Jacobsen, David Schnasa, editor.

Title: Theologies of the gospel in context : the crux of homiletical theology / edited by David Schnasa Jacobsen.

Description: Eugene, OR: Cascade Books, 2017 | Series: The Promise of Homiletical Theology | Includes bibliographical references.

Identifiers: ISBN 978-1-4982-9925-1 (paperback) | ISBN 978-1-4982-9927-5 (hardcover) | ISBN 978-1-4982-9926-8 (ebook)

Subjects: LCSH: Preaching. | Theology. | Hermeneutics. | I. Title.

Classification: BV4211.3 T50 2017 (paperback) | CALL NUMBER (ebook)

Manufactured in the U.S.A.   08/07/2017

New Revised Standard Version Bible, copyright 1989, Division of Christian Education of the National Council of the Churches of Christ in the United States of America. Used by permission. All rights reserved.

Contents

Contributors | vii

Acknowledgments | ix

Introduction | 1
   —David Schnasa Jacobsen

1 Do You See This Woman? A Little Exercise in Homiletical Theology | 15
   —André Resner

2 The Gospel of Prosperity: Jesus, Capitalism, and Hope | 42
   —Debra J. Mumford

3 Deconstructing a Gospel of Reconciliation: Locating Trouble and Grace in Postcolonial Preaching | 65
   —Sarah A. N. Travis

4 One Nation, Two States, and Two Words of God? The Gospel of Reconciliation and Theological Tasks of Preaching from a Korean Perspective | 84
   —Yohan Go

5 When Our Words Fail Us: Preaching Gospel to Trauma Survivors | 113
   —Joni S. Sancken

6 Gospel as Transfiguring Promise: The Unfinished Task of Homiletical Theology in a Context of Disestablishment, Empire, and White Supremacy | 138
   —David Schnasa Jacobsen

Bibliography | 157

Contributors

André Resner, Professor of Homiletics and Church Worship, Convener for the Department of Pastoral Theology, Director of the Seminary Chapel, Hood Theological Seminary

Sarah A. N. Travis, Sessional Lecturer and Minister in Residence, Knox College, University of Toronto

Yohan Go, Doctoral Student in Homiletics and Practical Theology, Boston University School of Theology

Debra J. Mumford, Frank H. Caldwell Professor of Homiletics, Associate Academic Dean, Louisville Presbyterian Theological Seminary

Joni S. Sancken, Assistant Professor of Homiletics, United Theological Seminary (Dayton, Ohio)

David Schnasa Jacobsen, Professor of the Practice of Homiletics and Director of the Homiletical Theology Project, Boston University School of Theology

Acknowledgments

I wish to thank the Academy of Homiletics for continuing to host the Consultation on Homiletical Theology at its Annual Meeting in Nashville in December, 2015. It is the commitment of the Academy of Homiletics that both inspires and enables our work of rethinking the discipline of homiletics in a more self-consciously theological mode.

I am particularly grateful to the members of this year's consultation for their hard work on this collection of essays. I have argued that the task of homiletics is not centered so much on a rhetorical move from text to sermon as on a theological naming of the gospel through a text and in light of a situation. Because the gospel is not a fixed entity, it involves renewed discernment in every time and place, just as theologian Edward Farley challenged us homileticians to do twenty-five years ago in the pages of *Theology Today*. I am so pleased that my colleagues André Resner, Debra Mumford, Sarah Travis, Yohan Go, and Joni Sancken who have helped me in this task in all their different ways and from their different perspectives. While we may not all hold the same notion about "the gospel in context," the dialogue around the consultation table in Nashville was rich and a challenging one for those of us in the field of homiletics who see the value of having a decidedly theological conversation about our work.

I wish finally to offer special thanks to my doctoral student, Rev. Yohan Go, for all of his help on this project. Yohan is an excellent homiletics graduate student who has already demonstrated talent as a teaching assistant at Boston University School of Theology. In these pages, you will get to see his great promise as a researcher. He has not only written a chapter of this book, but has assisted me with its preparation for publication. I am grateful for his work and excited about the way he has already begun to make his own contribution to the field of homiletics. His work and his commitment to being a contextual, homiletical theologian make me hopeful for my field and for the wider church.

Pentecost, 2016
David Schnasa Jacobsen
Boston

Introduction

—David Schnasa Jacobsen

Preaching is a theological act. It is theological precisely because it requires preachers to reflect on how to speak gospel in light of a specific text, a specific situation, and in a specific context. This third volume in the series, *The Promise of Homiletical Theology*, takes up the central theological task of preaching the gospel in context. The book offers a platform to leading and emerging scholars in the field of homiletics to do the theological work of naming gospel and invites others, whether teachers or practitioners, to go and do likewise. Preaching in these pages is not just a technical adjunct to exegesis, it is rather itself a thoroughgoing theological activity that requires naming gospel while honoring the otherness of texts, the uniqueness of situations, and the particularities of context. This important work is a central feature of what this whole series has been calling "homiletical theology."

This particular collection of essays also arises out of a context. The chapters in this volume represent the work of the third Consultation on Homiletical Theology at the Academy of Homiletics in Nashville, Tennessee in December, 2015. The group was convened to develop and discuss papers based on the following research problem:

> *How should we understand the relationship of gospel and context in homiletical theology?*

Contemporary homiletics explores context in relation to matters of identity, social-political world, ecclesial interpersonal realities, and shared situations, among others. What impact do these important studies have on theologies of the gospel for today in all their diversity? Assuming gospel is not some fixed, unchanging entity (Farley, *Practicing Gospel*, 2003), how does the gospel unfold historically and in the presence of our diverse hearers, contexts, and situations? How does that gospel relate to the scriptures and tradition that precede and underlie the church, hearers, and concrete communities in context? Papers that do theological reflection on the gospel with reference to theories of culture, identity, context, and situation are strongly encouraged.[1]

The contributors to this consultation largely try to take Edward Farley's notion seriously: that the gospel emerges differently in contexts over time and cannot be reduced to a fixed formula.[2] We do not all agree about what the gospel is or how to go about discerning its naming in context. Still, we gather to try to help our field of homiletics and the practice of preaching to see theological reflection more centrally related to how preaching exegetes Scripture faithfully and addresses situations truthfully. This means for homiletical theologians, like the six you will read in the collection of essays to follow, the theological task will be to reflect on what the gospel sounds like in context and in relation to specific texts and situations.

KEY TERMS GOING FORWARD

We begin by setting out the context for the way we are using our key terms: *gospel*, *context*, and *situation*. Again, while all the contributors to this volume are not using the terms in exactly the same way, a brief history of scholarship in the field will at least help to situate the framing of the central research question for readers who are new to this unfolding conversation.

Gospel

This part of our conversation has been shaped profoundly by the work of theologian Edward Farley. In a seminal article first published in *Theology Today* in the 1990s, Farley took on the "bridge paradigm" that predominated in the literature of homiletics at the time.[3] Farley lamented that preaching viewed its task primarily as that of "transferring" content rhetorically from the Bible to the present using various homiletical theories. Farley took issue with the reigning presumption that the task of preaching could be limited to such a technical enterprise as "bridging" the world of the Bible and our world today. This "bridge paradigm" presupposes, for example, that the good news

1. See #4 at www.bu.edu/homiletical-theology-project/research-questions.
2. Farley, *Practicing Gospel*, 80.
3. Farley, "Preaching the Bible and Preaching the Gospel." This article was reprinted in *Practicing Gospel*, 71–82. What follows is a summary of some of Farley's primary points.

of preaching, the gospel that it names, could be found equally distributed throughout the two-part canon. But Farley was also not willing to leave the gospel as a kind of reified essence that simply ran roughshod over biblical texts or contemporary contexts. Instead, he argued that the task of preaching was to name gospel. Its focus should not be the "world of the text," but rather the "world of gospel." The fact that Farley uses the term *gospel* without a definite article is not insignificant. Gospel, or the world of gospel, is something that must be named anew: not the transferring of a content across a bridge but an act of discerning theologically the mystery of salvation in this time and place.

For this reason, readers will notice that the scholars in these pages seek to name gospel differently in light of their contexts, situations, and texts. Just as Farley argues that there is no simple formula for gospel reducible to a given phrase across all times and places ("Christ and him crucified" or "Jesus is Lord"), so we struggle together in this volume to develop contextual understandings of gospel. In fact, in the pages to follow gospel is explored alternatively as liberation; prosperity; reconciliation; the life, death, and resurrection of Jesus; and promise. The goal is to open up rather than close off theological discussion, both among preachers and homileticians. Gospel as a term will be no "empty cipher"—something invoked yet not described—but its naming will vary contextually and thus be the object of critical theological reflection. In this way, these chapters take up both the opportunity and the challenge that Farley's reflections on gospel call forth.

Context

The term *context* has been used in various ways in the field of homiletics. Historically, context has been treated as a field of application in many practical-theological subdisciplines, and here homiletics has not been much of an exception. Within such a view, context is relevant to the extent that it is the realm where truth is applied concretely. The theological movement is top-down. The goal is translating the content of that which is stipulated as revelation in the hopes of rendering the text's transferred message more relevant.

With the rise of more complex models of reading and interpreting contexts, however, the otherness of contexts is seen as more than just a field of application, but a viable and important entity in its own right—and in a way that fundamentally reworked the application model. In some ways, this was made possible by the use of anthropological theories of the symbolic-interactionist type. Following the work of Clifford Geertz, for example, homiletician Lenora Tubbs Tisdale seeks to bring the theology of the preacher into dialogue with the local theology of the congregation.⁴ Just as an anthropologist uses multiple means to interpret a context by means of "thick description," so does Tisdale seek to show that congregations are more than blank slates on which preachers write (or texts are "applied"), but places where theological understanding already has a local color and shape. Tisdale desires to describe and interpret such local theologies as a way of making a real dialogue possible—a dialogue that goes beyond mere application.

In a similar vein, James Nieman uses the resources of an ethnographer to consider how preaching might relate in a more thoroughgoing way to its context in a congregation. With his appeal for the use of frames, tools, and signs in congregational analysis, Nieman argues that preachers can become more self-disciplined in the way they think about discerning their context so that preaching can be both fitting and use indirect means of persuasion that allow for genuine insight and transformation.⁵ While Nieman does a great service for the field of homiletics and the work of the preacher in a deeper form of contextualization, his model suffers from two limitations. First, context, as it was with Tisdale, tends to be described more or less monolithically. If the focus is discerning the ethos of a congregation through its tools (artifacts) and signs (disclosures of its dispositions in practice and common life), it is still a focus on one thing. His view, though exceedingly helpful for communicating in a congregation, also tends to a view of context that assumes a congregation is a bounded whole.

For this last reason in particular, Eunjoo Mary Kim begins to broaden the notion of context to include what she calls "transcontextual" elements.⁶ In an age of globalization, contexts are places where perspectives are not monolithic at all, but where multiple contexts meet. With her concern for globalization and an aesthetic orientation to the "kaleidoscope" of lenses that multiculturalism affords, Kim manages to describe context in a way that is both more dynamic and less "intracontextual" than some of the ways described above.⁷

Most recently Adam Hearlson has sought to bring a Bourdieuian perspective on practice to bear as a way of talking about context in preaching.⁸ Hearlson argues that contexts are not monolithic at all, but places where practices both replicate and transform understandings of context from both

---

4. Tisdale, *Preaching as Local Theology and Folk Art*.
5. Nieman, *Knowing the Context*.
6. Kim, *Preaching in an Age of Globalization*.
7. Kim considers her movement beyond the "intra-contextual" to be one of the distinguishing features of her work, *Preaching in an Age of Globalization*, 16.
8. Hearlson, "Preaching as Sabotage," 3.

more centered and marginal positions.[9] Hearlson writes, "For Bourdieu, the field of the congregation can be envisioned as a field of political struggle for power, where the actors are bound by their shared interest in the field but divided by their location within the field."[10] Context, in other words, is not some unified, reified reality, but a place of differing perspectives that both receive and alter the local landscape in practice, and in light of their own competing interests. The result is a view of context that moves beyond symbolic-interactionist theories of culture, or even intracontextual visions of context, to more conflict-oriented models. Such a view also requires a more thoroughgoing self-reflexivity on the part of the preacher who investigates context. This latter concern for self-reflexivity will surface in more than one of the essays in this volume.

Situation

In some ways, it may seem superfluous to separate out notions of context and situation. In fact, some of the writers in the essays to follow use the terms in almost synonymous ways. Context and situation sound like they refer to identical entities.

However, the language of situation can allow preachers who wish to articulate a gospel in context to identify how they interrupt the more ordered and consistent life of contexts. Edward Farley himself argues that the heart of the practical-theological task is what he calls a "hermeneutic of situations." In Farley's view the nature of a situation is that it places us in a moment of demand and response. In light of this, Farley describes the theological task of reflecting on situations thusly:

> A theological version of this task cannot avoid the insights of its own mythos into the corruption and redemption of human beings. Because of that corruption, human beings shape the demand of the situation according to their idolatries, their absolutized self-interests, their ethnocentrisms, their participations in structures of power. Faith, then interprets situations and their demands as always containing this element of corruption and redemption. Situations pose to human beings occasions for idolatry and redemption. The discernment of the demand-response is at the very heart of a theological hermeneutic of situations.[11]

9. Bourdieu, *The Logic of Practice*.
10. Hearlson, "Preaching as Sabotage," 3.
11. Farley, *Practicing Gospel*, 14.

In situations, there is something at stake. Precisely for this reason, situations call forth a gospel word in context.

From the standpoint of Farley's hermeneutic of situations, it becomes easier to see that situations describe something that interrupts or disrupts the settled ways we know and order our lives. At the same time, there is overlap between the ways in which we preachers talk about contexts as more settled "fields" and situations in which an event shakes things up. For this reason, Jacobsen and Kelly have tried in their own research to separate out situation from context in a way that acknowledges the validity and usefulness of both terms for preaching. Their distinction allows for a more differentiated mode of theological reflection that accounts first for synchronic in context and diachronic understandings in situations.[12] For this reason, context refers to the more or less enduring features that shape who we are and how we understand. Situations, by contrast, represent those *kairos* moments where a gospel in context needs to be articulated anew. Here Jacobsen and Kelly borrow from David Buttrick's notion of limit and decision moments in his "preaching in the mode of praxis."[13] Situations interrupt the normal flow, the order of things and call forth some kind of dialogue or engagement with the gospel. Situations are what Farley calls the "in light of which" of preaching the world of gospel in context.[14]

GOSPEL AND CONTEXT IN DIALOGUE

Along the way the reader may have noticed that straining out the differences between gospel, context, and situation has not been easy. It may be tempting to treat gospel, context, and situation as pure and distinct entities, like fruit in a basket. The relationship between them, however, is more complex than can simply be argued—whether from purity of the gospel as received deposit of Truth or from purity of context as a kind of unadulterated identity which can be idealized. It is hard to think one without the other—especially if we are committed *a priori* to keeping some term in the relationship "pure." The gospel is not some pure reality kept apart from context, nor is it merely an epiphenomenon of that which already is given in culture or context.

The first notion of purity is best refuted by the classic claim of Feuerbach who argues that all of our language about God is a mere projection of our

---

12. The distinction between context and situation comes initially from Jacobsen and Kelly, *Kairos Preaching*, 9, 38–41.

13. Buttrick, *Homiletic*, 408–11

14. Farley, *Practicing Gospel*, 91.

humanity, our culture.¹⁵ In this sense, any claim of a pure gospel as a separate entity will always actually be a cultural construct incapable of escaping its cultural determination. To try to push back at Feuerbach in the name of gospel *purity* is a fool's errand that crashes ultimately on the rocks of human language, culture, and yes, context. Conceptions of gospel cannot be kept pure by abstracting them apart from culture or context. There is no true acultural place to stand.

The second notion of the purity of a community of practice is challenged deeply by Ted Smith's description of the struggle around *gemeinschaftlich*-oriented interpretations of community. The argument is that ideal communities of practice serve as the basis for determining some "true gospel" by extrapolating from that ideal community or practices that can embody a pure gospel.¹⁶ In *The New Measures*, Ted Smith rightly argues for a view of ordinary life that pushes back on idealizations, whether of pure community or pure gospel.

Trying to find the gospel based on an internal purity that is applied to ordinary life or an idealization of community life that gives practical shape to a truly pure gospel is to confuse the "is" of human life with the "ought" or "may be" of theological norms or claims. Such attempts to maintain pure communities and/or stipulate some pure gospel founder on the critical rocks of Scylla and Charybdis.

What we are given as preachers, as homiletical theologians, is something different. To be a preacher is not to be the answer man or woman, nor is it to offer some endless stream of utterly relativized hunches from the pulpit. Preaching is rather a constructive-theological enterprise that brings into dialogue provisional understandings of gospel with contexts and situations. The conversation is one that cannot escape the cultural determinism that the Barthians fear, nor is it one that allows postliberals or radical orthodox theologians to posit either an ideal past or community that somehow provides a bedrock for a bounded whole with a derived pure gospel. To say that gospel is in dialogue with contexts and situations is to acknowledge the piecemeal way that homiletical theologians work this side of heaven.

One of the contributors to this volume, Dr. André Resner, has come up with an intriguing designation that helps to explain both the provisionality and recognizability of our work in preaching gospel in context.¹⁷ He argues that preaching is constantly bringing into relationship with its texts and contexts/

---

15. Feuerbach, *The Essence of Christianity*.

16. Smith, *The New Measures*, 16–22.

17. Both terms, *provisionality* and *recognizability*, proved important in the initial volume in this series on homiletical theology, *Homiletical Theology: Preaching as Doing Theology*, 54.

situations some working gospel that is ever tested and revised. Perhaps this is precisely the provisional space where homiletical theology can be conducted. Thanks be to God, we do not start from scratch, though we do think critically about the good gifts we have received in Scripture and tradition. Thanks be to God, our job is not simply to apply the truth to some fixed cultural norm either. Preaching is freed to engage culture critically even while being deeply enmeshed in it through language, symbols, and practices. The key is the dialogue between gospel and context, a dialogue that animates preaching and grounds its constructive-theological pulpit task in every time and place.

This dialogical notion about gospel and context is one reason why preaching can be much more than conveying information, i.e., again, picking out the fruit in some basket of objects, as it were. The language of knowledge, certainty, and authority that goes with such ways of thinking seems far from the realm of faith and critical engagement. In light of this need for something beyond flattened certainty and information, Paul's notion about apostolic preaching offers a more helpful theologically oriented vision: we are servants of Christ and stewards of the mysteries of God (1 Cor 4:1). Stewards receive something of great gospel value, especially in Scripture and tradition, for which they are held accountable.[18] In fact, it is the fact that preachers are theological stewards of the mysteries of the gospel that makes their work recognizable among the people of God in context. Yet, the object of their stewardship is more than what is, but also *what will* be. Mysteries in Paul's sense are not utterly inscrutable, but something *being revealed* in Jesus Christ. We are in this sense eschatological stewards of a mystery both given and being revealed. Such a way of thinking about preaching gospel requires critical thinking, to be sure, but here it takes the form of theological *discernment* that squares both with being servants of Christ and stewards of the mysteries of God. This is what preaching gospel in context is all about: discerning theologically how to name gospel with these people, in this place, at this time, and in light of some certain text and/or situation. This requires something more than information, but searching, discerning dialogue and reflection.

Of course, there does not seem to be much consolation for the preacher as steward of the mysteries. What is a constructive-theological task may seem daunting and runs the risk of ending up reinscribing our best human guesses and haphazard hunches for the divine. In such an event, Feuerbach wins. Homiletical theology, like any theology, runs the risk of projecting its theology onto an otherwise indifferent cosmos. Theologians, however, understand the fragility of their work through both its human and divine elements. While

---

18. Biblical scholars argue that Paul's language of "mysteries" in 1 Cor 4:1 refers to the gospel, e.g., Soards, *1 Corinthians*, 89.

we cannot presume to speak for God because we possess a superior wisdom (we certainly do not!), as stewards of the mysteries in the gospel we can trust that God the great Mystery can use our human failings to divine ends. Peter Berger, in a remarkable appendix to his great work on the sociology of religion, *The Sacred Canopy*, puts it this way:

> ... sociological theory must, by its own logic, view religion as a human projection, and by the same logic can have nothing to say about the possibility that this projection may refer to something other than the being of its projector. In other words, to say that religion is a human projection does not logically preclude the possibility that the projected meanings may have an ultimate status independent of man [sic]. Indeed, if a religious view of the world is posited, the anthropological ground of these projections may itself be the reflection of a reality that *includes* both world and man, so that man's ejaculations of meaning into the universe ultimately point to an all-embracing meaning in which he himself is grounded.[19]

This warning about the mixing of the is and the ought, the empirical and the normative, offers only little relief to homiletical stewards of the mysteries, but does open up a promise that the work is not utterly in vain!

Yet one more thing needs also to be acknowledged. Preachers as stewards of the mysteries remain throughout *servants of Christ*, too. What we do claim is at the very least *subject* to Paul's crucified risen one. Our best speculations, our deepest reflections, are always necessarily done in the deepest shadows of the cross and in the dawning light of resurrection. This, in itself, is an important caveat for our work. In 1 Corinthians 1–4 Paul's language about the cross puts to rout any conception of wisdom that is tied to a preacher: whether Paul himself, Apollos, Peter, or any other. It is a cross that cannot be contained in human conceptions of power or wisdom either. If there is a centrality here, it is a center of negation. Theologian Miroslav Volf calls the cross of Christ the decentering center, the "scandalous particularity of the suffering body of God's messiah."[20] Even Bultmann, the champion of translation and interpretation through demythologization, held to the importance of the scandal of the cross as the *real* stumbling block.[21] To be a steward of the mysteries of the

---

19. Berger, *The Sacred Canopy*, 180.

20. Volf, *Exclusion and Embrace*, 70. I am grateful to my student, Yohan Go, for pointing out to me the implications of this insight for homiletical theology. See chapter 4 for more detail.

21. Bultmann, *Jesus Christ and Mythology*, 36.

gospel and a servant of Christ, as a homiletical theologian and preacher, is to recognize the limits of our constructive-theological work as well.[22]

In the end, what matters is not the apprehension of gospel or context as objects. Instead, what really matters is the dialogue between them, a dialogue that—subject to the crucified, risen One—is ever dislocated in a desire to discern the mystery of salvation, the word of the gospel in context, in this time and place. Again, we do not do this in the same way, or even with the same explicit theological criteria, but we are convinced this represents an important center for the work of homiletics going forward: a field that sees itself as attending to a powerfully theological act called preaching.

SUMMARY OF CHAPTERS

The six chapters to come represent work from colleagues who wrestle deeply with what the gospel sounds like in context, and in relation to specific texts and/or situations. The hope is that you, whether homiletician or advanced practitioner, will see yourself primarily as a theologian in the way you engage in the task of preaching. The variety of perspectives also aids in envisioning the complexity of contexts in which gospel proclamation takes place. Here the idea is that reflection on a context, even one different from one's own, will pry loose the presuppositions that keep preaching from engaging its work with greater theological depth and fit.

Chapter 1 comes from the aforementioned Dr. André Resner, whose work invites us even more deeply into the notion of "working gospel," a provisional understanding of gospel that functions in dialogue with context. The essay, "Do You See This Woman? A Little Exercise in Homiletical Theology," does two important things. First, it reflects on matters of method and homiletical theology by considering the domains that shape its task: Bible, rhetoric, liturgy, context, preacher, and of course, "working gospel." Readers along the way will glimpse the homiletical-theological frame that animates Resner's work. Second, Resner invites the reader to join with him in seeing the conversation play out between his working gospel of liberation, the situational context of particular community called *Tierra Nueva*, and the biblical text about Jesus' anointing by a woman called a sinner when Jesus dines at the home of Simon the Pharisee in Luke 7:36–50. In addition to a stunning close reading of the text and an accompanying insightful dialogue with what Resner calls his situational context of *Tierra Nueva*, he shows the theological

---

22. Biblical scholar Patrick Miller describes this well in his thoughtful sermon on 1 Cor 4:1–5 in *Stewards of the Mysteries of God*, 82–87.

David Schnasa Jacobsen—*Introduction*

work of the preacher of the gospel in context in full view. Along the way, theologians like David Tracy and Charles Wood help him in his deeply discerning work. As part of the process, Resner argues the text functions in a theologically productive way both as window (to a perspective) and mirror (to us). Although Luke 7 in this case functions more in the mode of window, it does so in homiletical-theologically powerful ways to help discern through likenesses *and* differences a gospel of liberation in context.

In chapter 2, "The Gospel of Prosperity: Jesus, Capitalism, and Hope," Dr. Debra Mumford treats in a more historical and descriptive form the prosperity gospel from the context of American history and the rise of the Black middle class. Using a key scriptural text, "I came that they might have life and have it abundantly" (John 10:10b), Mumford demonstrates the deep roots that the prosperity gospel has in American life across African American and Euro-American religious communities over time. Far from isolating the prosperity gospel in certain groups or periods, Mumford shows the pervasiveness of the prosperity gospel in an American world marked by chattel slavery, capitalism, and "new thought" theologies—it is a deeply inscribed theology across North American traditions. Some contemporary interpreters may be inclined toward a reification of prosperity gospel that isolates it in certain social groupings. Yet, as Mumford shows, the resilience of the prosperity gospel across ecclesial communities should give preachers pause about how they use doctrines like divine providence and Christian vocation in every context. More than that, the prosperity gospel's broader pervasive influence should also goad preachers to think about how they articulate hope over nihilism and engage in a prophetic task in the complicated, capitalist context in which we all find ourselves. Mumford succeeds in complexifying both our understanding of the prosperity gospel and the ways we respond to its challenges and seek to make meaning in a capitalist context today.

In the next couple of chapters two contributors to this volume struggle with a similar sense of the gospel, albeit in different contexts. For chapters 3 and 4 the focus is the gospel of reconciliation that thankfully allows us to bring two understandings of the gospel in context into cross-contextual dialogue (please note the dialogue that takes place between the authors of these two chapters even in the footnotes!). We take here, then, a brief digression into understandings of the gospel of reconciliation, both of which have been impacted by postcolonial theory.

In chapter 3, Canadian homiletician Dr. Sarah Travis contributes helpful insights about reconciliation in her essay, "Deconstructing a Gospel of Reconciliation: Locating Trouble and Grace in Postcolonial Preaching." Building on her work in *Decolonizing Preaching*, Travis tries first to separate out understandings of gospel that leave it a monolithic, non-perspectival reality.[23] Gospel with a capital G is for Travis the good news of God in Christ crucified and risen in the power of the Holy Spirit. The gospel with a lower case g is reserved for our human understandings of the experience of the gospel of God's work in the world, which when not critically checked can easily go awry in contexts of privilege and desperation. Travis urges the use of postcolonial theory and theology, especially for those in contexts of privilege, as a way of understanding Gospel and in turn contextualizing gospel. When in a postcolonial context persons of different places in the colonial order relate, the terms of articulating gospel become deeply problematized. Nowhere else is this clearer than when persons of differing social locations meet to work through matters of reconciliation. Here Travis highlights the residential school crisis that has so impacted the Canadian context in the last several years. Through this very local example of white church complicity in the forced relocation of First Nations children into government-sanctioned residential schools, Travis seeks to invite us to revisit Gospel and gospel, to rethink even fellow Canadian homiletician Paul Wilson's distinction of "trouble" and "grace."[24] Drawing on Wilson's "tensive metaphor" of trouble and grace and the third identity that it posits, Travis offers along the lines of Homi Bhabha's "third space," a place for Travis where trouble and grace in all their dialogical complexity can be named in the midst of wounds yet to be healed. She notes the limits of the language of reconciliation and gospel even while seeking to find space to articulate a more contextualized and fluid gospel anew in the presence of neo-colonial "others."

In chapter 4 Yohan Go considers the problem of a gospel of reconciliation, both similarly and differently, in light of the contemporary Korean context. His article, "One Nation, Two States, and Two Words of God?: The Gospel of Reconciliation and Theological Tasks of Preaching from a Korean Perspective," seeks to explore this as a problem of both a colonized context in the age of the Japanese empire *and* a politically divided people on the Korean peninsula in a neo-colonial US-dominated reality today. Key for Go is the notion that gospel and culture/context were already in dialogue before Western missionaries arrived in Korea. While the missionaries' influence on Korean Christianity cannot be disputed, this early dialogue is especially important for indigenous Korean and neo-Confucian transformations of both gospel and context. While culture/context takes the lead in the dialogue, the relationship is one of mutual transformation, as the gospel itself continues to dislocate culture/context. The focus on reconciliation is in part a recognition of the struggle to continue to revise the gospel/culture relationship through

---

23. Travis, *Decolonizing Preaching*.
24. Wilson, *The Four Pages of the Sermon*.

dialogue. Because of the unique configuration of power on the divided Korean peninsula, an antagonized sense of identity has emerged—one which needs to be reconstructed in light of the gospel of reconciliation. Here Go finds postcolonial theory especially useful for his reconstructive efforts, particularly in light of the binaried identities fostered by the contemporary neocolonial context. To do this, Go draws on the theology of the cross of Mirsolav Volf to recognize the ways in which self-giving cruciform identities make room for one another and how the decentered center of the cross of Jesus Christ aids in the process—and in concert with the indigenous understandings of the too-long sublimated Korean interreligious context. The result is a gospel of reconciliation that makes room for the other, does not deny traumatic memories, but seeks to make space for identities in the process of being healed together, both intra-ecclesially and publicly—and in this sense the gospel reconciliation in context calls forth a profoundly religious *and* political engagement.

With chapter 5, we leave the gospel of reconciliation proper, but not the contextual problems posed by trauma. In a stunning essay, "When Our Words Fail Us: Preaching Gospel to Trauma Survivors," Dr. Joni Sancken takes up a profound pastoral problem. Drawing on the distinction of Jacobsen/Kelly around context and situation, and basing her reflections on the important work in a theology of trauma by Dr. Shelly Rambo, Sancken embraces the notion of Holy Saturday as a means of thinking about the necessity of preaching a fitting gospel word in the context of trauma that brings entailments with it. A breezy move from cross to resurrection will not suffice—something of the problem of the situation of trauma itself must form the way gospel is named. In light of this, Sancken proposes a gospel of the reconstruction of self through the preaching of Jesus' life, especially as exemplified in the christological section of the Apostles' Creed. For Sancken, the text of the Apostles' Creed and its christological claims become a locus for reforming traumatized identity in light of Christ's identity, as so much of that identity is tied up in a promise that is not yet fully realized, even while embracing, as Rambo does, God's revelation *and* God's hiddenness. What Sancken envisions is a gospel not yet fully named, but a chance to "begin to testify to that which may lie beyond words."

In chapter 6, "Gospel as Transfiguring Promise: The Unfinished Task of Homiletical Theology in a Context of Disestablishment, Empire, and White Supremacy," David Schnasa Jacobsen seeks to relate an understanding of the gospel as promise to the disestablished context of the white mainline church, characterized as a wound. Yet the more Jacobsen unpacks that context's relation first to colonialism and then to the recalcitrant reality of white racism in the now disestablished mainline Protestant churches, the more it seems this wound of disestablishment has complications and enduring scars. Jacobsen's hope is that the mystery of gospel and the mystery (or even mystifications) of context can profit from mutual dialogue. Carrying forward Sancken's interest in trauma, he argues that the wound that is both the Christian tradition of the gospel as articulated after the destruction of the temple and the recalcitrant form that wound takes in the rise of colonialism and racialized identities calls forth a gospel word of promise that does not so much erase, but transfigures the wound. Here the work of philosopher Richard Kearney and theologians Shelly Rambo, J. Kameron Carter, and Willie Jennings prove most helpful in promoting dialogue between gospel as transfiguring promise and wound. Along the way, Jacobsen breaches issues of identity, which are in mainline churches in deep dispute especially since the rise of postliberal and radical orthodox theologies. The wound, therefore, of a disestablished church issues in a faulty sense of identity, but also calls forth by means of promise a more fluid identity capable of engaging others publicly and talking about the world differently than it has in its wounded, self-protective identity as "exiles."

CONCLUSION

On behalf of the Consultation on Homiletical Theology, I commend these insightful essays to your reading. They represent a rich conversation that preaching as a theological discipline needs to have. All of them are focused on naming the gospel in context and seeing the two in deep relation. So whether the gospel is understood as liberation, prosperity, reconciliation, the life of Jesus, or promise, homileticians and practitioners alike will benefit from seeing the kinds of contextual reflection homiletical theologians do *as* theologians.

Yet there is more than one way to profit from a collection of essays like this. Those curious about the notion of working gospel and a dialogical conception of theological reflection with context will see this method most explicitly focused in the chapters by Resner, Go, and Jacobsen. Those wishing to go deeper into prosperity gospel and the language of blessing in preaching will be enriched by reading Mumford, Travis, and Go in particular. If articulating gospel in the face of trauma and memory are important, the essays by Go, Sancken, and Jacobsen will engage you in multiple ways. The goal of this collection is not to set out definitive pieces that settle this matter of gospel or context once and for all, but to invite preachers and homileticians to enter their contexts more deeply and name the gospel more discerningly wherever they are. In these pages, we are, in other words, inviting you to be a homiletical theologian, too.

— 1 —

Do You See This Woman?
A Little Exercise in Homiletical Theology

—André Resner

We are trying to understand just what sort of thinking is homiletical thinking, i.e., the thinking that preachers and homileticians do theologically. The matter is made complex because of the differing, overlapping, interpenetrating domains that pertain. I will first sketch those domains then conduct a case study in homiletical theology with a text from Luke and a contextual situation, *Tierra Nueva*.

DOMAINS PERTAINING TO A HOMILETICAL THEOLOGY

Bible

Homiletical thinking includes uses of the *Bible* and thus it requires hermeneutical activity. Still, the practice of preaching is not simply the interpretation of biblical texts but a particular kind of interpretation with a particular end, and contextual situation in view. Texts are never interpreted in a vacuum. They are interpreted with a "use" in sight. For preachers that use has to do with a "sermon" that the preacher will orally deliver in, most likely, the context of a worshipping congregation. That is one end, but the other has to do with preaching's message: what is its desired end? We will get to that in a moment.

It is enough now to note that the preacher's interpretive use of the Bible is a unique kind of hermeneutical activity, different from that of a biblical scholar preparing, say, a presentation for a Society of Biblical Literature section. In this example, audience, context, and *telos* affects the way we think of the difference between what the biblical scholar does with the Bible and the presentation, and what the preacher does with the Bible and the sermon.

Rhetoric

The consideration of *audience* illumines another domain that pertains, that of *rhetoric* or communication studies. This domain is a social science with its own history, canons of inquiry, goals and norms, and guidelines for practice and criticism. Preaching as a form of communication can be and is evaluated and assessed from the rhetorical frame of reference. Yet, preaching is more than a rhetorical discourse because of its subject matter, its liturgical and theological frame or context, and arguably, its end. There have been attempts to reduce preaching as a sub-genre to the primary rubric of rhetoric, but such attempts fail precisely at the thorny point of preaching's message, preaching's ends, and preaching's context.

Liturgy

Typically, the preacher presents the sermon to a congregation gathered for a service of *worship*. The sermon comes at a certain point in the flow of the liturgy. Contextual matters of the liturgy—prayers, oral interpretation of Scripture, singing, Holy Communion, calls to worship, benedictions, baptisms, confessions, assurances of pardon, interactions of passing the peace of Christ—all these frame and inform how the sermon is heard, understood, and experienced. Moreover, the liturgical elements do not simply frame the sermon, but conceptually and experientially overlap and interpenetrate the sermon and its message. When well-planned these overlaps and interpenetrations not only reinforce the sermon's message, but contribute to the message being heard, received, experienced via differing media—media as varied as the liturgical artistry available to the planners, performers, participants, and setting.

Context

Congregations are each unique entities in their own right. Each exists within a particular denominational stream of history, theology, and liturgy. Each also exists within a particular sociocultural *milieu* where economy, race, ethnicity, and politics pertain to the community's life and identity. Polity, the way a "church does church," and history dictate to a degree the expectations for worship and the sermon, but particularity—the way in which *this* congregation at *this* time and place with *these* particular people involved—must also be considered with profound seriousness.

Preacher

Finally, there is a preacher. The preacher is both a free and a constrained agent, embedded, so to speak, in all these domains, at the same time that these domains operate within the consciousness of the preacher. The preacher is constrained by matters that pertain to the preacher's family of origin, as well as his or her ecclesial family of origin. The kind of genogram work that systems theorists do can help preachers understand better how they are parts and outgrowths of the systems, familial and ecclesial, that they have grown up in.[1] Preachers are constrained by matters pertaining to the denominational system of which they are a part, a constraint that influences their theology, and their understanding of the relationship of the sermon to the liturgy. Each tradition's understanding of what it means to be ordained influences how preachers carry out their ministries. Constraints of gender, ethnicity, social and economic situation, mental and physical health, history of loss, success, and failure, all come into play for how preachers conceive their roles, how preachers perceive what preaching is and what it ought to do.

One of the results of these influences on the person of the preacher has to do with how the preacher conceives the gospel. It is not monolithically the same. Every preacher has what I call a "working understanding of the gospel." This is an always in-process perception of the ultimate message of preaching, a synopsis of the faith, an encapsulation of the whole point of Christianity, Christian community, of what difference God makes in and for the world. The preacher's working gospel entails a sense of ecclesiology, what the church is, what it is for, and what its mission is in God's economy in the world.[2] I contend

---

1. Jordan, *Reclaiming Your Story*. See also Wood, *Vision and Discernment*, 70: "Personal fears, inhibitions, prejudices, and preoccupations can have a great impact on one's understanding of the gospel."

2. I have elsewhere developed the idea of the preacher's working gospel. See Resner,

that the preacher's "working understanding of the gospel" is the imaginative theological and hermeneutical force that drives the way the preacher conceives, plots and delivers sermons, structures worship services in which those sermons live, move, and have their being. The preacher's "working gospel" mediates and guides how the preacher moves within each of the realms that pertain to preaching: Bible, rhetoric, liturgy, context, and self. The preacher's "working gospel" guides how the preacher conceives and uses the Bible, conceives and uses rhetoric, conceives, plans, and performs liturgy, conceives and challenges context, and reflectively, critically, pastorally engages, and sometimes tames (and sometimes frees) the self for witness. The preacher's "working gospel" adjudicates fitting and appropriate uses of the Bible, rhetoric, and self for preaching in the contexts of worshipping communities embedded in denominational and sociocultural contexts.

The preacher is constrained by many things, but not ultimately circumscribed. This is because of the theological character of preaching. For the preacher is free because of the power of God, the risen Christ, the impetus of the Holy Spirit, and the call to be the agent of God's gospel in his or her particular context, a context that has affirmed that call by means of a "setting apart" of the person for the ministry of the Word. Theologically speaking, ordination is a sign of the church catching up with what God has already decided. It is God who has chosen to use preachers and the means of preaching to elongate the gospel in the world through time. Preaching is not the only means of the gospel's extension in time, but it is one means. Because God so chooses to use it, it cannot receive its definitive description by mere sociohistorical, political, or psychological determinations or interpretations. Something about preaching always transcends the mundane, the human, the time-and-culture–bound conditions surrounding the gospel's proclamation.

The sense of freedom, even amidst all the constraints, needs to be examined and stated starkly. No one, week to week, is telling the preacher what to say or how to say it. There are expectations, yes, and there are all those constraints, personal and communal, which I have detailed. But there is also scandalous choice—of text, of image, of story, of a particular refraction of the gospel. There is an awful freedom to that. That freedom exists, as I have described, within streams of tradition, yet preachers' words, if they participate in that thing we call the Word of God, remain in some important sense unbounded even by the constraints of time and culture. That seems impossible, even counterintuitive. Yet the doctrine of incarnation points to both realities, that of the constraints of the flesh and that of the freedom of the Eternal Word. Word made flesh is perpetually mysterious, reducible to neither flesh nor to

---

"Preacher as God's Mystery Steward."

Word alone, expandable to the highest heavens beyond human language and reason, because God is not ultimately contained, but free. Yet covenant keeps, by God's mercy and grace, "binding" God to God's creation and creatures in a free, yet tenacious engagement that leads to both creation's and the creature's ultimate freedom—life, love, shalom, wholeness. Thus there is a certain irreducibility to the gospel, even when it is humbly enfleshed in the limited vocabulary, diction, and body of the stammering human who preaches. Perhaps it is in the spaces between our words and punctuation that the Spirit flies between the preacher's mouth and the hearer's ears to make the connections of faith in the unseen realms of the heart and soul.

"Working Gospel"

Edward Farley was the catalyst for my thinking about the gospel in relationship to the Bible.[3] He rightly challenged the prevailing paradigm of preaching that uncritically seemed to assume every passage from Scripture that comes to the preacher by means of the lectionary or by means of "preacher's choice," every 6–12 verse unit, necessarily contains the preachable "X" of preaching. He was right to say that it would take a fundamentalist assumption to make that logically work. It could just as well take a historical-critical mind-set to make it work, one that approaches each discrete passage with a view to preaching that passage's "theme" or "claim."[4] Farley asked, is that what preachers are called and sent to preach, namely the "preachable X" to be found in individual passages of the Bible? Or are Christian preachers called and sent to preach the gospel? If the latter, can we assume that the gospel that Christian preachers are called and sent to preach is to be found *ipso facto* in every 6–12 verse passage of the Bible? The question thus becomes in Farley's critique: if preachers are to preach gospel and not just the content of biblical passages, then how should the Bible be used to achieve preaching's true end?

Farley may have overstated his case somewhat in the sense that Christian preaching certainly does preach the gospel, but it also may have occasion to do many other things that may not be specifically construed as "*gospel* proclamation." One of those things may be characterized as preaching and teaching the Bible or Christian doctrine, though a case for why those should count

---

3. Farley, *Practicing Gospel*, 71–82.

4. See Miller, *The Way to Biblical Preaching*; Keck, *The Bible in the Pulpit*; Best, *From Text to Sermon*; and Long, *The Witness of Preaching*. Also, see Kuruvilla and his notion of pericopal theology that essentially holds that preaching's preachable "X" is to be found in any and every pericope, or passage, in the Bible no matter the length. See his *Text and Praxis* and *Privilege the Text!*.

as Christian preaching should be made rather than assumed, which I cannot do here. Nevertheless, Farley's challenge is an important one for preachers to wrestle with and it has led me on a journey to clarify just what it is that I mean by gospel.

That may sound rather strange because can we not as Christians and as Christian preachers assume that we know what the gospel is? I do not think so. In fact, I think it is one of the dirty little secrets about homiletics, the discipline that studies, writes about, and teaches preaching—that there is no consensus on what preachers and homileticians mean by the word *gospel*, and there is very little discussion about how a preacher's construal of gospel functions hermeneutically as the preacher engages the Bible with a view to its use in preaching. When Farley issued his challenge to the discipline of homiletics, few actually responded. Farley's own attempt at a reconstruction of homiletics fell short precisely at the point of trying to define and describe gospel and how it functioned in relationship with the Bible.[5]

In the introductory preaching class that I teach each spring semester I conduct an experiment with my students. The first week of class I give the next week's assignment: "Next week, each student will, in small groups of four to five, preach the gospel in eight minutes. Any questions?" Then I get the quizzical facial expressions and the usual queries: "Do we use a biblical text?" My response: "If for you to preach the gospel in eight minutes you feel you should use a biblical text, then use a text." "Can we use a manuscript?" "If for you to preach the gospel in eight minutes you feel you should use a manuscript, then use a manuscript." "May we include a video clip or some form a media, even a PowerPoint slide?" "If for you to preach the gospel in eight minutes you feel you should use some video clip or some form a media, even a PowerPoint slide, then you should use that form of media." That's the moment they realize that I'm going to answer every question the same way. Then they ask, "Are we getting a syllabus for the course?" I say, "Well, not yet. I need to hear from you first."

Now, I have a pretty good idea what we will be covering in the course, especially the pertinent domains that I described above: Bible, rhetoric, liturgy, context, preacher, as well as working gospel. But I truly want to hear what they bring to the preaching class first. I have learned that they bring a lot and it is powerful to hear that first, before I begin to tell them what I think about these things. I think the exercise does other things as well. It forms a bond between

---

5. Farley took three swipes at reform. In the first he decried homiletics' bridge paradigm but tried to replace it with his own version of a bridge system, "the bringing to bear a past event onto the present so as to open up the future." His second and third attempts became less clear and impractical for actual use. See his *Practicing Gospel*.

the students in the small groups, one that sometimes lasts all the way through seminary. It honors what they bring to seminary as valuable. We are not starting from scratch with the people that populate our classrooms. They have been shaped before they got to us. To state it confessionally, God has been at work in them for a long time before they get to me. My aim is to be one strong link in the chain of God's development of them for the ministry of the gospel.

Though I cannot hear all of the eight-minute gospel proclamations, I do visit each group and hear at least one sermon from each group. Having them preach right out of the chute gives them a concrete, confessional investment in the course and they feel I am investing in them by hearing what they have to say before I tell them what I think about preaching and the gospel. It also drives home to them in a powerful way just how diverse are the perspectives on gospel, and the varieties of ways that preachers use texts to preach the gospel. As a result of this exercise, I am beginning to imagine a more inductive approach to teaching and learning preaching.[6]

My idea of a "working gospel" first came to me when I read David Tracy's critique of the idea of a "canon with the canon." Tracy argued that no one really operates with such a wooden or fixed concept. Neither does anyone operate in theological thinking with the entire Bible at work in one's thinking. Rather, what Tracy observed was that theologians have as it were a "working canon," an in-process, biblical perspective, shaped by certain texts and ideas that, to the theologian, more aptly express the heart of things. In the same way, a "working gospel" implies this same synoptic view of what it is that God has done, is doing and will complete in the consummation (even that displays something of my working gospel that may not be embraced by others who operate with a different theological conviction about the gospel). One's working gospel is theologically constructed, biblically influenced, and bears the fingerprints of one's ecclesial and liturgical heritage. It operates in some ways like the *discrimin* that David Kelsey describes, those imaginative pre-decisions that shape the way we actually use the Bible in making our theological assertions.[7]

Though they do not use the term *working gospel*, the same idea is to be found in several theological works and approaches. Charles Wood, for example, develops two dialectical ideas that he believes must work in tandem as one does theology, "vision" and "discernment." "'Vision' is, at its most comprehensive, the quest for a coherent understanding of the Christian witness

---

6. See Resner, "No Preacher Left Behind." This is my proposal for a homiletical prolegomena of sorts where students of preaching work from sermons back to all the elements that make them up.

7. Kelsey, *The Uses of Scripture in Recent Theology*.

as a whole."[8] Discernment on the other hand looks for the specificity in individual situations. "If vision sees the totality, discernment is the grasp of the individual."[9]

Wood uses these two terms to describe and define the task of theological reflection. Vision and discernment must work in tandem and in dialectical correction of the distorting tendencies of each. For when vision takes over, it can require conformity of all details in every situation. On the other hand if discernment gains rein, it can fragment vision into peculiar details of any given situation. "There is no vision without discernment, and no discernment without vision."[10]

There is an analogy just here with the hermeneutical circle in the sense that the whole helps us to discern the meaning of the parts, but only the study of the particularity of the parts leads us to the synoptic understanding of the whole. I see a further analogical connection in preaching, and I will call it the homiletical circle. A synoptic perspective of the gospel, one's "working gospel," functions to discern gospel in the particular, whether in a text, a narrative, or a situation. This is equivalent to one's vision. The particular situation, narrative, or text requires the studied, particular, gaze of discernment, or as Wood also says, "paying close attention." Using Iris Murdoch, Wood says that this aspect of discerning attention "consists in 'a just and loving gaze directed upon a person, a thing, a situation.' Such attention—'really looking,' as Murdoch says . . . is not easily achieved."[11] In fact, such theological activity is a kind of spiritual discipline and practice, something akin to Farley's notion of "*habitus*," the habits of mind, soul, being that develop in persons given over to practices of Christian *phronesis* and praxis. Disciplined, patient discernment requires self-involvement, not detachment, and may require the re-evaluation of one's own self, soul, and faith. The homiletical circle is to be seen as a revisionist methodology where one's working gospel engages specific biblical texts and particular situations with a view to the preparation and delivery of a sermon, a word on target in light of one's working gospel, one's text, and the situation. The entire process through to post-sermon theological reflection leads to revision in one's theological thinking about gospel, texts, situation, and proclamation with a view to the next cycle.

John Barton has an important perspective to consider just here. He believes that for Christians to call themselves "a" or "the" "people of the book" is a bit of a misnomer. For one thing, the phrase comes from the Quran. In

8. Wood, *Vision and Discernment*, 69.
9. Ibid., 68.
10. Ibid., 76.
11. Ibid., 75.

addition, Christians owe their birth not to an exegesis of Scripture, but to the Holy Spirit-prompted preaching of the gospel of Christ crucified and risen on Pentecost.

Certainly it is false to say, as Paul Ricoeur (for example) has done, that the early Christian message is *primarily* or predominantly a hermeneutic of the Old Testament. For the first Christians, what happened in Christ was not an exegesis of Scripture, not even a strikingly original exegesis of Scripture, but a completely new, unprecedented, and irreversible event in the external world. It was not primarily something that had happened inside a tradition of textual interpretation. The interpretation of existing Scripture had to limp along as best it could to catch up, and it had no power to annul the new thing that God had done.[12]

This is especially true of the gospel's apocalyptic dimensions. In this case, the gospel may have arisen, from a historical perspective, out of the soil of first-century Jewish apocalyptic, but it cannot be reduced to that influence. Many have not taken seriously the apocalyptic nature of the gospel we see in the New Testament (especially Mark and Paul), dismissing it as merely remnants of an ancient, woolly Jewish ideology borne of the oppressed conditions of an occupied people. But what if the gospel is what it claims to be: *Revelation*, God revealing God's invasion and necessarily hostile (God's fierce love will not allow evil forever) takeover of a demonically stolen creation in the person, life, death, resurrection, and promised return of Jesus the Anointed One? This is but a partial glimpse into an aspect of my own working gospel.

To return to Barton, he helpfully affirms Farley's position that it is by means of an understanding of what God has done in the gospel—the new and unprecedented thing done in Jesus' death and resurrection—that we read and use the Bible in our theological thinking. Barton's chief concern has to do with describing the way in which the Bible functions as authority for Christians, and he rightly begins with a sense that ultimately what is authoritative is Jesus Christ himself as the Word of God, not a book per se. It is the "matter" of Scripture, the "center" of Scripture, or the "gospel," which is, for Barton, "an encounter with a gracious God," fundamentally an encounter with the faithful love of a God who takes back a broken creation in the work of Christ, that is the orienting presupposition for using the Bible for any sort of theological reasoning, including preaching. When we engage the Bible by reading, studying, worshipping, "we come face to face with the gospel and respond to it with our whole lives. If that is not to accord authority to the Bible, I do not know what would be."[13]

12. Barton, *People of the Book?*, 7.
13. Ibid., 89.

J. Christiaan Beker has argued similarly for the continuing efficacy of the biblical witness (its authority) on the basis of a catalytic relationship between the heart of the gospel (its "coherent core") and the many "time-bound, culturally specific situations into and for which the gospel is addressed."[14] The gospel never comes to us in a vacuum; it is always enfleshed in a situation. Paul's letters reveal the dynamic of coherent core and contingent situation achieving their catalytic effects in Paul's pastoral reasoning. Each situation demands a varying refraction from the core of the gospel. For Beker, "the abiding, constant, and normative elements of the gospel . . . focus on the apocalyptic-eschatological interpretation of the life, death, and resurrection of Christ."[15]

Like Barton, Beker turns to Martin Luther to illustrate how his understanding of the gospel functions hermeneutically when engaging all parts of the Bible, including the Old Testament. "The coherent framework of Scripture, that is, its normative pattern for Christians, must be located in and derived from the gospel of God's saving purpose for the world. Thus, the norm and center of Scripture is to be stated in terms of Luther's criterion of *'Was Christum treibet'*: 'All the genuine sacred books agree in this, that all of them preach and inculcate Christ.'"[16]

GOSPEL, SITUATION, AND TEXT IN CONVERSATION: A CASE STUDY

What I will do now is a case study in my way of conceiving and doing homiletical theology. The preacher is always engaged in a kind of hermeneutical "cross-fire" in the sense that s/he reads texts with two concerns always pressing on the consciousness: the concern of the people who will hear the sermon (a theo-rhetorical concern) and the concern about why the things in this particular biblical text should matter to these people *in light of the gospel* (a *kerygmatic* concern). So, gospel, hearers, and text(s) all fly about the preacher's consciousness in mutual conversation, sometimes creating a cacophony in the process, but by the time of the sermon preparation and delivery, hopefully creating a symphony of meaning, purpose, and experience.

The idea for the sermon can begin anywhere, but once it begins, all aspects of the investigation—Bible, rhetoric, liturgy, context, preacher, and

---

14. Beker, "The Authority of Scripture," 381.

15. Ibid. As Barton points out, the early church's designation of gospel, what I would call "working gospel" was "the rule of faith." That was not a list of books, but a summary sense of the new thing God had done in Jesus Christ. See Jenson, *Canon and Creed*.

16. Beker, "Authority," 382. See Beker's *Paul the Apostle* for a full development of his coherency/contingency schema.

working gospel—are kept actively engaged in the conversation.[17] Older homiletical theory seemed to assume that if we kept the process pure, moving in a linear fashion from biblical text to sermon, that we could keep the message pure and uncontaminated by extratextual concerns or pressures. It was an illusion. No method can guarantee hermeneutical purity. No preacher can truly shut down the voices in his or her head from self, hearers, or the sense of gospel that the preacher brings to any text or situation.

In the present case, my experience at *Tierra Nueva* (to be described below) came before my engagement with Luke 7:36–50. In fact, that experience came several years before I engaged the Luke text when preparing a sermon to preach in the chapel of the Boston School of Theology at Boston University. I found that when I began engaging the narrative in Luke, that the people from *Tierra Nueva* began to show up between the lines of the Lukan narrative. And now, populating the text, they made Jesus' question to Simon pop: "Do you see this woman?" My experience of seeing Bob Ekblad with the "invisible people" (especially to the established, well-heeled church) of the migrant farmworker community and the "invisible people" of the prison system made Jesus' question ring out with clarity. Of course these people are seen, but how? To what end? Does the gospel have anything to say to their invisible visibility?

Though no commentary on Luke I have read makes much of Jesus' question, "Do you see this woman?," preferring instead to concentrate on the "main point" of the narrative, namely the contrast between those who love much and those who love little and why that is so, in light of the *Tierra Nueva* experience Jesus' question now revealed another possible center of gravity in this narrative. What shifted the gravity point was the contemporary experience, the point of contact with the hearers from the vantage point, or perspective, of the woman on the floor. This reader, troubled by the situation of the frequently abused, exploited, rightless migrant farm workers in Washington state, brought that lens to the Lukan story. To use Ricoeur's metaphor, if the text is a musical score, my pre-experience at *Tierra Nueva* caused me as conductor of the orchestra to emphasize and "do a run," an improvisation, on a

---

17. A common fear just here is that of the preacher committing "eisegesis," the reading into the text the preacher's concerns to such a degree that the text becomes a mere hand-puppet of the preacher's rather than the text's message. I argue that the nature of reading the text for preaching the gospel requires that we bring not only the concerns of our situation into the text, but also the presupposition of the preacher's working gospel. Thus, I posit that all engagement with the biblical text for the purpose of preaching the gospel is a kind of eisegetical activity. I differentiate two kinds of eisegesis, one that violates or overrides the text's message—this type is obviously problematic and should be avoided. The other, though, brings the preacher's concerns and working gospel into active conversation with the text, seeking mutual illumination.

particular line of the score that may not have been developed quite that way before.

SITUATIONAL CONTEXT: *TIERRA NUEVA*

A conversation with Don Mowatt at Laity Lodge, a retreat center in southwest Texas, prompted him to invite me to Washington state to encounter a very different kind of world. When I went to visit Don's friend, Bob Ekblad, in Seattle, I did not know what to expect. Bob and Gracie had started *Tierra Nueva Del Norte* five years earlier. *Tierra Nueva* (New Earth) is a ministry that seeks to share the good news of God's freedom in Jesus Christ especially with people on the margins of our affluent, North American society and culture—immigrants, undocumented seasonal farm workers, prison inmates, ex-offenders, and the homeless. Through Bob's theological training in Montpellier, France and experience in working side-by-side with impoverished field workers in Honduras, he became passionately dedicated to proclaiming through word and deed the good news of God's reign "on earth as it is in heaven" with especially the oppressed in his region, for everyone's mutual liberation, healing, empowerment, and total salvation.[18]

We started at Bob's office, a simple, storefront space that served as many functions as presented themselves on an almost daily basis. The first day I sat with Bob and four Honduran friends who had come north for the berry season. Bob had known them for almost twenty years, since the early eighties, when Bob worked beside them in the fields in Honduras. They were poor farmers, then and now, but each was now an evangelist, too, with a deep faith and powerful connection with God, the gospel, and the Scriptures. We sat on couches and, with Bob translating, one by one they told me the story of their lives. The fabric of their very selves, relationships, work, and faith unfolded before me and I began to experience a profound humbling, though I had no words for what I was feeling.

From there Bob and I went to the jail for the Spanish Bible study. We sat in a room with nine inmates dressed in bright orange jumpsuits with "SKAGIT COUNTY JAIL" stenciled on their backs. Bob began the time by asking how things were going with the men. Feeling an obvious sense of ease with Bob, something nurtured through many such visits, they poured out their concerns and issues. Bob listened intently to each, then led a prayer and laid his hands on each man, praying specifically about the concerns that each

---

18. See, http://www.tierra-nueva.org/core-values/. For a brief history of the migrant farm worker movement in Washington see http://depts.washington.edu/civilr/farmwk_intro.htm.

man had voiced. After the prayer, Bob sat back in his chair and opened his Bible to a text from Exodus. Before he could begin, however, one of the men, José, who had been studying the Bible with Bob for several weeks now, had a question about the Samson story. The hour-long study now shifted its focus to Samson, his birth, God's unlikely choice of Samson's mother, and God's setting apart of the boy for God's work even before he was born for purposes that God had in mind. Prodding them through back-and-forth dialogue, Bob helped them to see how each of them could be just as unlikely a choice for God to call and use for God's purposes. The time ended with each man embracing Bob and me, then all Bibles were collected and stacked at the back of the room. The chairs were put back in order for the next meeting in the room.

For four days Bob and I went from one such meeting to another. Another day in Bob's office, settled back in the rough tweed couch, a woman named Rocio told me what it was like to have committed the worst sin of her life without even knowing she had done so, namely, by being born with brown skin, brown eyes, black hair, in an impoverished, Spanish-speaking–only home in America. She told us what it feels like to be in the grocery store or a department store and being watched closely by security guards and store clerks who assume she will steal if they look away. The aisles of the market seemed to close in on her as she pushed her cart around and between other mothers who pulled their children closer and patted their purses just to make sure that neither was vulnerable to Rocio's possible reach. She described the judgmental faces of other shoppers as they looked into her cart and sized up the kinds of food that she was intending to buy. She could not get used to being pulled over by the police simply because she was a Hispanic woman driving a car, having her license and registration meticulously studied, even though she had done nothing wrong. She had only been who she was, trying to survive another day in a place and among people who kept making it abundantly clear that they wished she was not there.

Bob asked her what her image of God was. She told of the God who had been brokered to her by the dominant culture around her, a God who looked like a larger-than-life elderly white man with a snowy white, flowing beard, stern expression, and a stick in his hand to strike at the slightest of wrongdoing. She had grown up believing that anything bad that happened to her was God's will, and anything good that happened was dumb luck. God was on the side of the cultural powers—the police, the courts, and judges in black robes—and was himself a kind of divine lawgiver and law enforcer. Church was a place for people who had figured out how to be good all the time and never did or thought anything wrong. It was also officiated by authority figures whose robes looked alarmingly similar to the stern judges in the courts where nothing good would ever happen for her or her friends and family.

Something had happened to her, however, that had begun to alter all of her preconceived ideas about God and church. Though she worked in a fish-packing plant from 4 PM to 4 AM, six days a week, she somehow had met Bob and Gracie and began meeting with them and studying the Bible with them. Hearing some of the issues she was having, Bob had stepped into her legal life as an advocate.

Over the years Bob has put together a team of helping associates: medical doctors, lawyers, entrepreneurs, police officers, firefighters, and others who believe in Bob, the work of *Tierra Nueva*, and ultimately that the promises of God in the gospel can come to pass in this age, even if only in some temporary and partial ways, here and now in the lives of the oppressed. When Bob and Gracie start walking alongside someone, each person experiences the grace of the "kingdom come, on earth as it is in heaven." Rocio testified as to how her life had changed because of what she experienced in relationship with Bob, Gracie, and the others who were part of the *Tierra Nueva* ministry. Her view of God, of white people, of grace, mercy, justice, and the possibilities for Christian community beyond traditional church had been transformed. She was a different person as a result of these relationships. Integral to her new perspective was the Bible study that Bob led them all in, one always tilted in the direction of a liberating, freeing gospel.

Reynalda, with her eight-year-old daughter sitting silently close by, told of how everyone in the town was more stringent on the Hispanic population: the police, the doctors, the businesses. She felt unvalued as a human being. She said, "You could even have the winning lottery ticket, but they wouldn't let you collect. They would figure out a way to keep you from the money."

Jorge was a migrant farm worker in the Seattle area for the berry-picking season. Bob had known him in Honduras and Jorge was supposed to have returned home the night I arrived, but Bob had arranged for Jorge to be examined by a local doctor. Predictably, Jorge had a severe hernia and needed surgery urgently. The doctor was going to require Jorge to stay for three weeks of recovery after the surgery, which he was performing *gratis*. Jorge told me of the many fellow field workers in Honduras who had hernias. He said that they would take pieces of wood and put them on top of the hernia then wrap a belt around the wood, pressing the hernia in so it wouldn't protrude, just so they could keep working in the fields. Sometimes it worked. Other times their hernias burst and they died in the fields.

Each told what it was like to live on the marginal outskirts of society in northwest Washington state. They felt God-forsaken, like beggars with no rights. Every day was a fight to climb out of their plight. They felt isolated, ghettoized, and a nuisance, that is unless they were needed to do something that the dominant culture would rather not do, like pick berries and vegetables in a hot field with backs bent, working for wages that sometimes were withheld at the end of the day by a capricious boss who knew that his conscripted laborers had little recourse to justice. In the four days I was there we went to more than one meeting with field bosses where Bob demanded cash in hand for some shorted field workers whom he had come to know at *Tierra Nueva*.

LUKE 7:36–50

"One of the Pharisees asked Jesus to eat with him, and he went into the Pharisee's house and took his place at the table. And a woman in the city, who was a sinner, having learned that he was eating in the Pharisee's house, brought an alabaster jar of ointment."

The Gospel According to Luke is often referred to as the gospel of the marginalized. That word, *marginalized*, is a powerful metaphor. It refers to those who are on the outskirts of the main story line, those not usually part of the primary plot. But in Luke's alternative version of reality those in the margins are transported to a place in the text, eclipsing the big-name movers and shakers who usually account for the story of humankind. In Luke 7, one such mover and shaker, a Pharisee named Simon, a man with education, accomplishment, and sociocultural cachet, is displaced in the story of God's alternate realm of reality by a nameless "sinner woman."

Almost everything in this story that Luke tells is strange to our twenty-first-century eyes and ears. Yet, Luke is setting a powerful contrast. We have an elite male: powerful, rich, a homeowner, with a circle of powerful, male guests, including the current cultural phenom, celebrity, curiosity, and crowd sensation—the invited guest, Jesus. Then we have a woman from the city, whose only identifying characteristic (at the beginning of the narrative) is that she is a sinner. We are not told the sin, or sins, that led to this being the way she was known by others in this city. Many have surmised that she was a prostitute in the town. That is possible, perhaps even probable, and would, if true, accentuate the divide and double-standard that was in place in first-century Palestine.[19] She was the "sinner" in this situation, after all, not her clients, cer-

---

19. New Testament scholar Bradley Trick writes: "Sexual is most likely. As an identifiable group, 'sinners' seems to have designated those who were publicly living their lives in conscious rebellion against God and his ways. Hence, the only two groups that the New Testament pairs with 'tax collectors' other than 'sinners' (e.g., Luke 3:30, 7:34) are 'gentiles' (Matt 18:17; cf. Gal 2:15: 'gentile sinners') and 'prostitutes' (Matt 21:31–32). The

tain men of the city, even though it definitely takes two to tango. It is a curious thing how Simon was so aware as to exactly who she was, and, "what kind of woman this is who is touching him—that she is a sinner."

We might think it bold and brazen of her, with her reputation, to show up at Simon the Pharisee's house in the midst of a crowded dinner party. What moxie! But in that day and time, it was almost inconceivable. What could possibly make a woman, who was viewed the way she was, put herself in a place of humiliation and perhaps even deadly harm by interrupting a Pharisee's dinner party, especially one where he was hosting a special guest such as Jesus. Her actions crossed serious social and religious boundaries and not only put Simon and his household to shame, but her actions also risked charges of defilement of the innocent and "clean" against her. This latter matter was no small thing in first-century Jewish culture. As New Testament scholar Marcus Borg has pointed out, just about every issue in that time and place boiled down to a purity issue.[20] Her presence at his party flew in the face of such grave concerns.

But Luke has already clued us into her mission. Somehow she knew that Jesus was going to be there that night, and she has come with an alabaster jar of ointment for him. "She stood behind him at his feet, weeping, and began to bathe his feet with her tears and to dry them with her hair. Then she continued kissing his feet and anointing them with the ointment." To us as privileged readers of this scene, we have what seems to be an unconscious, overwhelming display of emotion—gratitude, joy, and love mingled with tears over something that has transpired between her and Jesus. We will find out later in the story what that is: forgiveness, release, and acceptance of her as a person. It was an experience so overpowering that it had *dis*empowered any fear she had about being in the presence of the judgmental Pharisee, Simon, and his colleagues and their moral fastidiousness. Her freedom, and her desire to show Jesus her gratitude tangibly, overcame the social and religious implications of her invasion of Simon's home and dinner party. But Simon did not see it that way. "Now when the Pharisee who had invited him *saw it*, he said to himself, 'If this man were a prophet, he would have known who and what kind of woman this is who is touching him—that she is a sinner.'" Simon is appalled. We note Luke's careful phrasing: "Now when the Pharisee who had

---

big sins—i.e., the abominations that pollute the land with moral impurity—are primarily idolatry (hence gentiles become 'sinners' by definition), murder, and sexual sin. The setting in a small Jewish town (so she's not likely gentile), the fact that Jesus describes her sins—seemingly in contrast to the Pharisee's sins—as many (so it's not that she once killed her husband, e.g.), and the fact that it is a man who is categorizing her as a sinner (lacking sympathy because he cannot identify) all would fit well with her having been a prostitute." Personal email correspondence, January 20, 2015.

20. Borg, *Conflict, Holiness, and Politics in the Teachings of Jesus*, 8.

invited him saw it...." It is his title and position, his place of authority and his religious stature in the community that are first highlighted; Luke does not use his name. If anyone ought to know what is going on, if anyone should be able to discern and interpret rightly the situation, it is the professional interpreter and spokesperson for God and the tradition. Secondly, he is the one who had invited Jesus to his home, and now here is this intruder. Not only is the woman in the wrong for horning in on Simon's home and invitation-only dinner party, Jesus shows poor form in allowing her time, space, and audience on Simon's turf, table, and clock. Lastly, Luke zeroes in on the objectified optics of the situation. These nearly silent actions of the woman had created quite a scene for everyone to see. "It" was Luke's way of summing up the entirety of the spectacle before them all.

Simon. Saw. It.

"It" was the scene in front of him, the display now on show for everyone. The weeping, the bathing of his feet with her tears, the letting down of her hair, and her wiping his feet to dry them with her hair. The kissing, the anointing, and Jesus is at the center of it all, for God's sake, permitting *it*.

Simon and his guests could not but be revolted, disgusted, and dismayed by *it*. Jesus may have been the unknown entity in the room, but she was the known. Now, what they knew about her revealed to them what they were to surmise about Jesus.

It would have been probably impossible for them to have seen anything other than something sensual, even erotic, going on in this intimate exchange between the woman and the now discredited prophet—a fact that makes what Jesus does next so remarkable. Simon saw *it*. And *it* not only horrified him, but became the hermeneutical key for Simon's delegitimizing the potential prophetic status of Jesus.

> Jesus spoke up and said to him, "Simon, I have something to say to you." "Teacher," he replied, "Speak." "A certain creditor had two debtors; one owed five hundred denarii, and the other fifty. When they could not pay, he cancelled the debts for both of them. Now which of them will love him more?" Simon answered, "'I suppose the one for whom he cancelled the greater debt." And Jesus said to him, "You have judged rightly." (Luke 7:40–43)

Simon must have felt like he was being set up by Jesus' simple riddle, a common mealtime activity. It seems so innocuous and obvious. Simon answers Jesus' question as one who seems to know that this whole scenario Jesus has created is too easy, a ruse. "I suppose the one for whom he canceled the greater debt." The Greek phrase for Jesus' response to Simon is perhaps best translated, "Bingo!" But then comes the not so obvious question: "Then turning towards the woman, he said to Simon, 'Do you see this woman?'"

What kind of a question is that? To Simon it must have seemed like the dumbest question he had ever heard in his life. "Do I see this woman?! Are you kidding me? Do I see this *sinner* woman who has had the gall, the nerve, to barge into my house in the middle of my invitation–only dinner party with my colleagues from the synagogue and with my specially invited guest? What do you mean, Do I see her? *I have not been able to see anything else since she dared enter my home uninvited.* My eyes saw every step she took across my floor from the door to the table, every one of her unclean footmarks on my floor rendering everything in her path ritually unclean, every step—Unclean! Unclean! Unclean!—until she got to you and put on this embarrassing and sordid display at your feet with her crying, her putting her hair down, her kissing your feet, and her anointing them with the ointment . . . . *Do I see this woman?* My God, I haven't been able to see anything but this woman ever since she invaded my private space and imposed her presence, her filth, her sin, her shame on my home. How could you possibly ask me if I see this woman? Are you out of your mind?"

Just for a moment, dear reader, shift your focus, and your position in the room. We have been looking from Simon the Pharisee's perch, down at this woman and Jesus' feet. But now I want you to come over to her, down on the floor, at the end of the table. I want you to see what she sees. Glance with her over to Simon. What does she see when she sees Simon's face looking down at her? She cannot look long at Simon. She flinches, turning away from his harsh gaze the same way you flinch when someone suddenly throws a sharp, blunt object at you. You take cover, hoping the object will miss, or at least not leave too deep a mark or permanent scar.

Simon's penetrating gaze is like a pressure, pushing her down, down into a sinkhole where she has been for years, so long that it is a socially constructed reality that defines who she is: "loser . . . scum of the earth . . . sinner . . . whore . . . ." She is rejected and judged aberrant and immoral by these ruling, elite men, who also, conveniently, speak for God.

They do not mind using her when they want to. But somehow they never sink. They throw their bodies at her, and their dirty coins. Then they leave, only to return when they need to impose on her their rage and lust. They can come to her whenever they choose, but she must not come to them, at their homes. They leave her to her place, down there, beneath human dignity, little more than a waste can for their excess. Simon's gaze holds her down, keeps her down, forces her lower, never to rise. It reminds her how things are in this world. Some are righteous, some are sinners. Some are blessed, some are cursed. God knows who is who, and Simon and his colleagues inform the people of God's thoughts on the matter. Simon's gaze leaves its impression in no uncertain terms: "Remember who you are, sinner woman. Look away, stay away, for you there is no hope."

But now, look with her, with the woman there with Jesus, as she flinches away from Simon's condemning glare, and turns toward Jesus' face. I imagine that Jesus had turned his face away from Simon and toward her when he asked Simon the question, "Do you see this woman?" Now, she looks full into his face, into his eyes. What does she see? Light, joy, freedom, forgiveness, hope. He is a man, but no man has ever looked at her this way. No man has ever seen her for her own sake instead of what she could be for him. In her life a man's gaze has only meant a pending business transaction, manipulation, exploitation, abuse, torment—but not this man. From the moment he first saw her, his gaze felt like a burden lifted, a hand reached out toward her to lift her out of the sinkhole of her life to a newness of being she did not know was even possible—a cool breeze in a scorched life, a drink of fresh water for a parched soul. His countenance was for her a lifeline out of a hell she had always known.

At first I am sure she feared believing this man's face, mistrusted her own judgment that he might be different—he was still a man after all, but his face didn't change. It never mutated into a sales pitch. His expression never shifted, never angled to take advantage of her and her trust. She let herself believe him. Perhaps in that release of all the cautions and skepticisms she had layered over her heart, she experienced freedom, lightness, and life. That was why she was here at Simon's, risking what appeared to be everything in front of Simon and his guests, but really, since experiencing what she had in Jesus' presence, felt no risk, she feared nothing.

Perfect love had cast out fear, and she was freed, and thus now empowered to love.

There was nothing a man like Simon could do to her now that she had seen the face of non-manipulative, freeing Love. How does one get to such a place? How does one get to the place of freedom where this woman now found herself, no longer stuck, as we now see poor Simon to be, in his judgmental, countenance-destroying gaze? We have to go back to Jesus' little parabolic riddle to Simon. Which of the debtors, the fifty denarii debtor or the five hundred denarii debtor, will love the man who forgave both debts more?

An unexpected $5,000 repair bill to our house, car—you name it—would impose a serious crimp in most of our budgets for perhaps even a few years. But a sudden and unanticipated $50,000 bill would affect most of our lives permanently. To have someone come along and wave a magic wand so that both bills disappeared would create a definite party for the first person, but something of a life-altering celebration and awe for the second.

Jesus says to Simon, "That's the difference between you and her. For you, Simon, there is not much change when you meet God in worship. Everything is pretty much the same. You go through the motions, even offer the right sacrifice for your sins, and *voila*, all is taken care of, then back to life as usual. For her, everything has changed. An insurmountable mountain has been removed. And, interestingly, you were a big part of that mountain."

> "I entered your house; you gave me no water for my feet, but she has bathed my feet with her tears and dried them with her hair. You gave me no kiss, but from the time I came in she has not stopped kissing my feet. You did not anoint my head with oil, but she has anointed my feet with ointment. Therefore, I tell you, her sins, which were many, have been forgiven; hence she has shown great love. But the one to whom little is forgiven, loves little." Then he said to her, "Your sins are forgiven." But those who were at the table with him began to say among themselves, "Who is this who even forgives sins?" And he said to the woman, "Your faith has saved you; go in peace." (Luke 7:44b–50)

Simon saw *it*. Jesus saw *her*. The first leads to death. The second to life.

The power of Simon's judgmental gaze kept her down, stuck, and bound. The power of Jesus' gaze conveyed forgiveness, freedom, and a reciprocal love.

REFLECTIONS OF A HOMILETIC KIND

A challenge in our world is to continue Jesus' freeing presence through our fallible lives. All of us suffer from self-interest. None of us, after all, is Jesus, with 100 percent pure motives. Yet ministry in the name of Jesus compels us to see in and through these stories in the gospels our world and the way that the gospel might similarly change our world, and the lives we encounter in our world, into one where heaven's agenda meets and eclipses, or perhaps better, transforms the earth's agendas.

The preacher engages a biblical text to discern and feel the gospel pulse of a story. The preacher reads for the gospel pulse embedded in context and situation. Early in my engagement with this story in Luke, the characters from *Tierra Nueva* began to appear between the lines, in the gaps between words and punctuation. I could see their faces, hear their voices. To find the gospel pulse one typically starts with the God figure in the scene, in this text Jesus, and in the situation of *Tierra Nueva*, Bob Ekblad. One then observes what that character does and says, watching closely for the effects that those words and actions have on the other characters. As the God figure here, the preacher privileges Jesus' and Bob's actions and words as gospel actions and words, unless they can be proven to be in conflict with what God's predominant actions and words are elsewhere throughout the biblical witness.[21] In this case, the preacher focuses on the difference between what Jesus sees when he looks at the woman and what Simon sees.

The preacher here also engages in some between-the-lines "sanctified imaginings" of what it would feel like to be under the contrasting gazes of Jesus and Simon. One could say that Luke does not develop this theme overtly, and thus question whether the preacher should develop this theme in a sermon. This raises one of the most interesting questions for homiletical theology as it thinks about the preacher's use of biblical texts for preaching. If one's conventional exegesis leads the interpreter to conclude, in this case, that Luke did not develop the theme of what the woman felt under the gaze of the two men in the story, on what grounds would the preacher make much of it in the sermon? Might we not be imposing a psychological interpretation on the text that the text itself does not generate?

This is where the audience for the sermon comes in. The preacher stands between the text (and the gospel claims that the text exerts) and the potential listeners to the sermon. Thus, the sermon and preacher serve a mediating position. I would argue that if the preacher senses a need in the hearers to hear a word that the text whispers (rather than shouts), then the preacher is justified in teasing out implications of the text that the text's author or editor may not be seen to fully develop. If the preacher chooses to follow this path, s/he must still be fair to the text, by which I mean, the preacher must develop the text's subsidiary message within the larger concerns of the text and not in ways that conflict or contradict those larger aims.

That requires the preacher to think in a series, first about the text's varying emphases, then about the implications of those emphases on the hearers. The hearers in my case will also be invited to imagine themselves from each

---

21. In the New Testament, Mark 7:24–30 is a notable text in this regard. Jesus there refers to the gentile woman begging for Jesus to exorcise a demon from her daughter as a dog and thus unfit for kingdom's benefits. Jesus' words are disturbing, and thus raise serious questions about the anti-gospel words and actions of the God figure, Jesus, in this text. My own reading of that text leads me to surmise that Mark was addressing a church in the aftermath of the fall of the Temple that was excluding gentiles based largely on race or ethnicity. Mark's risk is to portray Jesus this way in order to hold up a mirror to his community and challenge them to loosen their grip in light of the larger claims of the gospel, a gospel in this case forced upon Jesus (and Mark's church) by the gentile woman who "gets it."

character's vantage point, and assess the impact of the gospel for them in each case.

Homiletical theology is partly a hermeneutical activity. Two metaphors will help us see how that is the case: the text window, and the text as stained glass window.

Text as "Window" and "Picture"

Two metaphors may prove useful in thinking about how the biblical text serves the preaching of the gospel: text as window and picture. Imagining the text as a window helps us see ways in which characters and situations may be interpreted by means of analogy.[22]

Envisioning the text as a window is not a new idea. In the history of interpretation of the Bible, some presumed that a historical critical study of the Bible would permit the interpreter to see through the text and into the mind of the original author to discern his or her intentions.[23] Others more cautiously believed that the text could serve as a window on the ancient world behind the text. The text as window thus yields up historical information, layered with the ideological viewpoint of the writer. It could also give us a glimpse into the lives of the communities behind the text.

Certainly, the biblical texts are not only historical, but they render a kind of history in the sense that they reflect the past situations, people, places, and things of an ancient time. But they are far from doing history the way that moderns think of history from a post-Enlightenment perspective. Working from the vantage point of Meir Sternberg, Thomas G. Long has identified three key strands in biblical narrative: the historical, the ideological, and the artistic.[24] Long, following Sternberg, sees biblical narrative weaving these three into the tapestry that we now see. Long elegantly sums up how he sees these three elements relate to one another: "When history is seen as theologically shaped, it takes an artist to tell the story."[25]

The reliability of the biblical text to clearly show us anything behind the window is always open to question. Because of that, I like Phyllis Trible's image of the text as a picture.[26] This metaphor allows that history, ideology, and

---

22. This is an exercise in analogical reasoning. See Farris, *Preaching That Matters*.

23. The most thorough argument for this approach is to be found in the work of the literary critic E. D. Hirsch. See his *Validity in Interpretation*.

24. See Long, *Preaching and the Literary Forms of the Bible*, 68–69.

25. Ibid., 68.

26. Trible, *Rhetorical Criticism*, 97–99.

artistry are at work, but the opacity is questioned: do those elements show us clearly something in the external world, or are they a depiction of things as the writer characterized them? Probably some of both in most cases, but all we have is the picture, the depiction, of the text itself.

So, I am not using the metaphor of the text as window to describe a feat of historical inquiry, whereby we can see through the text to things as they really existed in the ancient world. Rather, starting with the metaphor of picture, I see the text as depicting a perspective. The text is thus similar to an impressionistic artist. The biblical narrative serves up a kind of rhetorical impressionism, where accuracy of historical detail is less important than the emotive effect of color and light. Monet's painting, "Water Lilies," is clearly about water lilies that exist in the real world. But his painting is a perspective that he takes on them. Engaging what the text gives us (rather than trying to drill down under or behind the text), allows us to engage the perspective of the text, one that is especially driven in the case of the Gospels, by concerns about the identity disclosure of the main character, Jesus, his message of the kingdom of God, and what it means to be human beings in relation to both Jesus, the kingdom of God, and potentially competing empires.

One's exegetical study achieves its ends for the preacher when that exegesis renders to the preacher the pictorial dimensions of the text so that s/he can now look from the text's vantage point out into his or her world. This is where the metaphor of window comes in for me. I want to see my world in light of the colors and emotive expressions and depictions of the text. In a sense then, to claim an opacity for the text is to say that it colors the way I look at my world. Insofar as we trust the ideological brush strokes of the text—its theology, its gospel, its depictions of power relations—these brush strokes help us interpret our world in the new light provided by the text.[27] The reliability of the text's depiction is always engaged critically by the working gospel that the preacher brings to the text. In turn, the text's theological and gospel contours critically engage the preacher's antecedent working gospel, forcing a reevaluation and possible revision. This might be termed a "homiletical suspicion," a healthy suspicion that the text's construal of the gospel may actually be a problematic

---

27. This raises the very large issue of reliability of texts to always or mostly render to us good or sound theology, and truly gospel depictions, rather than slants of the domineering power structure at work to maintain the status quo. See especially Fiorenza, *Wisdom Ways*. Fiorenza (4) rejects the metaphor of text as window when it is used in the sense of accurately depicting the world behind the text. "*Wisdom Ways* challenges you to give up long-held convictions, such as the views that the biblical text is an unclouded window to the historical reality of wo/men, that G*d has written it, that it is the historical source-text providing data and evidence which document wo/men's reality, or that it contains biblical injunctions and prescriptions as timeless revelation and fixed norms given for all."

disfigurement of the gospel. Homiletical suspicion works both ways, however, for the preacher allows the text's gospel overtones to interrogate the preacher's antecedent working gospel, testing it for its Christianness, its coherence to truth, and its fittingness in this particular context.[28]

In the Lukan text we have the Pharisee who is the image of a judgmental religious orientation that ironically functions to keep those who need God, love, freedom, and forgiveness most, stuck in their places of victimization. We have the unnamed woman, the image of a victim of a society, a culture, and a religious system that has a double standard firmly in place.[29] We also have the God figure in the person of Jesus who breaks convention, crosses boundaries, breaks religious rules, all for the purpose of reaching and freeing the most vulnerable in the situation, in this case the woman. Jesus also exposes Simon the Pharisee for his hypocrisy, his arrogance, and his toxic religious system and practices. This is the work of justice—the exposure of exploitative acts and systems that hurt and discriminate against the innocent, and that keep them stuck in the sinkhole of despair and shame, while those who operate the system reap the benefits of a society that rewards them and honors them as righteous, good, and godly.[30]

The preacher now looks through these portraits from the text at his or her world to explore potential analogies. The operative question becomes, who are these characters in my world? Have I ever seen in my own experience, in cinema, literature, or elsewhere, any similar characters and situations so that my hearers can more fully identify and "get it," because the situations and claims in the text and the text's characters are visible and active in their world? This look at the world through the window of the text's portrait for the purpose of preaching the gospel means that we are not just looking at the

---

28. These are Charles Wood's tests for the authenticity and integrity—"the validity"—of Christian witness. See his *Vision and Discernment*.

29. She is usually characterized as "the sinful woman." How might it change our perspective to instead call her "the woman who loved much?"

30. Due to the constraints of space, the current study will not examine the domain of "liturgy" explicitly. However, one important liturgical consideration in that regard in light of this text and the context of *Tierra Nueva* would be the relationship of liturgy to justice. This has to do with the worshipping congregants' Monday through Saturday lives, certainly, but it also has to do with the way in which justice informs the liturgy (through readings, prayers, litanies, sermon, etc.) as well as the space wherein worship is experienced (arrangement of space, issues of access, use of paraments, banners, use of the arts, etc.). See these useful resources: Wolterstorff, *Hearing the Call*; Junker, *Prophetic Liturgy*; Westermeyer, *Let Justice Sing*; Walton, *Feminist Liturgy*; Duck, *Worship for the Whole People of God*; Hessel, *Social Themes of the Christian Year*; and Koester, ed., *Liturgy and Justice*.

world blindly. The text has ground lenses for our perception of our world and its characters and their actions and words.

We are, thus, looking very specifically for distinct analogies, and we are interpreting what we see in our world in terms that the text helps us see and interpret. The text colors our viewing of our world and in this sense the text is not just any window, but a stained glass window of sorts. For as Long intimated, the Bible isn't telling us just any story, it is telling us a theologically shaped story. Just as the church through the ages has annealed glass with colors to depict a particular snapshot-in-time of the story of the gospel, when the biblical text becomes the window that the preacher holds up to the contemporary world to understand it, to interpret it in terms of the text and the gospel reflected in the text, the text, and ultimately the gospel to which it bears witness, become the hermeneutical *discrimin* for our perception of the world.

A stained glass window is a freeze-framing of a moment in time. It is a depiction of that moment in a partially opaque window. The stained glass metaphor is one particularly fitting for a homiletical theology. Because what I imagine the preacher attempting to do in a particular sermon, is to freeze-frame the gospel moment that the text depicts. Texts potentially render numerous split-second moments that could be annealed into glass and thus become visual witnesses of God's interrupting our world with redemptive grace. For me, I freeze-frame the moment where Jesus asks Simon the question, while looking at the woman bowed down at his feet, hair down, drying his feet from her tears: "Do you see this woman?" The question then becomes: what does that gospel moment that I see in the text look like in my world?

Looking at my experiences in Seattle at *Tierra Nueva*, the jail, the fields, the churches, and the courthouses through the stained glass window of Luke 7:36–52, I cannot help but see the characters in Washington take alignment with the characters in Luke's narrative. José, Rocio, Reynalda, Jorge, the Hondurans, the other men in the prison, all refract the profile of the "sinner woman." They are objectified, victimized, judged harshly, and they feel the gaze of the dominant culture on them constantly, wishing they were not there, suspecting the worse in them. Nobody's place can change in such a caste system. All are stuck, to the benefit of the powerful and to the demise of the vulnerable. They are contemporary "sinners" in the sense that they should be quarantined from the "righteous" perhaps especially in relationship to worship, but also in daily commerce, unless we need them to serve our needs in some way.

Lurking around them in the sociocultural environment are the churches, the legal system, the penal system, the medical establishments. Most of the people in these realms fit the profile of Simon the Pharisee: accomplished in power, self-assured, and often arrogant and judging. These usually keep their distance from the "aliens," though they do not consciously calculate this fissure in the social fabric when they prepare and eat their fruit salads.

There are, however, exceptions. Just as in the Gospel accounts, here and there, a Pharisee (like Joseph of Arimathea and the Pharisee that Jesus praises as being not far from the kingdom of God) shows himself to be genuine and compassionate, a person of God open and willing to connect with a fellow human being in need. Bob and Gracie have been able to enlist such people to help in their ministry. They become the advocates in the courts and before the field bosses for those without voice. They become the surgeons wielding their healing arts for the injured and ill who have no insurance or money.[31]

Bob and Gracie and the *Tierra Nueva* ministry align in the Lukan stained glass window with the person of Jesus and the freeing, life-altering way that he is with people, especially the most vulnerable. But they also embody his prophetic presence in the churches, in the courts, at the prison, and in the everyday commerce in the fields. They call people out and through their parabolically lived existence. They embody a revelatory, apocalyptic exposure of inequity, racism, and any of a number of other God-denying, hypocritical, blasphemous, and self-serving and Godforsaking social actions by often and otherwise church attending, tax-paying, America-loving citizens.

CONCLUDING REFLECTION FOR HOMILETICAL THEOLOGY

The biblical text in the Gospel narrative serves as a window for hearers to see themselves in the story, even taking turns looking at each character and seeing likenesses and differences.[32] The text serves as a window through which we

---

31. It can be a little too easy to come down hard on the Pharisees as a pigeon-holed type in the Gospels, and such readings can suggest an anti-Judaism bias. In Luke 7:36–50, the Gospel writer is, I believe, clearly contrasting the judgmental and non-merciful attitude of Simon the Pharisee with the unnamed woman who loved much. Simon, a Pharisee in the narrative, represents someone in the sociocultural situation who misuses power and lacks self-awareness before God, self, and his community such that those without power, like the woman in the story, are harmed and kept in their place. Interpreters, preachers, and teachers in the church must be careful not to convey however, even unintentionally, anti-Jewish sentiment in the use of texts like Luke 7. For further reflection see, Reuther, *Faith and Fratricide*; Stendahl, *Paul Among Jews and Gentiles*; Sanders, *Paul and Palestinian Judaism*, xiii; Melcher, "The Problem of Anti-Judaism in Christian Feminist Biblical Interpretation"; and Nirenburg, *Anti-Judaism*.

32. When looked at from the vantage point of the hearer, it could appear that the text is functioning more like a "mirror." But because it is the preacher who is communicating the message of the text, and hopefully the gospel to which the text bears witness, it is actually

as preachers can see in our world analogous characters, actions, and words. When the preacher uses a scenario like that of the ministry of *Tierra Nueva* in order to show what the theological and missional implications of the text look like in our contemporary world, the concretization—the narrated, lived experience in our world—becomes a window too.

The characters in the *Tierra Nueva* story help hearers identify themselves, and thus evaluate the narrative's and the gospel's implication for their own lives. But the contemporary story also becomes a window through which we approach the Lukan text. The "sinner woman" in Luke 7 does not display all the characteristics of the people to whom Bob and Gracie minister in Skagit County. Yet her character is malleable enough to contain the variety of characters, all under the rubric of the poor and marginalized. So too with the figures in power in both the biblical text and Washington context. There are no literal Pharisees in Bob's world, but that image and character construct is flexible enough to adapt to the many powerful people in his sphere. Some of them even turn out to be good, kingdom-of-God–seeking Pharisees, seeking God's justice, grace, and shalom.

This little exercise shows one way of holding text and context in tension with one another while allowing each to mutually illuminate the other. As such, my hope is that the preacher's task as a steward of God's mysteries of the gospel in context is made a little more clear, a little more complex, or a little more arduous, depending on the needs and orientation of the preacher who reads this.

---

the imaginative angle of vision of the preacher projecting onto the imaginations of the hearers these textual and Gospel portraits, thus "window" and "stained glass window" seem to be better metaphors for this process.

—2—

The Gospel of Prosperity

Jesus, Capitalism, and Hope

—Debra J. Mumford

*I am come that they might have life,
and that they might have it more abundantly.*

(JOHN 10:10B)

Abundant life—life in which basic human needs are not only met but are exceeded. Life that encourages human flourishing.[1] It was in search of abundant life that this nation was founded. It is in search of abundant life that people continue to immigrate to the United States from all over the world. Therefore, it is no surprise that what has come to be known as prosperity gospel originated in the capitalistic context of the United States. Prosperity gospel is Christian preaching in which listeners are not only taught about the death and resurrection of Christ, but are also taught that God wants them to be materially prosperous.[2]

---

1. This definition of *abundant* is taken from the Greek word περισσός (*perissos*), which means "exceeding some number or measure or rank or need"; "over and above," "more than is necessary," or "superadded."

2. In this chapter, *gospel* is defined as the content of Christian preaching including Jesus' death and resurrection. Gospel also includes the benefits bestowed upon believers who have faith in Jesus. See Powell, "Gospel," in *The HarperCollins Bible Dictionary*, 337.

As a result, it important to understand that the prosperity gospel did not emerge *ex nihilo* with the beginning of the Word of Faith movement in the preaching of Kenneth E. Hagin in 1962. Long before Hagin began preaching his message of financial prosperity, preachers of many different Protestant sects, as well as movements outside of Protestantism, integrated their faith with capitalism, thereby laying the groundwork for the emergence of Hagin's brand of prosperity gospel. Through the years, each iteration of prosperity gospel sought to fulfill the human longing for abundant life.

In *The Protestant Ethic and the Spirit of Capitalism*, Max Weber contends that the groundwork for the marriage of capitalism and Protestantism was first laid in Europe during the Reformation. Many sects such as the Puritans, Calvinists, Pietists, and Quakers brought their commitment to asceticism with them to the New World. A commitment to asceticism necessarily meant keeping all of the bodily passions and desires in check. A person with an idle body and mind was more likely to fall into sin.[3] In order to avoid falling into sin, everyone was required to work in the particular labor to which he or she was divinely called.[4] Puritans, for example, believed that God provided each person with a calling in which they were required to labor even if they were already wealthy.[5] The work into which one was called had to be done to the glory of God. As a result:

In this section Powell presents three other possible definitions of "Gospel" found in the New Testament. One refers to the message Jesus shares of what God is about to do as it relates to "impending salvation." Another is a combination of what Jesus said about God and what followers of Jesus said about him as is found in Acts 10:34–43 when Peter has the epiphany that God shows no partiality and in Mark 14:9 when Jesus interprets the actions of the woman with the alabaster jar of ointment. The final definition of *gospel* refers to books that include what Jesus says about God and what people such as Paul say about Jesus.

3. Weber, *The Protestant Ethic and the Spirit of Capitalism*. This work was first published as a two-part article in 1904.

4. Ibid., 40–41. Weber credits Martin Luther with developing concepts of *calling* and *asceticism* that were very different than the traditional monastic view. Weber believed that Luther grew to believe that monastic life was an abdication of worldly responsibility. However, one of Weber's most prominent critics, H. R. Robertson, demonstrated that the concepts of calling and worldly asceticism that Weber attributes to Luther's actually existed long before Luther's time. For example, Franciscan Friars were sent out into the world to spread the gospel beginning in the twelfth century. Robertson also contended that the Calvinist positions were misrepresented in Weber's analysis. Not all Protestants, in particular the Calvinists, valued the worldly work of the laity as highly as they did the work of ordained ministers. See Mentieth, *Aspects of the Rise of Economic Individualism*.

5. Weber, *The Protestant Ethic*, 106.

> The power of religious asceticism provided [employers] . . . with sober, conscientious, and unusually industrious workmen, who clung to their work as to a life purpose willed by God.[6]

For Weber, the Protestant ethic also offered an explanation for the unequal distribution of wealth. Some had more worldly goods than others because of "special dispensation of Divine Providence."[7] Only God understood why some were allowed to have more than others. As it relates to the potential pitfalls of wealth, acquiring wealth just for the sake of acquiring wealth was frowned upon. However, acquiring wealth while fulfilling one's calling was acceptable as long as it did not lead to unrighteous behavior.[8] The search for abundant life in Weber's scenario could be realized more for some that others. Because of Divine Providence some would realize more financial prosperity than others. All people could please God by working hard and avoiding personal sin.

The marriage between Protestantism and capitalism was colonially consummated within the institution of chattel slavery. Perhaps it was the belief that God provides every person with a specific calling and in the special dispensation of Divine Providence that enabled Protestants seeking religious liberty to enslave other human beings. Protestants of various stripes made their way to North American from England fleeing religious and political persecution in pursuit of liberty.[9]

Africans first arrived in Jamestown, Virginia as indentured servants in 1619.[10] In 1643, Puritans in the Plymouth colony joined with Puritans in the Massachusetts, New Haven, and Connecticut colonies to form the New England Confederation. Though the primary purpose of the Confederation was to protect themselves from their common enemies, they also made laws

---

6. Ibid.,120.

7. Ibid. Weber attributes this particular perspective to John Calvin. However, he provides no citations as evidence of his contentions. Critics like David Little posit the Weber's contention that Calvinist doctrine such as Divine Providence was the basis for a new social order ignored the development of Puritanism that took place between Calvin (1509–1564) and the Puritan Richard Baxter (1615–1691) whom he cited so liberally. See Little, *Religion, Order, and Law*.

8. Weber, *The Protestant Ethic*, 109–14.

9. Quakers, for example, whose beliefs differed greatly from the doctrines of the Anglican Church, were being persecuted because they denied the existence of the Trinity, refused to swear oaths, and espoused a doctrine of inner light. They also believed the individual's moral conscience was the moral authority for the individual rather than the Bible. These and other beliefs and practices made them the target of political and religious persecution. See Penn, *The Political Writings of William Penn*, § 6.

10. Thirteen/WNET, "Slavery and the Making of America," lines 1–3.

legalizing slavery and managing fugitive slaves.[11] Quakers like William Penn established colonies by insuring all "freemen" who lived in their Provinces and territories and who believed in Jesus Christ, would be free from political and religious persecution.[12] While Penn and other Christians were committed to religious and political freedom, they had no issue with slavery.[13]

After arriving in the New World, the colonists used slave labor on farms to yield a variety of food crops, tend livestock and in urban settings as tradesmen, coachmen, gardeners, and extra help in kitchens, stables, and laundries.[14]

However, many Protestant newcomers to the colonies not only embraced slavery personally by becoming slave owners, they used the Bible to justify the institution of slavery and developed their own *slave prosperity gospel* for the benefit of all of those who would profit financially from slave labor. The *slave prosperity gospel* had two main goals: convincing slave owners that Christianized slaves made better slaves (than those left unconverted), and indoctrinating African slaves with select biblical passages to shape them spiritually and emotionally into profitable commodities.

In an essay entitled: "The Negro Christianized: An Essay to Excite and Assist that Good Work, The Instruction of Negro-Servants in Christianity" Puritan minister and Harvard graduate Cotton Mather responded to reservations of slave owners about converting their slaves.[15] He reminded them of the biblical mandate to share the gospel with their slaves and to attend to their

11. Elson, *Chapter VI, Colonial New England Affairs.*

12. Penn, *Pennsylvania Charter of Privileges.*

13. The Quakers are known for being abolitionists. However, the Quakers participated in the slave trade for many years. It was not until 1758 that they prohibited their members from buying and selling slaves. They were unable at that meeting to get a consensus to mandate slave owners to free slaves they owned at the time. In 1776, they officially prohibited their members from owning slaves altogether. See Angell, "Quakers: From Slave Traders to Early Abolitionists."

14. "Introduction to Colonial African American Life." Slavery existed throughout the colonies including the northern colonies of Massachusetts, Rhode Island, and Connecticut. *The Boston Globe* reported how Puritan governor of the Massachusetts Bay Colony, John Winthrop, helped to write the first law in North America sanctioning slavery in 1641. See Manegold, "New England's Scarlet 'S' For Slavery."

15. Smolinski, *Biography: Cotton Mather.* Cotton Mather was a Puritan pastor, philosopher, and scientist who wrote over 450 books and pamphlets during his lifetime. His unusual name was a combination of his maternal grandfather's name (John Cotton) and his family name (Mather). He was the pastor of Boston's Second Church (Congregational). Among his many publications is included one of the most comprehensive medical handbooks in colonial America, *The Angel of Bethesda*. He also published more than fifty works related to eschatology. Mather's many scientific and theological achievements have been eclipsed by his role in the Salem witch trials, in which he had people investigated for witchcraft.

spiritual well-being. Early in the essay, Mather's belief in Divine Providence became evident. He argued that Negroes had a "low" place and function in the world that could not be changed. What could be changed was their destiny in the world to come.

> The State of your *Negroes* in this World, must be low, and mean, and abject; a State of Servitude. No *Great Things* in this World, can be done for them. Something then, let there be done, towards their welfare in the *World to Come*.[16]

Mather also addressed the concern of some slave owners that slaves would have to be set free after baptism. Mather assured them that baptism was not a license for manumission. Indeed, quite the opposite. Christianizing of slaves had benefits: better and more financially profitable slaves. Mather used the words of the Apostle Paul in Philemon to justify his contention that Christianized slaves could be profitable:

> Your *Servants* will be the *Better Servants*, for being made *Christian Servants*. To *Christianize* them aright, will be to *fill them with all Goodness. Christianity* is nothing but a very Mass of Universal Goodness. Were your *Servants* well tinged with the Spirit of Christianity, it would render them exceeding *Dutiful* unto their *Masters*, exceeding *Patient* under their *Masters*, exceeding faithful in their Business, and afraid of speaking or doing anything that may justly displease you.[17]

> *Onesimus* was doubtless a *Slave*: but this poor *Slave*, on whose behalf a great Apostle of God was more than a little concerned; yea, one Book in our Bible was Written on his behalf! When he was *Christianized*, it was presently said unto his *Master*, Philem. 11. *In time past he was unprofitable to thee, but now he will be profitable*.[18]

Mather was obviously attempting to sell the slave masters on the concept of Christianizing their slaves by convincing them that Christianity could help their slaves become the slaves of their dreams: "dutiful," "patient," "exceeding faithful," and "afraid of not pleasing their masters." To seal the deal, Mather wrote that, according to the Bible, their Christianized slaves would be more profitable than non-Christianized slaves.

---

16. Mather, *The Negro Christianized*, § 9. While Mather advised slave owners to treat their slaves well, he also believed that slaves could be made better slaves if they were indoctrinated with select biblical passages and teachings.

17. Ibid., § 13.

18. Ibid., § 14.

After selling the slave masters on the merits of Christianizing their slaves, Mather then instructed the slave masters on how to sell Christianity to their slaves. It is in the section of the pamphlet leading up to the catechisms that Mather further confirms his Protestant theology, anthropology (Divine Providence), and ethic. Africans were slaves because God called them to be slaves. If they served Jesus Christ faithfully in their calling and lived Godly lives by not sinning against God, they would be rewarded with eternal happiness in heaven. It was only in heaven where they would enjoy rest from all of their labors and troubles.

> Tell them; *That if they Serve God patiently and cheerfully in the Condition which he orders for them, their condition will very quickly be infinitely mended, in Eternal Happiness.* Show them, that it is GOD who has caused them to be *Servants*; and that they Serve JESUS CHRIST, while they are at Work for their *Masters*, if they are *Faithful* and *Honest Servants*, and if they do cheerfully what they do, because the Lord JESUS CHRIST has bid them to do it ; and that, if they give themselves up to JESUS CHRIST, and keep always afraid of Sinning against Him, it won't be *Long* before they shall be in a most *Glorious Condition* ; It can't be *Long* before they Dy, and *then* ! they shall *Rest* from all their Labours, and all their Troubles, and they shall be Companions of a*ngels* in the Glories of a *Paradise*.[19]

It is important to note that Mather advised slave masters to teach their slaves not only how to do their work, "faithfully" and "honestly," but also the countenance with which they should do their work, "patiently" and "cheerfully." As a result slave masters would not only benefit from industrious slaves, but they would also experience slaves who were happy about their work. Happy slaves were less likely to try to escape their enslaved condition.

Mather's belief in asceticism was demonstrated in his admonition for slaves to give themselves up to Christ to keep from sinning. If they immersed themselves in their work, they would live lives that were pleasing to God and be rewarded for their labor in heaven.

Left out of Mather's *slave prosperity gospel* are sections of the Bible that would lead slaves to believe that they should be free, such as the entire book of Exodus or Luke 4. Passages such as Ephesians 6:5 (slave, obey your masters . . .) were highly recommended. The Ten Commandments were part of the catechism with slight modifications such as:

Q. *What is the Tenth Commandment?*

---

19. Ibid., § 21.

A. Thou shalt not Covet.

Q. *What is the meaning of it?*
A. I must be Patient and Content with such a Condition as God has ordered for me.[20]

In this *slave prosperity gospel*, faithfulness to God was conflated with service to the slave master so that slaves could only please God when they pleased the slave master. They could only be rewarded by God when they met the many standards of the slave master. Slaves who pleased their slave masters were financially profitable to the slave masters as well. Therefore, abundant life, or life in which human needs were not only met but exceeded, could only be realized by the slave masters. Slaves supposedly benefitted spiritually by being introduced to the gospel of Jesus Christ and receiving the reward of being with God in the afterlife. Slave masters experienced abundant life on earth. Slaves experienced abundant life in heaven.

NEW THOUGHT MOVEMENT

Abundant life was also pursued outside of Protestantism. In 1802, a quiet movement began in New England under the leadership of a clockmaker named Phineas Parkhurst Quimby—a movement that would prove foundational for what would become known as the Word of Faith movement or contemporary prosperity gospel. This movement is New Thought metaphysics or, more simply, New Thought. The term *metaphysics* indicates a belief that individuals can control the circumstances of their lives by controlling their thinking.

Quimby, born in 1802, was particularly interested in mental healing. After being healed of tuberculosis, he was inspired to better understand the relationship between a person's physical illness and his or her thoughts. He began to study and practice mesmerism (hypnosis) and eventually developed his own healing theories. For example, in a short essay titled "Is Disease a Belief?"[21] Quimby wrote of the relationship between the mind and disease:

> If I am sick, I am sick for my feelings are my sickness, and my sickness is my belief, and my belief is my mind; therefore all disease is in the mind or belief. Now as our belief or disease is made up of ideas which are matter, it is necessary to know what ideas we are

---

20. Ibid.
21. Mumford, *Exploring Prosperity Preaching*, 10–11.

in; for to cure the disease is to correct the error; and as disease is what follows the error, destroy the cause, and the effect will cease.[22]

Quimby felt that by discovering the connection between the mind and disease, he had rediscovered the healing technique of Jesus. Out of the New Thought movement grew several other movements. Quimby's best-known student was Mary Baker Eddy, who founded Christian Science. In turn, some of Eddy's students included Charles and Myrtle Fillmore, who founded the Unity School of Christianity; Malinda E. Cramer, who cofounded Divine Science; and Ernest Holmes, who founded Religious Science. Over the years, proponents of New Thought taught that changing one's thinking could not only affect one's health but every aspect of one's life, including financial well-being. New Thought metaphysics was believed, by some, to be the path to abundant life. New Thought has a humanist, rather than Divine, orientation.

Almost one hundred years after Quimby developed New Thought, those teachings somehow found their way into the preaching and teaching of a Methodist minister named Essek William Kenyon.

KENYON, HAGIN, AND CONWELL

Though Kenneth E. Hagin is often credited with being the father of the Word of Faith Movement, it was Essek William Kenyon who developed the theology upon which the movement is based. Kenyon was an evangelist, pastor, and teacher who was born in a lumber camp in Hadley Hills, New York, on April 24, 1867.[23] Because of his family's poverty, at the age of twelve, Kenyon began to work at a carpet mill twelve hours a day. During his teen years, Kenyon dreamed of becoming an actor. However, upon converting to Christianity at the age of seventeen while attending services at a Methodist church, Kenyon discerned that he was called to preach. He was given an exhorter's license by the Methodist Episcopal Church in Amsterdam, New York. At the age of nineteen, he preached his first sermon. His intellectual curiosity led him to explore philosophy and metaphysics. He attended services of a Unitarian minister and also received training at Emerson College of Oratory in Boston.

With very little formal education and a great zeal for preaching and teaching the word of God, Kenyon pastored several churches and preached as an evangelist throughout the United States. His utmost concern was for Christians to live victorious lives. Kenyon believed that once Christians understood the rights and privileges that the death, burial, victory over hell,

22. Ibid.
23. Ibid., 13–14

and resurrection of Christ afforded them, they would no longer live defeated lives—lives contaminated by sickness, disease, and poverty. When believers embraced the truth of the Bible, they would become the supermen and superwomen God intended them to be. The biblical truths believers needed to embrace include material prosperity, physical healing, and authority to obtain whatever they confess in the name of Jesus. There was no doubt in Kenyon's mind that Jesus intended all believers to live lives of abundance and prosperity.

Evidence of New Thought in Kenyon's theology was present in his teaching about positive confession. Kenyon taught his followers the law of positive confession, which has two aspects. First, believers must confess that they have something (e.g., healing, material goods) *before* it is manifested in their lives. When believers make confessions such as "I am rich," they must believe that they *are* rich before wealth materializes in their lives. The second aspect of positive confession is that, since believers will never rise above their confessions, they should never make a negative confession. For example, they should never say they are poor or cannot find a job even after looking for work unsuccessfully for months. By talking about their poverty or lack of success in their job search, they are glorifying Satan, who has the ability to deprive them of blessings. Because God has redeemed believers from Satan's reign, it is imperative for Christians to confess that Satan has no right to reign over them with poverty, weakness, or failure. When Christians make positive confessions, even after experiencing defeat or failure, they are embracing God's promise for health and wholeness and rejecting Satan's right to affect their lives.[24] The law of positive confession applies to every aspect of believers' lives.

Other Protestant preachers like Russell Conwell (1843–1925), a Baptist pastor and founder of Temple University, combined their Protestant work ethic with the belief that God wants God's people to be materially prosperous.[25]

---

24. Ibid., 86–87. Prosperity preachers teach their followers that sickness and disease do not belong in the body of Christ. In fact, according to prosperity theology, sickness among the people of God is evidence of lack of knowledge, lack of faith, or broken fellowship with God. Many Word of Faith preachers believe, as E. W. Kenyon also taught, that it is abnormal for Christians to go to physicians for healing. There are no cases of sickness and disease that God does not want to heal. Indeed, it is not the will of God for anyone to die of disease. Today's Word of Faith preachers have adopted Kenyon's teaching, which connects sin to sickness and disease. Just as Jesus' resurrection settled the problems of sickness and disease, it also settled the problem of sin. There is no sin problem. Sin has been handled. Sin and sickness come from the same source—Satan. Therefore, just as Jesus' resurrection took care of the problems of sickness and disease, it also took care of the condemnation of sin. When a person is born again, all sins are forgiven and the sin nature is replaced by the nature of God. Moreover disease is eradicated along with the sin.

25. "Russell H. Conwell," lines 56–86. Conwell was the pastor of the Grace Baptist Church in Philadelphia. He began what would become Temple University in 1884 by tutoring people who had little money and little formal education in his church study. The

In a sermon/lecture/dramatic presentation entitled "Acres of Diamonds," Conwell told story after story of people who traveled far and wide looking for treasure in foreign lands when everything they needed to make their fortune was already in their own backyard (sometimes literally). In the sermon, Conwell argued that Christians must get rich if they can in ways that still honor God because "money is power":

> Love is the grandest thing on God's earth, but fortunate the lover who has plenty of money. Money is power: money has powers; and for a man to say, "I do not want money," is to say, "I do not wish to do any good to my fellowmen." It is absurd thus to talk. It is absurd to disconnect them. This is a wonderfully great life, and you ought to spend your time getting money, because of the power there is in money.... We ought to get rich if we can by honorable and Christian methods, and these are the only methods that sweep us quickly toward the goal of riches.[26]

In the sermon, Conwell makes it clear that he believes there is nothing honorable about being poor—especially for those who do not have to be. For Conwell, abundant life includes power. People with money have the power to make their lives and the lives of people in their communities and nation better. Therefore, the person who has an opportunity to become rich but does not take it is not living within the will of God for herself or himself.

POSITIVE CHRISTIANITY

More than one century after Quimby made his discoveries about the mind and disease and several years after Essek William Kenyon and Russell Conwell began preaching a gospel of power and money, Norman Vincent Peale (1898–1993) combined New Thought with his Methodist evangelicalism, Calvinist language, and belief in the American dream to develop positive Christianity.[27] His quintessential text, *The Power of Positive Thinking*, sold over five million copies. Building on earlier books *The Art of Living* and *You Can Win*, Peale defined power as the ability to control one's own life, health, and destiny. Throughout the book, Peale offers stories and practical advice about

---

number quickly grew from one to six and then to forty. In 1887, Conwell announced the formation of Temple College. The first commencement was held in 1892. It was incorporated as a university in 1907.

26. Conwell, *Acres of Diamonds*. Conwell claimed to have preached this sermon more than 6,000 times.

27. George, *God's Salesman*, 135.

how to tap into the power of God through Jesus Christ to change one's life and circumstances and thereby realize a life of abundance.[28]

Peale grew up in poverty in Ohio. He was the son of a Methodist minister and a faith-filled mother. Peale earned a bachelor's degree at Ohio Wesleyan and a master's degree from Boston University School of Theology. While serving as a pastor in the 1920s and '30s, Peale surveyed the culture and observed that church attendance was in decline. Many people were growing disillusioned, bored, and frustrated with church. Gradually allowing New Thought to inform his ministry, he published *The Power of Positive Thinking* in 1952, a time when the United States culture was embracing religious authorities who were addressing needs and concerns of the masses in unique ways. Reinhold Niebuhr and Paul Tillich had become public intellectuals and celebrities. Billy Graham and Rabbi Joshua Liebman wrote books that were accessible to the public.[29]

Peale's positive Christianity did not promise adherents that they would be rich. However, he did teach that no one had to live in poverty or lives of defeat. If they put their faith in God and believed in the power of God at work in them, there was nothing they could not accomplish.

THE WORD OF FAITH MOVEMENT

For Kenneth E. Hagin (1917–2003), best known as the father of the Word of Faith Movement, the 1960s were a time of new beginnings. Hagin, a Southern Baptist, converted to Pentecostalism because he wanted to fellowship with people who believed in divine healing.[30] Hagin's belief in divine healing was undoubtedly influenced by his own divine healing at the age of seventeen. He had suffered from a deformed heart and incurable blood disease all his life. However, after reading Mark 5:34, wherein Jesus healed the woman with the issue of blood, he believed he was completely healed.[31] Soon after his healing, Hagin began to preach.

---

28. Peale, *The Power of Positive Thinking*. Throughout the book, Peale tells stories about people who have changed their thinking and thereby changed their lives. In many chapters, he offers step-by-step instructions about how to change particular ways of thinking or adopt new spiritual practices. For example, in the chapter entitled "Believe in Yourself," he offers ten ways to build one's self confidence such as: picture yourself succeeding, cancel negative thoughts with positive ones, don't build up obstacles in your imagination, and repeat ten times a day "If God be for us, who can be against us?" (Rom 8:31.)

29. Ibid., 128–29.

30. Hagin, "Healing and Miracles through United Prayer," 4–8.

31. Hagin, *New Thresholds of Faith*, 3–4.

In 1962, Kenneth Hagin began preaching and teaching that reality is "created in the minds and affirmed in the speech of believers."[32] Hagin founded the Kenneth E. Hagin Evangelistic Association, which was the beginning of the Word of Faith Movement.[33] Though Hagin claimed that his teachings were inspired by the Holy Spirit, it is believed that he actually plagiarized his teachings from Kenyon, an independent evangelist and Bible teacher.[34] In turn, Kenyon is believed to have adopted many of his teachings from Christian Science and New Thought.[35] Central to Kenyon's message was practicing positive confession; and experiencing material prosperity and physical health as divine right.[36]

Hagin advanced Kenyon's argument that poverty is abnormal by declaring poverty to be a curse. Kenyon taught that it was abnormal for believers to be in poverty and that believers should have success and victory in their lives because they share in God's creative ability. In his sermon, "Redeemed from the Curse of Poverty," Hagin contends that Christ has redeemed Christians from the curse of the law. The curse of the law is threefold: poverty, sickness, and second death.[37] Under the New Covenant, the blessings of Abraham belong to Christians. The blessing is also threefold: material, spiritual, and physical. In the sermon, Hagin preaches that it is not wrong for the Christian to have money. But it is wrong for money to have the Christian. If the believers' material possessions, or desire for material possessions, are preventing them from serving God with their whole hearts, then believers are misdirected. Hagin is also clear that God's promise to meet all of believers' needs according to God's riches does not relieve believers of responsibility to work and make an effort to earn a living.

---

32. Harrison, *Righteous Riches*, 6.
33. Ibid.
34. Ibid, 5–6.
35. McConnell, *A Different Gospel*, 30.
36. Harrison, *Righteous Riches*, 8.
37. Hagin, "Redeemed from the Curse of Poverty," 173–86. Hagin cites Deut 28:16–19, 38–40 as evidence of the curse of the law which would befall those who did not obey the law of God, "Cursed shalt thou be in the city, and cursed shalt thou be in the field. Cursed shall be they basket and they store. Cursed shall be the fruit of the body, and the fruit of the land, the increase of thy kind and the flocks of thy sheep. Cursed shalt thou be when thou comest in, and cursed shalt thou be when thou goest out . . . ."

BIBLICAL INTERPRETATION FOR PROSPERITY PREACHING

Kenyon, Peale, and Hagin each had literal views of Scripture. During Kenyon's lifetime, forms of biblical exegesis that were dominating European theology made their way into theological seminaries and divinity schools in the United States. Kenyon and many other evangelicals of his day rejected biblical exegesis because they felt the Bible should not be treated like a secular document by subjecting it to scientific inquiry. Therefore, Kenyon rejected biblical exegesis. By rejecting biblical exegesis, he and other evangelicals were attempting to defend the Bible from assaults of outsiders whom they felt were decidedly un-Christian.[38] Like Kenyon, Peale and Hagin also believed the Bible meant exactly what it said (or should be understood exactly the way it was read) without need of observing the contexts. Another way of explaining their perspective is that they believed the Bible was God's *propositional revelation* that God supernaturally communicated to chosen people in the form of "cognitive truths."[39] In propositional revelation, every sentence of the bible stands on its own as a divinely inspired truth. The context surrounding the verses does not matter. No sentence in the Bible contradicts any other sentence. Their belief that the Bible is God's propositional revelation explains why they approached preaching by first choosing themes and then finding verses that contained words or phrases related to their themes to support their main points. However, as with much literal interpretation, their use of Scripture often did not support their contentions when they were read in-context.

SEED-FAITH DOCTRINE

An essential tenant of Hagin's prosperity gospel is Oral Roberts's doctrine of seed-faith. Oral Roberts (1918–2009) was licensed as a minister in the Holiness Pentecostal tradition. Born in Pontotoc, Oklahoma, Roberts was healed of tuberculosis during a revival meeting at the age of seventeen. His healing was the beginning of a ministry in which people were encouraged to believe in miracles.[40]

Roberts' doctrine of seed-faith is the basis of the Word of Faith teaching of the *divine economy*. The divine economy is an economic system based on

---

38. McGrath, *A Passion for Truth*, 59.

39. Henry, *God, Revelation, and Authority*, vol. 6, 456.

40. Harrell, *Oral Roberts*, 37. Roberts was ordained in the United Methodist Church and considered himself an independent evangelist.

the belief that God wants to provide God's people with material prosperity.[41] An alternative to the secular economy, the divine economy is activated by faith in the goodness of God and the law of sowing and reaping or seed-faith.

Robert's doctrine of seed-faith is composed of three core principles that, if applied properly in the life of the believer, can ensure that she or he will have abundant life or a life of prosperity.[42] The first core principle is that Christians should turn their lives over completely to God by recognizing that God, not humanity, is the source of all their needs.[43] People who help Christians at various points in their lives are instruments of God but they are not the source of any blessings. God is the source.[44]

The second core principle is the principle of sowing and reaping.[45] Whatever the believer gives freely to God becomes a seed for God to multiply back to the believer in the form of their needs. When the believer sows seed of any kind by giving of their talent, time, love, compassion, or money, they will receive those things in return. If believers want God to supply their financial needs, they should give seed-money to God for God to reproduce and multiply.[46] Roberts is very careful to differentiate seed-faith giving from tithing. Seed-faith giving is done before the miracle is manifested or the need has been met.[47] Tithing is giving after one has been blessed by God financially.

Roberts is also clear that giving to God means Christians give to the church or they give to someone to whom God has directed them.[48] For ex-

---

41. Perriman and World Evangelical Alliance, *Faith, Health and Prosperity*, 51.

42. Roberts, *The Miracle of Seed-Faith*, 37. This book, like many of Roberts's books, is written in a narrative form. Though he presents a doctrine, he does so with testimony or stories of his own personal experiences and with the experiences of other people. When sharing his personal experiences, he depicts himself as a regular guy, someone who steps out on faith and is rewarded by God for doing so. The struggles that he and his wife Evelyn go through are stories to which his readers can relate. The lesson for the readers is, therefore, just as God blesses Oral Roberts for his faith, God will bless anyone who acts in a similar way. Though he does not tout himself as a spiritual superhero, the testimonial nature of his writings nevertheless bolsters his spiritual credentials. To readers he is a man of faith. But rather than being a man of faith to be idolized and put on a pedestal, he is a man of faith to be emulated.

43. Ibid., 15.

44. Ibid.

45. Ibid., 23.

46. Ibid., 21. Roberts cites Luke 6:38 as evidence of the need to give, "Give, and it shall be given unto you; good measure, pressed down, and shaken together, and running over, shall men give into your bosom. For with the same measure that ye mete withal it shall be measured to you again."

47. Ibid., 27–28.

48. Ibid., 57.

ample, there was a time when Roberts and his wife were struggling to pay their rent. Roberts was led to give a seed-faith offering to God. After he gave the offering, a man who was a member of the church Roberts was pastoring gave Roberts an amount seven times the offering Roberts had given to the church. As a result, Roberts and his wife were able to stay in the house.[49]

The third core principle of seed-faith is to immediately expect a miracle after the seed has been planted.[50] In order to expect a miracle, the believer must "release their faith" in God by truly believing that God is going to grant them a miracle.[51]

Though Roberts advises believers to plant seed like the miracle they need, for example, planting a seed of time if they need time, of love if they need love, he simultaneously espouses planting of money seeds to meet other types of needs. For example, he recounts a testimony of a young woman who planted a seed of faith for reconciliation in her marriage. When she decided to plant a financial seed, it was the point of contact she needed to release her own faith. She and her husband did reconcile. However, it would seem that if believers should sow like seed, rather than giving money she should rather have helped someone else reconcile their relationship as a way of mending her own.

Roberts cites Galatians 6:7 as evidence of the law of sowing and reaping, which is the central premise of his teaching, and Luke 6:38 as evidence of God's promise to give back to those who give. For Oral Roberts, abundant life can be realized when committed Christians surrender their lives to Christ, sow seeds into a God-approved ministry to a God-approved individual, and believe with their whole hearts that God will act according to Roberts's interpretation of the word of God.

PROSPERITY PREACHING IN AFRICAN AMERICAN COMMUNITIES

While Hagin and Roberts were continuing to develop their ministries, New Thought metaphysics was finding its way into African American religious communities. During the Great Migration (1915–1920), an estimated 1.5 million Southern blacks moved to Northern states to escape sharecropping, tenant farming, and abject poverty.[52] During this period, Chicago's black

---

49. Ibid., 18. Roberts also sees no conflict of interest in accepting a personal offering from a church member.

50. Ibid., 29–30.

51. Ibid., 30–31.

52. Mintz and McNeil, *The Great Migration*. The Great Migration occurred during a period of industrial expansion in the northern United States. African Americans hoped

population grew by 148 percent, Cleveland's by 307 percent, and Detroit's by 611 percent. Many blacks hoped to find employment in the North and new lives for themselves and their families.[53] One preacher who arose during this period was George Baker, better known as Father Major Jealous Divine or "Father Divine."[54] Father Divine (1877–1965) established the Peace Mission Movement in Sayville, Long Island, New York, in which he preached self-help and positive thinking; held his followers to a strict code of ethics including no drinking, smoking, or drugs; prohibited racial prejudice and discrimination among those in the movement; and established small black businesses while urging his followers to patronize those businesses.[55] Although Father Divine required his followers to maintain a strict standard of personal piety, he also encouraged a commitment to social justice. Divine's followers were urged to develop a plan for a "righteous government" in which equality for all would be realized and such practices as Jim Crow and lynching would be repealed.[56] Father Divine was known for his flamboyant appearance.

Another flamboyant preacher during this period was Charles Manuel Grace, also known as Daddy Grace or Sweet Daddy Grace. Sweet Daddy Grace (1881–1960) founded the House of Prayer for All People in 1919 in West Wareham, Massachusetts, in which he promised his people they could live the good life by "placing their trust, their faith, and most of their money in his hands."[57] Though the doctrine of the House of Prayer for All People is said to have resembled Pentecostalism, Daddy Grace also preached positive thinking.[58]

Rev. Dr. Johnnie Colemon and Rev. Dr. Frederick J. Eikerenkoetter II (Rev. Ike) were preaching messages of self-reliance and individualism while preachers of the civil rights movement preached messages about the need for solidarity and the power of unity in the face of injustice. However, the preaching of Ike and Colemon was more comprehensive that it appeared on the surface.

Rev. Dr. Colemon (1920–2014) was an ordained minister in the Unity tradition. After enrolling in the Unity School of Christianity and being healed of an incurable disease, Colemon began to teach Unity principles of healing and positive thinking. In 1956, Colemon founded the Christ Universal Temple

---

to find well-paying jobs and escape the oppression of the South.
53. Ibid.
54. Harrison, *Righteous Riches*, 133.
55. Simpson, *Black Religions in the New World*, 266.
56. Ibid., 268.
57. Harrison, *Righteous Riches*.
58. Simpson, *Black Religions in the New World*, 266.

in Chicago, which is currently the largest New Thought church in the world with 20,000 members.[59] Members are taught that a happy, healthy, and prosperous life is within reach of each individual who realizes that the kingdom of God is within her or him.

Dr. Frederick J. Eikerenkoetter II (1935–2009), better known as Rev. Ike, believed that all the problems of society began with the individual.[60] He preached a gospel of self-identity to get each person to believe in the "divinity or dignity within himself."[61] Rev. Ike founded the Miracle Temple in Boston in 1965 and the United Church and Science of Living Institute in 1969 to teach people how to live better lives through positive thinking. Though not formally a member of the New Thought movement, his teachings were an intersection between New Thought teachings and African American religious expressions.

While Father Divine, Sweet Daddy Grace, Rev. Johnnie Coleman, and Rev. Ike were among the first black preachers to formally incorporate New Thought metaphysics into their preaching, many of today's black Word of Faith preachers acknowledge the teachings and preaching of Kenneth E. Hagin as a major influence on their own preaching ministries. One of the first and most prominent African American preachers to be influenced by Kenneth Hagin is Frederick K. C. Price.

FREDERICK K. C. PRICE

Though the Word of Faith movement is a predominantly Euro-American movement, there are African American preachers who have founded and currently serve as senior pastors of large Word of Faith congregations. One of the black pioneers and most widely renowned preachers of the Word of Faith movement is Frederick K. C. Price. Price founded the Crenshaw Christian Center in South Central Los Angeles in 1973.

CCC currently has a membership of over twenty-two thousand.[62] Price readily admits that his faith was influenced by the teachings of Kenneth Hagin during a critical period of his ministry. "It was during this time that Betty (his wife) and I began to take the first steps to walk by faith, which has brought us to where we are today."[63] Price holds an honorary diploma from the Rhema

---

59. O'Connell, "Rev. Johnnie Colemon, Chicago Megachurch Founder, Dies at 94."
60. Hamilton, *The Black Preacher in America*, 204.
61. Ibid.
62. "Pastor Fred Price Jr." In 2009, Fred Price Jr., son of Frederick K. C. and Betty Price, was installed as the senior pastor of Crenshaw Christian Center.
63. Ibid.

Bible Training Center. Price even named one of the buildings on the Crenshaw campus after Hagin.[64] Price's theology is consistent with Hagin's theology of prosperity.

PROMINENT AFRICAN AMERICAN WORD OF FAITH/PROSPERITY PREACHERS

Though Price was one of the first African American preachers of Word of Faith movement, today he is one among hundreds. Some of the most well-known include: Creflo Dollar, Bill Winston, and Leroy Thompson Sr. Each of these preachers has fully embraced Hagin's theology of prosperity.

Creflo Dollar Jr., is the pastor of World Changers International Ministries of College Park, Georgia, which has a membership of twenty-three thousand. Dollar started his ministry in the Kathleen Mitchell Elementary School cafeteria in 1986 with six members. World Changers Church currently operates satellite campuses in Brooklyn and Queens, New York, and Carrollton and Norcross, Georgia.[65] Taffi Dollar, the first lady, serves as co-pastor, overseer of the Women's Ministry, and CEO of Arrow Records, a Christian-based recording company.

Bill Winston founded the Living Word Christian Center in 1989 in Oak Park, Illinois with fewer than fifty members.[66] Today the membership is more than nineteen thousand. In addition to operating a Bible training school and a Christian academy, Living Word also owns and operates two shopping mall in the Forest Park, Illinois area.[67]

Leroy Thompson Sr. is the pastor of Word of Life Christian Center in Darrow, Louisiana, which has seventeen hundred members.[68] Though his

---

64. Harrison, *Righteous Riches,* 163. Price is a role model for all Word of Faith preachers in general, and for black Faith preachers in particular. Though he has certainly thrived in the movement, he is not without controversy. The relationship between Hagin and Price changed when Price began a preaching series and wrote books that attacked racism in the Christian church. Price objected to Kenneth Hagin Jr.'s (son of Kenneth E. Hagin and heir of the Rhema empire) teachings against interracial marriage. The senior Hagin defended his son's stance. Price severed all ties to his former mentor. He even removed Hagin's name from the building on the Crenshaw campus.

65. In many Word of Faith churches, first ladies play a major role in the ministry. For example, Taffi Dollar serves as co-pastor, overseer of the Women's Ministry, and CEO of Arrow Records, a Christian based recording company.

66. Living Word Christian Center, "History," lines 1–4.

67. First lady Veronica Winston oversees the Prayer Ministry and the Women's Ministry.

68. Word of Life Christian Center, "Apostle Leroy Thompson, Sr.," line 104.

congregation is small compared to many other Word of Faith congregations, his books and videos entitled *Money Cometh* have been read and viewed by followers all over the world.

Price, Dollar, Winston, and Thompson teach and preach Kenyon's theology that Christians have rights and privileges that the death, burial, victory over hell, and the resurrection of Christ afforded them. The biblical truths believers need to embrace include material prosperity, physical healing, and authority to obtain whatever they confess in the name of Jesus. While some African American preachers of New Thought metaphysics admonished their followers to fight for social justice, contemporary prosperity preachers including Price, Dollar, Winston and Thompson deny that seeking social justice is a biblical mandate. For them, once all people are converted to Christianity, all of the social ills of society will disappear.

SUMMARY

From the time this nation was founded, preachers and pastors have combined their belief in material prosperity with their life experiences and Christian faith to develop several iterations of prosperity gospel. For Puritan minister Cotton Mather, belief in Divine Providence and asceticism culminated to form one of the first slave prosperity gospels. In the slave prosperity gospel, slave masters benefited financially and socially by getting "profitable," "dutiful," "patient," and "exceedingly faithful" slaves. Slaves supposedly benefitted by having a relationship with Christ and being freed from their personal sins. While slave masters received financial profit by enslaving Africans, the Africans themselves received the promise of heaven in return for their faithfulness.

Phineas Parkhurst Quimby believed he rediscovered the teachings of Jesus when he preached and taught that if people could control their thinking, they could control their circumstances. According to Quimby, metaphysical believers could relieve their bodies of all sickness and disease with their minds. Baptist minister Russell Conwell combined his Protestant work ethic with his belief that God wants all people to make a lot of money to preach about the power of money. After growing up in poverty and experiencing a call to ministry, Methodist pastor and evangelist Essek William Kenyon combined his Christian faith with New Thought metaphysics to develop a Christian theology that empowered believers to be the materially prosperous people God intended them to be. Kenyon also taught believers that they have victory over sickness and disease through the person and work of Jesus Christ. Pentecostal pastor Kenneth E. Hagin combined his belief in divine healing with Kenyon's

New Thought metaphysical theology to develop the Word of Faith movement. For Hagin, poverty was not only outside of the will of God, it was a curse.

Holiness Pentecostal pastor Oral Roberts rose from poverty and physical illness to develop the doctrine of the divine economy. In the divine economy God multiplies gifts of believers back to them in the form of their needs.

African American pastors such as Johnnie Colemon, Charles Manuel Grace, and Frederick Eikerenkoetter II developed sermons that spoke to the social and economic conditions of African Americans who were experiencing systemic racial oppression. The pastors combined their religious beliefs with New Thought Metaphysics to develop a theology that gave Africans Americans hope for attaining material prosperity in this life rather than having to wait for their Godly rewards in the life to come. Frederick K. C. Price was one of the first African American pastors to adopt Hagin's theology of prosperity. Today there are hundreds more.

IMPLICATIONS FOR A HOMILETICAL THEOLOGY OF THE GOSPEL: WHY PROSPERITY GOSPEL MATTERS TODAY

When presenting on contemporary prosperity gospel around the country, I encounter many people who look upon the prosperity preachers with disdain and contempt and who view adherents as gullible, stupid, or just plain naïve. They find it hard to understand how preachers can manipulate the gospel for financial gain and how people of faith in the pews can possibly believe that Jesus intends the gospel to be used for such an end. The first reason it is important to identify, acknowledge, and closely study prosperity gospel is to remind ourselves that the gospel of Jesus Christ has long been shaped by the cultures in which it is preached and taught. Some cultural adaptations have highlighted the gospel's liberative qualities or made it relevant or more meaningful. Other cultural adaptations, such as the slave prosperity gospel, have used it to oppress many for the benefit of a few. Prosperity gospel is a product of the North American capitalistic culture. Throughout the history of the United States, preachers have combined their personal experiences of religious persecution, poverty, sickness, and disillusionment with the religious establishment with their Christian beliefs such as Divine providence, Divine calling, and belief in money-as-blessing to develop sermons and theologies that reflected the cultures of their times.

Another reason to study prosperity gospel is to recognize that it is part of the theological lineage of many different Christian traditions. Therefore, when people of different denominations point their fingers at Hagin's brand of prosperity and declare it heresy, they are engaging in reification.[69] Reification, as it relates to Christian history, is the ability of some Christians to objectify prosperity gospel as if it was created by people who did not share some of their own values, traditions, and cultures. All Christian traditions in the United States are influenced by our capitalistic culture. Acknowledging prosperity gospel, past and present, provides us with an opportunity to examine our own theological beliefs for the ways they are shaped and influenced by capitalism and its many harmful manifestations.

By closely examining prosperity gospel we can acknowledge Divine Providence for what it is—a form of religiously sanctioned classism. Divine Providence contends that God created some people to occupy higher or lower social status than others while denying the role of oppression and social injustice in maintaining the reality of social class. Divine Providence presumes and supports a social hierarchy that privileges some while relegating others to second class status. By tying together work and sin with Divine Providence, the purveyors of the slave prosperity gospel in particular, and the Protestant work ethic in general, were able to connect life on earth to the afterlife in a way that was not just about personal behaviors/sins such as adultery, lying, coveting, etc., but also about daily vocation. If a person did not work in the station to which someone determined they had been called by God and do it cheerfully and faithfully, then she or he was taught they would go to hell. The guilt associated with this particular aspect of theology could be stifling at best and paralyzing at worse to aspirations of those who want to reach beyond the circumstantially inscribed status into which they were born.

The material promise of wealth was developed in prosperity gospel by interpreting each verse of the Bible as propositional revelation or without considering their contexts. Interpretation of biblical texts out of context has been used, and is still being used, to deny the ordination of women (1 Cor 14:34) and justify their subjugation to male authority (Eph 5:22–23). It has been used to deny the legality of interracial marriage (Gen 28:1) and support separation of the races (Acts 17:24–26). It has been used to justify the annihilation of indigenous people all over the world (Josh 1:3) and the murder of gays and lesbians (Lev 20:13). Literal interpretation of the Bible has been and continues to be a dangerous practice. There is no limit to the atrocities the Bible can be made to condone when preachers assert that the Bible is the dictated word of God and that every sentence in it reflects the will of God without regard to context. Preachers need to be reminded that they should never use the Bible to

---

69. Berger and Luckmann, *The Social Construction of Reality*, 106.

oppress or marginalize anyone. Preachers must always interpret biblical texts in context.

From New Thought metaphysics and prosperity gospel, preachers can be reminded of the importance of hope in their preaching. By orienting African American hope for happiness and peace in the life to come, the slave prosperity gospel deprived them of hope for happiness in their earthly lives. In his groundbreaking book, *Race Matters*, Cornel West wrote that the major enemy of black survival in America is nihilism or loss of hope:

> The major enemy of Black survival in America has been and is neither oppression nor exploitation but rather the nihilistic Threat—that is, loss of hope and absence of meaning. For as long as hope remains and meaning is preserved, the possibility of overcoming oppression stays alive. The self-fulfilling prophecy of the nihilistic threat is that without hope there can be no future—that without meaning there can be no struggle.[70]

Through the slave prosperity gospel, slave masters taught their slaves that God created them to be servants and that they would be rewarded for their faithful service in heaven. While slave prosperity gospel deprived many African Americans of hope that they could ever live abundant lives on earth, New Thought metaphysics and prosperity gospel restored hope that abundant lives were possible.

For African Americans relocating during the Great Migration, New Thought metaphysics was good news on at least two fronts: material and existential. When African Americans packed up their families and possessions and made the physical journey from Southern states and lives of abject poverty and servitude, they were doing so in hope of a more abundant life. Therefore, messages of New Thought metaphysics preached by Father Divine fed into the hope that was already present when he preached that African Americans deserved to be treated justly and humanely like all other people simply because of their humanity. Father Divine taught the people to start their own businesses and thereby create abundant lives for themselves. The preaching of Rev. Johnnie Colemon conveyed a message of independence, self-worth, and self-esteem. She taught the people that everything they needed to have an abundant life was within them. All they had to do was change their thinking. Missing from New Thought metaphysical preaching was divine sanction. When preachers like Frederick K. C. Price adopted the teachings of Kenneth Hagin, African Americans heard that it was God's will that they be materially prosperous in their earthly lives. They learned that they did not have to wait

---

70. West, *Race Matters*, 14–15.

until they died to receive a reward for Christian living. If they had the faith in Jesus Christ, they could experience material prosperity, peace, happiness, social, and spiritual well-being on earth.

Preachers who study prosperity gospel are reminded of the need for prophetic preaching. Prophetic preachers, including some evangelicals, agree that social ills of society do not disappear automatically when people convert to Christianity. Prosperity preachers need only examine the social interactions of the converted Christians in their own congregations to disprove their theory that individual conversion yields social perfection. While many people inside churches profess Jesus Christ as their Savior, lying, cheating, backbiting, power grabbing, adultery, domestic abuse, racism/ethnocentrism, ageism, and classism exist among the saints of God. Though Christians strive to be like Jesus, we fall short of Jesus' example every day. As long as humanity embodies flesh, we will need to intentionally address issues of social justice.

Christians are members of the body of Christ. That means that those of us who purport to follow Jesus are the hands, feet, eyes, and ears of Christ in the world. We should not only believe that Jesus is the Son of God and through him we have been given the gift of salvation, but we should also work to embody the salvation of which we are beneficiaries by being a justice-seeking people.

Studying prosperity gospel can provide preachers with an opportunity to revisit their conceptions of Jesus and what it is about his life, death, burial, and resurrection they need to proclaim. Jesus was ultimately crucified for being a social and political threat. He proclaimed a kingdom of God in which the poor, the hungry, the distressed, the hated, and the excluded are called blessed. In the same kingdom, the rich, the full, the laughing ones, and those of good repute are forewarned of ill-fated futures. In the kingdom of God as articulated by Jesus, poverty is no longer a life sentence to marginalization and condemnation (by God or humans). Wealth is no longer a sign of godly favor or divine sanction. In the radical kingdom that Jesus proclaimed, blessings were directly dependent on human interaction and the degree to which those interactions embody God's kingdom. Jesus sought to liberate humanity from its self-made systems of power and privilege. As the body of Christ, we must be about his work every day of our lives as we all seek to realize abundant life.

— 3 —

Deconstructing a Gospel of Reconciliation

Locating Trouble and Grace in Postcolonial Preaching

—*Sarah A. N. Travis*

INTRODUCTION

At mealtimes, my family prays a responsive grace which we learned from friends in Malawi: "God is good, all the time. All the time, God is good. Because that is God's nature." These shared words confess what my family—white, affluent, Canadian—understands about God in the world. This affirmation about God's goodness comes amid knowledge of a world that suffers, a world in which it is not always easy to see or interpret God's action.

The writers of the Gospels shared their particular visions of how the good news of Jesus Christ came alive in their own contexts. Preachers today continue the task of locating good news in both its generality and its particularity. Inspired by homileticians such as Paul Scott Wilson, we search this time and this place for trouble and grace in order to proclaim God's action in response to the sorrows and dis-ease of life. The gospel that is preached and heard is distinctly contextual. Gospel promises of life, power, victory, and blessing are interpreted according to historical specificity. While modernity assumed a universal human condition according to which the gospel is always and everywhere the same, postmodern hermeneutics challenge notions of universality.

It is a theological task to interpret gospel for this time and this place. So varied is the conception and expression of Gospel/gospel within the Christian experience that it is necessary to define the meaning of the term for my purposes in this chapter. Gospel (capital G) in simplest terms remembers God's action in Jesus Christ crucified and risen, revealed in Scripture and through the Holy Spirit. This is distinguished from gospel (small g), which here refers to human experience of God's grace, that is, how we name and interpret what God has done and is doing in the world. The fact of God's gracious nature and the incarnation through which it is revealed is in itself good news for all times and places; it is pure gift. The essence of God's good news in Jesus Christ is consistent in all times and places, but the experience and articulation of the gospel is dynamic and rarely straightforward. The manner in which we experience and respond to the implications of God-with-us is contextual.

There are times when the gospel will not initially sound like good news when received by particular populations. Consider Martin Luther's contention that the Gospel convicts us of sin before it offers us grace—thus it is experienced as bad news (*cacangelium*) before it is good news (*evangelium*).[1] "So the Gospel sounds most harsh in its strange tones, and yet this must be done, that it may be able to sound in its own proper tones."[2] The Gospel brings us into a new relationship with God, but in doing so it utters words that challenge our previous selves and relationships. In this sense, the good news of the gospel puts to death our familiar life and habits of relating to others and to the Divine. While the Gospel proclaims a new way of being that is entirely good, it also brings transformation that may be disturbing and difficult. Imagine the situation of a long-time prisoner who learns she is soon to be released, free to return to the world. We might expect that this would feel like entirely good news. However, this prisoner has no material resources or security, is aware that the world has changed dramatically during her time away, fears the response of her family, and does not have a home to welcome her. Freedom, in this example, will likely be experienced as a troubling reality rather than a gift. So too the gospel of Jesus Christ, and its ethical, relational implications may be troubling and disturbing for some individuals and communities, depending on circumstances.

While there are many circumstances that will affect the articulation and reception of gospel, this chapter considers the reality of colonialism has

---

1. Watson, *Let God be God!*, 157.
2. Martin Luther, from *Weimarer Ausgabe* 113.23, as quoted in translation by Watson, *Let God be God!*, 181.

problematized gospel as it is spoken out loud in particular worship settings. How may we understand trouble and grace in a postcolonial world? I urge preachers to revise their articulation of gospel in light of postcolonial insights, not just for the sake of novelty but in the belief that postcolonial insights will deepen the encounter between communities of faith and the triune God. Postcolonial perspectives attend to the local and global implications of uneven power relationships, and the shifting nature of power in a globalized world which bears the continuing effects of colonialism/imperialism.[3] While the age of formal colonization is over, the world is imperial in nature insofar as powerful nations continue to control resources and maintain power over others in a variety of ways.[4] In North America, we see evidence of the impact of colonial and imperial actions as they have negatively affected certain communities, for example economic and social disadvantages for particular races and ethnic groups. Colonialism has shaped, and continues to shape, both national and personal identity, as well as the relationships among nations and communities.

Both postcolonial theories and postcolonial preaching are "anticipatory discourses"—they are devoted to the transformation of the present toward a future reality that is unchained from the limitations of the past.[5] Postcolonial preaching reorients the Christian gospel away from the false gospels of empire, recognizing that these gospels have often been conflated historically. Searching history and the traditions of the church for instances of colonial and imperial power, postcolonial preaching imagines possibilities for healing, reconciliation and transformed relationships both among human communities, and in terms of human-divine relationships.[6]

Postcolonial preaching is theo-ethical discourse that is concerned with the well-being of all who are caught in the web of colonialism/imperialism. It is a relational discourse, and thus the preached gospel is not restricted to gathered listeners in their own context, but always also considers what is good news for others, elsewhere. In other words, what is the grace of this sermon for those who are not in the room, and in what way does that grace respond to the specific troubled faced by those who are not in the room? For those who live on the others side of the world? Even for those who live in a distant past or future? A problem arises for preaching when what is "good news" for others

3. The field of postcolonial studies is broad and encompasses a wide variety of perspectives and ideological commitments.

4. See McLeod, *Beginning Postcolonialism*, 8; and Segovia, "Biblical Criticism and Postcolonial Studies," 49–65.

5. The term *anticipatory discourse* is used by Childs and Williams to describe "postcolonialism." See Childs and Williams, *Introduction to Post-Colonial Theory*, 7. See also Young, *Postcolonialism*, 4.

6. For a fuller treatment of postcolonial preaching, see Travis, *Decolonizing Preaching*.

is not, or does not seem to be, good news for us. Or, conversely, when what we perceive as life-giving is detrimental to the lives of others. When preaching desires abundant life for all, that which is bad news for some is bad news for all.

Colonialism and imperialism in past and present have destroyed and divided humanity. In a globalized world, as geographic and social distance decreases, citizens of the world find themselves in close proximity to others. This proximity heightens the awareness of power differentials, historical engagements, and ongoing consequences of the struggle for wealth and resources. While discrimination and inequality are ongoing, there is a growing awareness that the time has come for public discourse to recognize and name certain injustices in order to restore, or recreate, relationships among victims and perpetrators. Following the formal end of the Apartheid system in South Africa, for example, a national process of Truth and Reconciliation was undertaken. From the perspective of Christian faith, reconciliation and the healing of shattered relationships become possible because of God's love in Jesus Christ. To proclaim such possibility is to name God's grace into deep trouble. Reconciliation, however, is not a straightforward process, and serves as an illustration of the challenge of articulating aspects of gospel in light of historical particularity. I have chosen to focus on one example of tragic suffering related to my own nation's colonial history—the situation of Canada's First Nations peoples with regard to residential schools.

Homiletic perspectives built on the interplay of trouble and grace exhibit theological integrity.[7] These perspectives maintain a tension between law and gospel, allowing the preacher to move between them in order to shed light on the brokenness of creation and the power of God in Jesus Christ. Paul Scott Wilson's *Four Pages of the Sermon* is perhaps the most fully articulated and theologically focused treatment of trouble and grace for preaching. According to Wilson, there are four theological functions which correspond to four "pages" of a sermon: Trouble in the Bible, Trouble in the World, God's Action in the Bible, God's Action in the World.[8] This manner of interpreting the gospel is a strong theological resource for preaching gospel in a postcolonial church. What requires more thought, however is the process by which we identify and name trouble and grace in a diverse and complex world. Trouble and grace are not necessarily straightforward, and require interpretation and attention to context.

---

7. See Wilson, *Preaching and Homiletical Theory,* for a description of the development of the law-gospel/trouble-grace school of homiletics.

8. Wilson, *The Four Pages of the Sermon.*

A focus on God's action is a strength of Wilson's model, but one of the realities of trouble is that it is sometimes hard to see what God is doing. It is also easy to misinterpret what God is doing—as demonstrated by those who have equated conquest with God's gracious action. What becomes challenging for preaching in a postcolonial world is not the balance of trouble and grace in a sermon, but rather the very understanding of what constitutes trouble and grace. From a postcolonial perspective, preachers will wonder: "this is good news for my community, but is it good news for others? And if it is not good news for others, is it still good news for my community?" What God is doing in the world does not always sound like good news for this particular gathered community. It must have been bewildering for listeners in slave-owning congregations in the American South in the era of emancipation, who had long heard slavery equated with gospel in terms of God's ordering of humanity. In terms of perception of the gospel, liberation belonged on trouble's page, if you were preaching to slave owners. And on grace's page if you were preaching to a slave. Perception of trouble and grace depends on who is preaching and who is listening. The cost and benefit of grace and trouble will depend on where you are standing.

Effective sermons accomplish something among the hearers, but despite the best efforts of the Holy Spirit, sermons do not always accomplish something that is good or synonymous with Gospel. Sermons can intentionally or unintentionally entrench existing power imbalances, cooperate with the powers that be, condone acts of discrimination or segregation. Thus our proclamation of "grace" requires careful thought. It becomes much more difficult to identify and proclaim good news insofar as what is good news for me might be the opposite for my neighbor. Any simple designation of trouble/grace is called into question.[9]

In what way can trouble/grace modes of preaching acknowledge ambiguity and tension amid trouble and grace? I begin by discussing gospel interpretation in light of postcolonial theological perspectives, and then turn to Luke 4:16–30 to provide a scriptural example of the gospel's double edge. Against the backdrop of the ongoing process of truth and reconciliation, I name the ambiguities inherent in preaching trouble and grace in a postcolonial context. Finally, I engage with trouble and grace homiletic perspectives in search of resources that can aid preachers to speak a more adequate truth about the world as it was, is, and shall be.

---

9. Wilson does not advocate a strict binary division between trouble and grace, but in fact sees a dynamic relationship between trouble and grace that is helpful here and will be discussed below.

Theologies of the Gospel in Context
THE GOSPEL AND POSTCOLONIALITY

Biblical texts are products of empire, as are the scriptural and theological traditions of the church. These have been inscribed and interpreted in a colonial world. This colonial situation has impacted the proclamation of the gospel in different ways depending on historical, social, and geographical location. In various ways, empire has successfully claimed and subverted the gospel. Colonizers from Christian nations have frequently acted in the name of Jesus Christ, with full participation of the church. Colonial seizure of lands, peoples, and resources has been viewed as providential—commanded and enacted by God. A victory of settlers over aboriginal peoples might be considered by the colonizers as an example of God's grace, and the conversion and Christianization of native peoples as a blessed fulfilment of Matthew 28 and its command to "make disciples of all nations." The conquest of North America by Britain, Spain, and France was very good news for those nations, and interpreted to be evidence of God's gracious care for the leaders of those lands. Conquest, however, was a violent and harmful process for the existing inhabitants and is certainly not to be equated with God's love in Jesus Christ. Good news for the colonizer has meant trouble for the colonized.

A postcolonial perspective will pry open interpretations of gospel, asking "is this good news? For whom?" A process of decolonizing gospel might argue that the gospel of Jesus Christ invites the church to occupy a marginal position and willingly concede both social standing and real estate. It might argue that the good news is found in service rather than conversion. It might argue that conquest is never synonymous with good news, and that imperial acts actually serve as a counter-gospel. This process of decolonizing gospel is painful because it signals the end of something for constituencies which have benefited and continue to benefit from colonial/imperial processes. In that sense, decolonizing is a sign of God's grace, but it sounds a lot like trouble for those who might lose standing, power, money, or control.

Filled with the Holy Spirit, Jesus entered the synagogue in Nazareth. Reading aloud from the scroll of the prophet Isaiah, Jesus said, "The Spirit of the Lord is upon me, because he has anointed me to bring good news to the poor. He has sent me to proclaim release to the captives and recovery of sight to the blind, to let the oppressed go free, to proclaim the year of the Lord's favor."[10] Isaiah's words take on renewed and urgent meaning for those gathered in the synagogue that day. Suffering under the weight of Roman authority, taxed to the hilt and treated as second-class citizens in their own home, we would assume that those who heard Jesus words would have felt

---

10. Luke 4:18–19.

relief and hope when hearing Jesus' words. Surely, Jesus' pronouncement that the prophet's promise was being fulfilled here and now would be good news—great news—for this oppressed community. However, as Jesus himself realized, no prophet is welcome in his hometown. The crowd did not hear this as good news, not coming from Jesus, a lowly carpenter's son. They did not accept his authority to proclaim God's word, and thus his words angered rather than encouraged. This "good" news in fact made these people so angry that they attempted to throw Jesus off a cliff. So we begin to see that good news is not always received as such. Even as we might have assumed that Jesus' words would be well-received by the poor, the captive, the blind, the oppressed, we will assume that these words were not good news for the rich, the captor, the ones who refused to see truth, the oppressors. The "year of the Lord's favor," would not have identical consequences for all. Some would be made free, and some would lose their slaves. Some would be given enough to eat, others would have less than what they were accustomed to eat. Some would grasp a small amount of power, and thus chip away at the great privilege of others. Jesus' words about freedom, about hope for the poor—these are gospel words. Yet hard words for some to swallow.

Two thousand years later, what do we make of Jesus' good news? Luke 4 has been called programmatic for Jesus' mission and ministry. If this is true, then this passage invites, or commands, a re-ordering of human community. The poor and the marginalized are clearly placed at the center of social priority—a move that pushes the privileged to the margins. This text will not sound like good news for those who are quite comfortably captive to empire—those who benefit consciously or unconsciously from the poverty of others, or those who close their eyes to injustice and are quite happy existing with the status quo. For a congregation that is wealthy and well-situated within the global scale of power, this text may sound threatening and uncomfortable, especially if this text is indeed central to how we understand Jesus' purpose. In fact, that congregation might rightly wonder where on earth the good news is for those who are not poor or knowingly oppressed.

It will be bewildering for some listeners today to be challenged with the negative side of their own blessing. For example, in the congregation in which I worship, there are several individuals who hold key positions in Canadian mining corporations. This is their livelihood, this is where they find their vocational purpose and earn the money that benefits their families. They will likely interpret this wealth as blessing, as the outcome of gospel for them. Yet consider a family at the other end of the spectrum—perhaps a family in a Nicaraguan mining town, perhaps one whose land has been confiscated under unfair terms. What is interpreted as gospel by the white executive in Canada is most certainly the trouble from which the Nicaraguan family prays for release. What is gospel in this situation? What is the responsibility of the preacher in terms of naming the trouble experienced by others, especially when that trouble is linked to grace in the experience of others?

A task of postcolonial preaching is to participate in the healing of relationships endangered or destroyed by colonial processes, in fact, to participate in a process of imagining and constructing a future that does justice within these relationships. While governments and national churches seek to redress the past and enact reconciliation in financial, material, and symbolic ways, preachers use words and theological imagination. In order to address the continuing effects of colonialism, it is helpful for preachers to consider the contextuality of trouble and grace. An example arises from an important Canadian social issue—the relationship of Canada's aboriginal peoples to the population at large.

TROUBLE AND GRACE IN CONTEXT: RESIDENTIAL SCHOOLS AND RECONCILIATION IN CANADA

Recently, a national process of Truth and Reconciliation has sought to understand the situation of Canada's aboriginal peoples. In a similar manner to the South African Truth and Reconciliation Commission, this process has named out loud the trouble caused by colonization, racism, and assumption of cultural superiority on the part of white, European settlers in relation to the original inhabitants of the land. The final report of the commission has received considerable attention from media outlets, and has prompted responses and resources from Canadian churches. It is a subject that will, and should, find its way to the pulpit. Canadian Christians are not easily characterized, but many belong to multicultural denominations that were established in a colonial age, participated in colonial projects, and continue to experience the legacies of the colonial past. Finding the words to articulate gospel amidst these multifaceted and disturbing realities, especially in proximity to aboriginal neighbors, will be a tremendous challenge for preachers. The articulation of trouble and grace is difficult, and becomes formidable when preachers participate in the process of reconciliation.

When European colonizers first landed on the soil that we now call "Canadian," the land was already occupied by a native population.[11] While

11. Canada occupies the northernmost portion of North America. Thirty-five million Canadians live in a land area of approximately four million square miles. It is important to note that Canadian identity is not monolithic. Canada's indigenous peoples are diverse, and represent a variety of geographic, historic, and social locations.

Canada's self-identity is rooted in a sense of tolerance and welcome, the opposite has been true in the experience of aboriginal peoples. As the fledgling nation of Canada was settled in an east-west pattern, the original residents were removed from the lands they called home, and relegated to reserve lands that were not able to support traditional livelihoods. "For over a century, the central goals of Canada's Aboriginal policy were to eliminate Aboriginal governments; ignore Aboriginal rights; terminate the Treaties; and, through a process of assimilation, cause Aboriginal peoples to cease to exist as distinct legal, social, cultural, religious, and racial entities in Canada."[12]

In the late 1800s, schools for aboriginal children were established with the aim of "removing the Indian from the child," in other words, assimilating them to the predominantly white Christian culture. These schools were part of a systematic act of cultural genocide. In the words of Canada's first Prime Minister Sir John A. Macdonald,

> When the school is on the reserve the child lives with its parents, who are savages; he is surrounded by savages, and though he may learn to read and write his habits, and training and mode of thought are Indian. He is simply a savage who can read and write. It has been strongly pressed on myself, as the head of the Department, that Indian children should be withdrawn as much as possible from the parental influence, and the only way to do that would be to put them in central training industrial schools where they will acquire the habits and modes of thought of white men.[13]

Canadian denominations, including Roman Catholic, Anglican, United, Methodist, and Presbyterian, were active participants in the establishment and operation of residential schools. The fact that former residents of these schools are generally called survivors gives some indication of the conditions within the schools. Harsh discipline, uncomfortable living conditions, and the suppression of aboriginal language were part and parcel of life in the schools. Children were separated from their parents and their culture, and often encountered danger and abuse. Some residential schools remained in operation until the 1990s, thus the memories are recent and the wounds are still fresh for many. The end of residential schools, however, does not signal the end of injustice for Canada's first peoples. Inequality in heath care and education continues, and aboriginal children are at significant risk. Hundreds of aboriginal

---

12. Truth and Reconciliation Commission of Canada, "Honouring the Truth, Reconciling for the Future," 1.

13. "Official Reports of the Debates of the House of Commons of the Dominion of Canada. First Session, Fifth Parliament, May 9, 1883," 1107–8.

women are missing or have been found murdered, a vast over-representation in relation to the population at large.[14]

The mandate of the Truth and Reconciliation Commission includes the words, "The truth of our common experiences will help set our spirits free and pave the way to reconciliation,"[15] and the report goes on: "The Survivors acted with courage and determination. We should do no less. It is time to commit to a process of reconciliation. By establishing a new and respectful relationship, we restore what must be restored, repair what must be repaired, and return what must be returned."[16]

The Truth and Reconciliation Commission acknowledges the difficulty of the term *reconciliation*, an acknowledgment shared by postcolonial theorists. From a postcolonial perspective, there is a suspicion that reconciliation processes, rather than seeking the good of those who have been victims of colonialism, are politically expedient or serve economic interests. Some anti-colonial leaders, such as Franz Fanon, have categorically denied the possibility of reconciliation in a postcolonial society.[17] The word *reconciliation* implies the restoration of a relationship to a former state, yet few would wish a return to historical modes of relationship among aboriginals and non-aboriginals in Canada. For the Commission, "reconciliation is about establishing and maintaining a mutually respectful relationship between aboriginal and non-aboriginal peoples."[18] This process has indeed begun to change the conversation about this relationship, and raise awareness among Canadians, many of whom are unaware of the degree of pain and destruction lurking in the seemingly benign halls of Canadian history.

The historical relationship among aboriginal peoples and others who dwell in this land has created a postcolonial situation that challenges the colonial question "who is 'savage?'" While white populations acted according to a belief that native peoples were savage because they were not Christian and did not follow European customs, their own behavior was truly savage and destructive. In the persistent attempt to civilize aboriginal populations, the Canadian government revealed itself to be mired in trouble. Those who perceived their own culture to be superior were in fact revealed to be unjust and irresponsible. Such ambiguity lies at the heart of all colonial relationships.

---

14. See the report of the RCMP, http://www.rcmp-grc.gc.ca/pubs/mmaw-faapd-eng.htm.
15. "The Mandate for the Truth and Reconciliation Commission," 1.
16. "The Mandate," 6.
17. Fanon, *The Wretched of the Earth*, 39
18. "The Mandate," 6.

The Canadian churches' response to the report of the Truth and Reconciliation commission acknowledges that churches "share a responsibility to ensure that the task of reconciliation does not end today."[19] This responsibility will play out through various channels, one of which will be preaching. I perceive reconciliation to be a gospel process—that is, a process that is enabled by God's action in Jesus Christ. It is, however, not a straightforward, easy process, but one that is forged amid tears and in the memory of blood.

While we as preachers desire to proclaim the grace of God working in all situations, it is difficult to name that grace out loud sometimes, especially in the presence of those who have long felt the absence of good news, and experienced "God's presence" not as a healing light but as a punitive weapon in the hands of colonial agents. Lurking at the back of our minds is the question that we dare not ask out loud—where was God when all this was going on? When wounds are so deep that healing is unimaginable, where and what is good news? What is good news in light of injustice? What is good news in light of cultural genocide? These questions might seem shockingly unfaithful, yet they signal an acknowledgement of the depth of the trouble caused by human abuse of power. To ask these troubled questions in the development of sermons and in sermons themselves is to wonder aloud what many listeners are already thinking. Acknowledging the experiences of abandonment, punishment, degradation enacted in the name of God is an important step on the path toward reconciliation. The proclamation of grace will need to untangle the actions of humanity from the actions of God, freeing God from colonial entanglement.

Preachers name our Creator as the One who calls us away from power abuses and the violent suppression of difference that are not permissible in the household of God. We proclaim God as the one who listens to desolate questions, embraces lament, comforts the broken-hearted. This aims not only at the healing of victims, not only the forgiveness of oppressors, but the restructuring of the relationships among those who exist in a colonized space.

Yohan Go offers the timely reminder that "although victims, perpetrators, or everyone in-between are all in need of grace, healing, and forgiveness, the kind of grace, healing and forgiveness that is needed for victims, perpetrators or bystanders cannot all be the same."[20] The place of forgiveness in this process of reconciliation is, and remains, difficult. The proclamation of forgiveness in a postcolonial age requires a commitment to deep theological struggle and to articulating the ambiguity inherent in this kind of "good

---

19. Hiltz et al., "Response of the Churches to the Truth and Reconciliation Commission of Canada."

20. Personal Correspondence from Y. Go, December 5, 2015.

news." As we preach the gracious act of God in forgiving our sins, it is also necessary to keep in mind that hearing that God forgives the sins of perpetrators may be very difficult for victims to hear. Does it sound like good news that God will forgive the vilest offender when you have been damaged by that offender? The gospel of forgiveness ceases to be gospel when victims are pressured to forgive, as when forgiveness is presented as a moral imperative. Individual preachers do not have the authority to offer forgiveness on behalf of a wronged community unless that preacher is specifically granted authority to speak for a particular group. There are few things in the human experience more difficult than to forgive another human being's grievous wrongdoing. This difficulty may be exponentially larger when an entire community, or religion or culture has been implicated in wrongdoing. Here we see again the blurred good news—forgiveness is gospel, a gift of God. Yet for forgiveness to become a reality in the human community takes a great deal of hard and painful effort. In reflecting on the relationship of preaching and forgiveness, Richard Lischer writes:

> At the heart of the Universe lies a mysterious, hidden Being whose very self is moved by love for all that he has created. In the ministry, death and resurrection of Jesus of Nazareth, the Being has been revealed as one who is perpetually turning toward us as if to welcome us home, the way a mother and father open their arms to a wayward child. Whenever we preach, our sermons participate in this, God's definitive gesture toward the world.[21]

It may be that the task of preaching when it comes to forgiveness is to hold open the possibility that forgiveness is possible, to point to a God that holds arms open for us. That is gospel, yet it does not banish the trouble in a manner that ignores or devalues the very real pain experienced in the crucible of human relationship. Such a space is opened when the preacher proclaims God's invitation to experience and share forgiveness, while at the same time not hesitating to name the way things are—the depth of the rupture and the seriousness of the sin.

To acknowledge a negative legacy of the church such as residential schools takes humility. This involves not only a true accounting of past wrongs, but also retracting past claims of superiority and arrogance. It is good for us as a Christian community to practice humility. But it may be "good for us" in the same way that eating broccoli and exercising are good for us. The gospel, the good news, is not preached effortlessly in this situation. The gospel of reconciliation, of equality, of reparation and truth—it is unpalatable for those who

---

21. Lischer, *The End of Words*, 133.

have the most to gain from injustice. It may also be unpalatable for those for whom words like *reconciliation* sound like a call to abandon just anger, or "get over it," or shake hands with the abuser, or to shut up. According to the Rev. Stan McKay, a residential schools survivor,

> [There must be] a change in perspective about the way in which Aboriginal peoples would be engaged with Canadian society in the quest for reconciliation.... [We cannot] perpetuate the paternalistic concept that only Aboriginal peoples are in need of healing .... The perpetrators are wounded and marked by history in ways that are different from the victims, but both groups require healing.... How can a conversation about reconciliation take place if all involved do not adopt an attitude of humility and respect? ... We all have stories to tell and in order to grow in tolerance and understanding we must listen to the stories of others.[22]

McKay names a repeated refrain of postcolonial theology—that both colonized and colonizer are in need of healing. All have been part of the process of trouble, whether as victims, perpetrators, or bystanders, and all are in need of grace. A challenge of preaching in postcolonial mode, however, is finding ways to articulate trouble and grace amid the complexities of woundedness, responsibility, and power.

PREACHING TROUBLE AND GRACE IN A POSTCOLONIAL CHURCH

Preaching in a postcolonial context calls for a more fluid, ambiguous, contextual view of trouble and grace. Gospel effectually contains both trouble and grace—it convicts us, challenges us, urges change, pries our fingers from beloved possessions, spins us out of our comfort zones, and then it forgives us, reorients us, embraces us, energizes us, recreates us. Trouble and grace, then, exist in a dynamic relationship. Paul Wilson characterizes this as a tensive metaphor.[23] "By juxtaposing trouble and grace, and by the power of the Holy Spirit, a third identity is generated, an identity of faith, hope, and love of God and neighbor. The result is far from a static notion of polar opposites, it is a generative postmodern tension...."[24]

---

22. McKay, "Expanding the Dialogue on Truth and Reconciliation—In a good way," 107.
23. Wilson, *Preaching and Homiletical Theory*, 92.
24. Ibid., 99.

The space between trouble and grace, then, is dialogical and productive—within this space, God produces something new. This brings to mind the postcolonial concept "third space."[25] Elsewhere, I have argued that a postcolonial sermon can function as a third space in which persons affected by colonial processes find space to encounter one another in the presence of the triune God.[26] Such a space honors the ambiguities of colonial relationship by conceding that there is more to "truth" than meets the eye. Listeners are given permission to ponder their own ambiguous location in the midst of empire, and to ponder the ambiguous nature of trouble and grace in their own lives. It is a space in which truth can be negotiated. Thus, in this sense, experiences of trouble and grace can be spoken, modified, discussed, and transformed. When the sermon functions as a third space, we listen more carefully to learn what constitutes trouble, and what constitutes grace in a particular setting. Most importantly, we can test our theological assumptions about what God is doing in the world, ensuring that we are not merely affirming human action and naming it grace.

Preachers, week to week and day to day, want to say something that is true about God and about the world. Postcolonial theology serves to remind preachers that the utterance of truth is complicated. Our utterance of truth is only partial, and more than one thing can be true in relation to any given text or contemporary situation. Modern truth and reconciliation processes demonstrate that multiple truths, even opposing truths, can be spoken simultaneously. As we construct sermons, we can fruitfully wonder where there is space for more than one truth to be spoken. Honoring difference in human experience is a key aspect of postcolonial preaching, and will include an openness to various experiences of trouble and grace. Honoring difference is a necessary stance for preaching toward reconciliation. "Writing and reading in the service of forgiveness and reconciliation require participants willing to risk vulnerability to the unfamiliar and unknown, and involve creating a narrative that forgoes univocal logic for the sake of promoting human renewal and advancement toward new horizons."[27] In the same way, postcolonial preaching invites vulnerability and acknowledgement of diversity, looking toward the horizon of God's future.

---

25. "Third space" is a metaphorical concept introduced by postcolonial scholar Homi K. Bhabha. When "colonized" and "colonizer" come into proximity, an opportunity arises to challenge assumptions about difference, cultural purity, and power. The encounter is potentially transformative, and the parties involved may be released from historical patterns. See Bhabha, *The Location of Culture*, 14.

26. See Travis, *Decolonizing Preaching*.

27. McGonegal, *Imagining Justice*, 11.

It is important to note here that it may be unfair to invite those who are already vulnerable to become even more vulnerable. Equally important is that those who have been marginalized by colonial processes should be free to actively resist ongoing domination.[28] The imagined "third space" of postcolonial preaching, instead of smothering resistance, should be a space in which victims can express discontent with the status quo. It may also be a space in which perpetrators and bystanders may support or participate in programs of resistance, at the invitation of those who have been marginalized.

Sermons that hold trouble and grace in tension offer several advantages for preaching that respond to colonial and imperial reality. First, these sermons allow for a sustained look at trouble. Rather than skipping over difficult realities in a rush to get to the good news of God's love, these sermons abide, for a long moment, on the pain and suffering. A sermon on Luke 4, for example, can examine the social and political realities underlying the text in the time of Isaiah, the time of Jesus and the biblical audience, as well as the way that those realities are replicated in the world today. In terms of the Canadian process of reconciliation, it's not about closing a chapter in Canadian history, but rather holding the book open so that we do not forget. The news is in fact so terrible that we want to glance at it and then shut our eyes to avoid the glare. However, in the postcolonial context, Christians are invited to confess their entanglement in colonial systems, and bear responsibility for the suffering and healing of others. This calls for sustained attention to trouble, especially as our attention is an act of grace toward those who suffer. In addition, a postcolonial sermon will explicitly includes colonialism/imperialism as trouble both in the biblical text, and in the historical and contemporary world. Naming trouble will affirm the experience of those whose lives have been negatively affected, and may educate those who are unaware of their own participation and responsibility.

Second, these sermons offer an opportunity to talk about the very nature of good news. We can challenge prevailing social conceptions of "good news." We can acknowledge that we may need time to adjust to good news. The redistribution of resources in pursuit of justice is certainly something advocated by Jesus, and is consistent with Judeo-Christian theological traditions. Luke 4 is certainly gospel, but it is not good news for those who stand to lose material resources, or power, or even to lose face. Postcolonial preaching involves wrestling "good news" away from predominant cultural forms. According to the gospel, humility, justice, loss, and dying to self are all good news. This is a stark contrast to the empire's gospel according to which power, wealth, and privilege are worthy goals. Thus, the proclamation of Luke 4 can be celebrated

---

28. My thanks to Y. Go for this insight.

even by a privileged community, if they are invited to perceive that it is good for the entire human community when the poor are fed and the oppressed are lifted up. It is good news when those who benefit from colonial entanglement realize that they too need to be freed from the chains of empire.

One of the most profound lessons of the trouble-grace mode of preaching is that human beings are not powerful. God's grace is always what gets us out of trouble. This is significant in the face of historical and contemporary manifestations of colonialism and imperialism, which reveals repeated attempts of various groups historically to seize power and control over other lands and peoples. Yet according to postcolonial theory, even colonizers are not as powerful as they think they are. All of us, whether we belong to more or less powerful groups, are still colonized by a system that is more powerful than any of us. No matter how faithfully we try to dismantle the imperial machine, history has shown that human community is powerless to extricate itself from the threads of empire. As a preacher I cannot address or redress the wrongs that have been done to aboriginal communities by generations of Canadians. My membership in the household of God means that I share responsibility even when I am not guilty. But there is nothing I can say or do that will restore what has been lost. In our search for a renewed and reconciled community then, we are thrown back on God's resources. This will not initially sound or feel like good news to people who are seeking control and influence over their own lives. It will not sound like good news for preachers who long to fix what is broken. Following the June 2015 shootings in Charleston, South Carolina, homiletician Sam Persons Parkes wrote:

> It is tempting for me to finish the sermon with the modal verbs of trouble—must, should, ought (e.g. "We must work toward reconciliation," or "We ought to do this or that."). These verbs invariable cast us back on our own feeble resources. Instead, employ the verbs of empowerment—can, may, might. What capacity for reconciliation has God opened up in us in light of the cross and resurrection that we could not muster ourselves? There, at that point, rests a gospel that is greater than our own power.[29]

It is appropriate to confess the limited power of the church given its historical inability to avoid entanglement with the powers fuelling colonialism/imperialism. "We" have not been able to prevent or adequately atone for the wrongs that have been, and continue to be. "We" can barely muster the vocabulary to name out loud our own complicity and responsibility. Postcolonial preaching will be most effective when it acknowledges the limitations of

---

29. Parkes, Facebook, June 21, 2015.

human power, and the destruction inherent in relying on human power systems. It is only divine, gracious power that will offer freedom from domination, and release communities for reconciliation. By putting God at the center of our sermons, we are dislocating the powers of colonialism that have divided communities in countless ways, and reminding ourselves and our listeners that abundant life will come not from misuse of power but from the creative power of Love. Problematizing the firm distinction between trouble and grace will hopefully not result in a murky proclamation, but in good news that is a more adequate and fitting response to trouble. It is the articulation of a gospel that speaks a fuller truth.

IMPLICATIONS FOR HOMILETICAL THEOLOGIES OF THE GOSPEL

Sermon by sermon, preachers practice the task of naming God's action in the world: The good news that God has come near to us in the person of Jesus Christ, in the presence of the Holy Spirit. We proclaim the end of death and suffering even as we see that dying and suffering is a reality here and now. Preachers utter gospel words that make a claim about God's action in the past, present, and future. We turn those words over and examine them, and contemplate what they mean in the context of our own woundedness and dislocation. Good news usually means change, transformation, newness—all of which are life-giving but rarely easy. The Gospel of God-with-us is urgent and essential. Yet like the scandal of particularity in the incarnation, the meaning and implications of gospel are particular and specific. Good news has a flip side. The promise of life is bad news for the powers of death. For those within the human community who are accustomed to aligning themselves with the powers of death, good news may not initially sound like good news. Naming gospel is an essential task of preaching but it is not a straightforward task. The gospel must intentionally remain "an object of sustained theological reflection, especially in light of the relationship of gospel and culture or context."[30] I have explored some of the complexities of gospel interpretation in light of the ongoing effects of colonialism and related power inequalities, and specifically in terms of the tragedy of residential schools in Canada. There are several insights which contribute to the study of homiletical theology.

As Eunjoo Mary Kim has written, globalization "has shifted the locus of theology. We ask, Where is God? What is God doing? To answer these questions, we need to look at the underside of history and the emancipatory

---

30. Jacobsen, "Introduction," 3–19.

struggles of dehumanized people everywhere."[31] The context of a homiletical theology of the gospel is a global context. Our textual interpretation and our interpretation of God's action in the world is accomplished in the presence of "others." This is true in literal and figurative ways. In a globalized, postcolonial world, our co-worshippers represent multiple geographic and ethnic origins. Our neighborhoods are shared with immigrants and with adherents of many religions. Globalization means that we are connected in significant ways through media to communities in every corner of the globe. Our context for doing theology, our context for preaching is not limited to a specific congregation or sanctuary. Our context encompasses all of God's people—those we know and those we do not. Thus, we engage in interpreting gospel not only for those who are physically proximate, but for those who are not in the room. Gospel, and the interpretation of good news, is not only for us, but for others. The interconnection among Christian communities is real not only from the standpoint of ecclesiology but through increasing awareness of the situations in which others find themselves. Thus, preachers will need to consider a multiplicity of others when interpreting good news—interpreting gospel is a glocal practice which takes into account both the local and the global, recognizing that one cannot be understood without the other.[32]

What constitutes good news, and in what way, will be dependent on context. In Luke's gospel, Jesus proclaims good news for those who are most vulnerable. This promise of freedom, however, is not without ambiguities when one considers the stakeholders. It is surely bad news for those who have benefited from the marginalization of the poor. It is satisfying news for those of us who occupy the centers of society but still long for justice and freedom for the oppressed. Yet also troubling, because we still wonder how on earth such freedom will be accomplished and at what cost. When it comes to the situation of residential schools in Canada, I hear Jesus' words amid the knowledge that damage has been done that cannot be undone. Despite a growing awareness on the part of Canadians that tremendous violence has been done to indigenous children, violence continues to plague indigenous communities.

These musings of the ambiguity of good news are deconstructive—they pull apart assumptions about gospel and risk losing sight of the very essence of good news. This may be especially true for the marginalized, for as Yohan Go has suggested, if the gospel is problematized for the wealthy and privileged then it is also problematized for the poor and marginalized.[33] The promise of

31. Kim, *Preaching in an Age of Globalization*, 66.

32. Kim's chapter "Globalization and the Context for Preaching" is helpful here. See *Preaching in an Age of Globalization*, 19–41.

33. Personal Correspondence from Y. Go, December 5, 2015.

life, the reality of Jesus Christ and the movement of the Holy Spirit, a kingdom of justice and joy, are aspects of gospel on which hope and resistance to evil are to be built. Problematizing gospel is not intended to shake these foundations, but rather to shake those interpretations of gospel that have clouded the essence of Gospel. For example, interpretations which have proclaimed white culture to be superior to aboriginal culture; or named colonization as a practice of God's kingdom; or benefitted the rich at the expense of the poor. These practices are not gospel. Gospel interpretations that untangle God from colonial participation will offer both hope and theological resources to those who long for freedom and justice. Those of us who are not poor will also be made aware of the ways we also are limited and oppressed by systems that undermine gospel. Deconstructively, we may say that gospel can be ambiguous. Constructively, we can say that gospel is flexible and dynamic and large. There is room enough to proclaim both freedom for the poor and freedom for the rich—we will require freedom in different ways. There is room enough to proclaim forgiveness for victims and perpetrators—although the nature of that forgiveness and the process by which it occurs may indeed be different. There is room enough to proclaim the possibility of reconciliation—although what is required for that to occur will depend on one's context—as victim, as perpetrator, as bystander. There is room enough within the gospel to find good news for all. The task for the homiletical theologian in a postcolonial context is to search deeply—to examine the nuances and contextual realities in order to locate the good news that will offer joy to those in the room, and to locate the good news that will mean life for others.

— 4 —

One Nation, Two States, and Two Words of God?

The Gospel of Reconciliation and Theological Tasks of Preaching from a Korean Perspective

—*Yohan Go*

TWO WORDS OF GOD FOR A DIVIDED KOREA?

My theological interest in the gospel of reconciliation for preaching began from my personal struggle to understand a strange experience that I had about two years ago. On July 26, 2014, I participated in an ecumenical event, "Korea Peace March and Vigil," organized by the United Methodist Church in Washington, DC. The main purpose of this gathering and peace march was to raise a voice for peace and the reunification of the Korean Peninsula. Since the Korean Armistice Agreement between North Korea and the United States (Not South Korea), on July 27, 1953, the two Koreas are still at war/in a state of conflict. During the peace march to Lafayette Park in front of the White House, about 300 participants shouted, "Peace treaty now. Peace for Korea now." The representatives of the meeting visited the White House and met the director for Korea at the National Security Council. They requested three things: lifting economic sanctions against North Korea that make North Koreans suffer, stopping US military training on the Korean Peninsula that aggravates military tension between North and South Korea, and taking the lead in forging peace between the two Koreas. While this event seemed to deal only with political issues, the fundamental motive for this ecumenical event was the Christian faith. In her speech at Lafayette Park, Bishop Mary Ann Swenson, ecumenical officer for the United Methodist Council of Bishops, said, "For us, this march is about being one in Christ, being one people, one land and truly having peace and reconciliation on the Korean Peninsula as a part of our Christian witness."[1] Hearing her speech was a very moving moment for me. After coming back to Boston, what puzzled me was a conversation with one of my church members who participated in a different peace march, which was held a week ago at the same place. The peace march was hosted by a conservative Christian organization, the Korean Church Coalition for North Korea Freedom, and the purpose of the peace march was to raise a voice for human rights issues in North Korea. One of the requests this group made to the US government was to pass a bill for the North Korea sanctions act in order to press the North Korean government to improve freedom and basic human rights for North Koreans. Both Christian groups made it clear that their motivations for these peace marches are rooted in their deep commitment to their Christian faith. However, what they requested of the US government was the opposite—as if they had heard different words of God. One group took God's peace and reconciliation as the central motive for their action while another group chose God's liberation from bondage as the core theological motive for their action. Many questions come to mind. Does God's peace with reconciliation contradict God's liberation? Is it legitimate to ignore human rights issues in North Korea for the task of peace and reconciliation in Korea? Is it ethical/moral to request using an invisible deadly weapon, namely, economic sanctions against North Korea for the sake of North Koreans? Why do we, Koreans and Korean Americans, have to protest for the reunification of Korea at the White House? What should be the theological tasks of preachers for liberation, peace, and reconciliation in the Korean peninsula? What does it mean to preach the gospel? All these questions have led me to the fundamental question: what is the gospel in a divided Korea? To answer this question, critical theological reflection on both gospel and context is necessary.

---

1. Worthington and Lee, "A Dream for Peace On the Korean Peninsula," line 20–21.

THEOLOGIES OF THE GOSPEL IN CONTEXT

TOWARD A CONTEXTUAL HOMILETICAL THEOLOGY OF GOSPEL

As part of his unfolding vision for homiletical theology, David Jacobsen offers a profound insight about how homiletics is a particular way of doing theology in relation to practices and theories of preaching and context. Homiletics does not merely use theologies. Homiletics itself is a place for doing theology in its conversational and rhetorical mode, constructing provisional theological understandings at a moment when traditions no longer speak all that is needed in that moment.[2] This "unfinished" or provisional character of homiletical theology partly comes from the contextual and provisional nature of the gospel itself. While Christian gospel is essentially linked to the past event of Jesus Christ, the gospel as good news is always defined in relation to a context and situation where it unfolds. In Edward Farley's words, preaching the gospel is "to bring to bear a certain past event on a present situation so as to open up the future."[3] To be good news, the gospel must be a response to the bad news in a particular place and time. The gospel cannot be defined acontextually because the bad news not only varies from place to place but it also always keeps changing. In this sense, the gospel cannot simply be identified with some biblical contents or doctrines. It is not a full-blown and unchanging belief system that the church possesses permanently. Rather, as Douglas John Hall argues, the gospel is something that the church has to discover, rediscover, receive, and rearticulate ever anew in its worldly context to be the church.[4] Further, the gospel named in a context is always interwoven with culture/context. In fact, every articulation of gospel, no matter how abstract, is gospel in a particular context, implying cultural elements and contextual concerns. Thus, it is difficult to reflect on the gospel without considering it in a particular context. This profound interwovenness of the gospel with culture/context calls for critical reflection on approaches to relating the gospel and culture/context for homiletical theology and how they interact with each other. This provisional and contextual character of the gospel requires a holistic approach to the gospel and context.

2. Jacobsen, "The Unfinished Task of Homiletical Theology," 47–53.
3. Farley, *Practicing Gospel*, 80.
4. Douglas Hall and Edward Farley share a similar view on gospel as mystery. Gospel is not fixed and unchanging entity, nor something that we can invent, master, or possesses permanently. For Farley, gospel is the mystery of God's salvific action in relation to the concrete human context with which we have to continue to struggle to fathom. For Hall, gospel is something that has been done for us by God and we have to discover and rediscover the gospel in ever-changing contexts. See Hall, *Waiting for Gospel*, 8–9, and Farley, *Practicing Gospel*, 81.

Therefore, I want to reflect on the gospel in the Korean context by examining how the gospel has interacted with the sociopolitical and religio-cultural context of Korea, shaping and being shaped by each other. I will also name what the gospel is in the contemporary Korean context, namely, the gospel of reconciliation, and offer a reflection on its implications for Korean preaching and North American homiletics. Since the purpose of this paper is not an extensive historical review of how the gospel has unfolded throughout Korean history, I will focus on two significant historical events that have influenced the formation of enduring patterns of Korean context: Japanese colonialism and the division of the Korean Peninsula. Two primary reasons for the historical review are to examine the relationship of Scripture/tradition and culture/context and to uncover "the disguised suppression of the past"[5] in the present situation in order to name the gospel in the contemporary Korean context.[6] But before moving to the historical review, I will begin with examining two conversion stories of early Korean Protestants to define the relationship between Scripture/tradition and culture/context. Defining their relationship will provide a basic framework for articulating gospel in context and a particular lens through which to see how the gospel has unfolded in the history of Korea and interacted with the Korean context.

THE RELATIONSHIP BETWEEN SCRIPTURE/ TRADITION AND CULTURE/CONTEXT

While the word of the gospel itself is *extra nos*, gospel is always incarnate in context when it is proclaimed. Gospel is always communicated through various religious and cultural media such as language, symbols, and narratives. However, cultural media themselves are not neutral. They are deeply entangled with whole systems of meanings, reflecting distinctive cultures, worldviews, and values. Further, context is not a passive recipient of the gospel. David

---

5. Farley, *Practicing Gospel*, 39.

6. In this article, I focus more on the relationship of the sociopolitical context of Korea and the gospel than the religio-cultural context for two reasons. First, the sociopolitical situation not only demands an urgent response from the church and calls for homiletical theological reflection on gospel in context, but also shapes a people's way of understanding of the world and sense of identity just as religion shapes the worldview of the people. Second, the relationship of sociopolitical context of Korea and the formation of Korean preaching has not been a major subject of research in the field of homiletics, in comparison to studies about the influence of traditional religious and cultural traditions on Korean preaching. For studies about the relationship of traditional Korean religious traditions and Korean preaching, see Lee, *Korean Preaching*. Also see Kim, *Preaching the Presence of God*, 15–33.

Theologies of the Gospel in Context

Jacobsen and Robert Kelly define context as "enduring realities of culture, society, and language that shape our understanding and orient, for good or for ill, the way in which we hear the gospel."[7] In other words, context shapes the interpretive lens through which we understand the world and the Scriptures, orienting our ways of hearing the gospel, while the gospel shapes and reorients our ways of interpretation. We can neither clearly separate the gospel from culture/context, nor simply identify the gospel with culture/context. What is at stake is how to define the relationship of the gospel and context. Because naming gospel in context is the moment of interaction between Scripture/tradition and culture/context, defining the relationship between them is the starting point for the articulation of gospel. I will elaborate on my own position by examining two historical accounts of early Korean Protestant converts and the role of Scripture in their conversion and delineate my understanding of gospel at the end of this section.

A unique historical fact in the Korean Protestant church was the presence of Korean Protestant Christians and the Korean Bible even before the first Protestant missionary arrived in the Korean peninsula. The early conversion of Koreans to Christianity cannot simply be attributed to the efforts of Western missionaries because early Korean Protestant converts actively received the gospel through the subjective reading of the Chinese Bible rather than through hearing Western missionaries' preaching and teaching. According to Duk-joo Yi, a Korean church historian, Baek Hong-jun, one of the first Protestant converts, became a Christian through the self-study of a Chinese Bible.[8] After three years of self-study of the Bible, he went to China and was baptized by John MacIntyre, a Scottish missionary, in 1879. He also participated in John Ross's Korean Bible translation work and volunteered to smuggle the Korean Bible and distributed it in Korean territory, risking his life in the process and contributing to the establishment of the first Korean Protestant community in Uiju area.[9] The conversion of Yi Su-jeong in Japan shows a similar pattern. Unlike Baek, who was a commoner, Yi Su-Jeong was a *Yangban*, a noble man, and sent to Japan to study Japanese modernization programs such as law, agriculture, and the postal system. During his stay in Japan, he received the Chinese Bible from Tsudasen, a famous agriculturist and Japanese Methodist, and studied the Bible with the occasional aid of Tsudasen.[10] After earnestly reading and studying the Bible, he was deeply touched by it, received baptism, and wrote a public confession of his Christian faith in

---

7. Jacobsen and Kelly, *Kairos Preaching*, 29.
8. Lee, *Han'guk Gyohye Yiyagi (A Narrative of Korean Church)*, 20–21.
9. Kim and Kim, *A History of Korean Christianity*, 58.
10. Kim, *History of Christianity in Korea*, 107–12.

1883. Yi contributed to establishing the first Korean Protestant community in Japan and sent a petition letter to the American Mission Board for sending missionaries to Korea, earning him the title "Macedonian of Korea" among early western missionaries in Korea.[11] He also translated parts of the Chinese Bible into Korean by himself.

From these two conversion stories, we can elaborate on the relationship between Scripture/tradition and culture/context for the task of defining the gospel in context. First, Scripture/tradition witnesses to the gospel but it is not the gospel itself. The gospel witnessed by Scripture/tradition is always to be offered as an invitation in a whisper, waiting to be discovered and rearticulated as the good news for the present context by those who read them with their own cultural lens and particular concerns. As Baek and Yi discovered the good news when they read and studied the Bible, the gospel in context emerges when culture/context encounters the gospel witnessed in Scripture/tradition through a mutual dialogue. Second, culture/context is prior to Scripture/tradition in defining the gospel in the present context because culture/context determines the initial orientation of the dialogue with Scripture/tradition. Culture/context not only brings its own concerns and questions that demand responses from Scripture/tradition, but it also provides a particular cultural lens and a semiotic system to reflect on Scripture/tradition on its own terms. For example, as a member of the educated elite in the Confucian tradition, Yi interpreted the Bible through a Neo-Confucian lens, producing a unique Korean Protestant confession of faith. Yohan Bae, a systematic theologian at Presbyterian University and Theological Seminary, Korea, has examined Yi's confession of Christian faith in relation to orthodox Neo-Confucian teachings, revealing a deep connection between Yi's reading and interpretation of the Bible and the Neo-Confucian conceptual framework. For Yi, the purpose of Christian faith at the utmost level is to be in perfect unity with God, which is similar to the Confucian ideal of being a sage who lives in a perfect relationship with heaven.[12] As Confucianism emphasizes self-cultivation toward becoming a sage, so also does Yi highlight the process of sanctification in order to reach the highest level of faith, being in perfect unity with God.[13] This does not mean that Scripture/tradition is a mere resource for interpretation, but rather, it is an active dialogue partner. Yi's reading of the Bible is a moment of active interaction between a Neo-Confucian worldview and biblical worldviews through which something new emerges. While Yi's understand-

---

11. Lee, *Han'guk Gyohye Yiyagi (A Narrative of Korean Church)*, 39.

12. Bae, "Lee Ju-Jeongeui sinanggobakmunaedaehan Yugyochulhakjuk boonsuk (A Confucian Analysis of Lee Su-Jeong's Confessional Essay)," 490–91.

13. Ibid., 494–5.

ing of Christian faith has many parallels to Neo-Confucian teachings, Yi acknowledges the significance of the grace of God received through faith in the process of salvation and self-transcendence in order to reach the utmost level of faith.[14] This is a profound shift from the Neo-Confucian perspective, which emphasizes only human agency and self-cultivation in the process of becoming a sage. Although Yi discovered the gospel in the Bible through his own religious and cultural interpretive lens, the encounter with the gospel witnessed in the Bible profoundly changed his way of understanding the world and self.

In short, culture/context takes the lead in the dialogue with Scripture/tradition in the initial stage, orienting the direction of dialogue between them. Culture/context provides its own interpretive lens through which one interprets the gospel witnessed in Scripture/tradition. Contextual concerns and cultural-religious perspectives already involve the interpretation of the gospel witnessed by the Scripture/tradition from the beginning. Scripture/tradition not only provides its own understandings of gospel, but also disrupts readers' cultural and religious worldviews and values. As mutual dialogue between culture/context and Scripture/tradition continues, the gospel for the contemporary context is dialogically discovered and articulated by those who read or heard the gospel witnessed by Scripture/tradition. The gospel is not a simple solution or answer to the questions from context posed at the beginning of the dialogue. Sometimes, gospel deconstructs questions themselves and changes the direction of discourse between Scripture/tradition and culture/context, opening a completely new horizon of meanings of texts and context, and offering a new lens to interpret both culture/context and Scripture/tradition.

On the basis of this preliminary understanding of the relationship between Scripture/tradition and culture/context, I define gospel as God's liberating and life-giving act for human flourishing, peace, and reconciliation, which unfolds and incarnates in concrete historical contexts without losing its eschatological and transcendent dimension. Gospel as God's liberating and life-giving act is always and already present in every culture/context even before Christianity reaches that culture/context. Because the Trinitarian God had already been present in Asian/Korean culture through the Spirit, Eunjoo Mary Kim argues, "The context for preaching is not merely an informative resource for preaching but is the concrete locus where the preacher finds the presence and work of God the Spirit."[15] In the same sense, the gospel as God's liberating and life-giving act is present in every context and is working to transform culture/context for human flourishing, peace, and reconciliation.

---

14. Ibid., 498.
15. Kim, *Preaching the Presence of God*, 5.

Gospel as witnessed in Scripture/tradition refers to revelatory movements of encountering God's liberating and life-giving action in history. Scripture and tradition as a witness to those moments of divine encounters and memories of the revelatory moments in human history represent God as a living reality here and now and reorient our attention to the gospel, namely, God's liberating and life-giving act in the contemporary context and situation. On the one hand, gospel witnessed in Scripture and tradition as an interpretive lens not only helps us to see more clearly God's liberating and life-giving act in context, to which we have been oblivious, but it also challenges the conventional values of society and its understandings of reality. On the other hand, a new revelatory encounter with God's act in culture/context sometimes calls for a revision and renewal of understanding of the gospel as witnessed in Scripture/tradition, which involves expanding previous gospel articulations in light of what God is doing here and now. Thus, naming gospel in context is a moment in the dialogue between gospel in culture/context and gospel as witnessed in Scripture/tradition. With this preliminary understanding of the gospel witnessed in Scripture/tradition and gospel in culture/context, I will explore how the gospel has unfolded and interacts with a wider sociopolitical context throughout Korean church history.

THE GOSPEL WITNESSED AND THE GOSPEL DISCOVERED IN THE TIME OF NATIONAL CRISIS

The late nineteenth century and the early twentieth century was a time of initial dynamic interaction between Scripture/tradition and Korean culture/context which shaped the basic ethos of Korean Protestant Christianity. It was also a period of national crisis and sociopolitical upheaval caused by the geopolitics of the region. In short, Korea was in rapid decline in all aspects while surrounding countries, especially Japan, wanted to take control of it for their benefit. Furthermore, Korea became the battlefield for two wars between rival countries (the Sino-Japan War in 1895 and the Russo-Japanese War in 1904) and a prize for the winner. After winning two wars, Japan declared Korea a protectorate in 1905 and annexed Korea in 1910. Koreans suffered from Japanese colonial rule until they were liberated in 1945. It is during this time of national crisis and rapid social change that Western missionaries arrived in Korea, proclaiming the good news since 1884. What was the gospel proclaimed by Western missionaries? Did Koreans hear the glad tidings? How did the gospel interact with the context?

Theologies of the Gospel in Context

Due to the theological and denominational diversity of early missionaries, it is difficult to find a monolithic understanding of the gospel among them. However, there were common theological threads that unified missionaries' differences, namely, puritanical zeal, pietistic faith, and nineteenth-century evangelicalism.[16] Depending on the denomination, a certain type of faith and theology is more prominent than the other two aspects. For Presbyterians, puritanical faith was the most prominent; while for Methodists, pietistic faith was the most prominent. Nevertheless, missionaries shared all three features. In this perspective, the general characteristics of missionaries' theology were a belief in the absolute authority of the Bible, christocentric faith, an emphasis on individual salvation by faith, and the importance of personal moral living. Furthermore, the separation between the church and the nation was missionaries' basic stance on the church-state relationship, keeping the church away from political affairs.[17] These characteristics of the missionaries' theology influenced their understandings of the gospel that were reflected in their preaching. Jangmyeon Jung analyzed some missionaries' sermons, which were published in journals of the three denominations, Presbyterian, Methodist, and the Holiness churches, during Japanese colonialism. He identifies the following characteristics of missionary preaching as shared among the three denominations: first, denominational differences were not clearly represented in sermons. Sermons commonly reflected evangelical theology emphasizing personal salvation through Jesus Christ by faith and highlighted strict moral living for Christians. Second, doctrines were the main content of sermons, particularly Christology, and the sermon form, in general, was deductive-topical preaching. Third, no sermon dealt with social and political issues. Sermons focus on individual moral transformation, not social transformation.[18] From these characteristics of missionaries' theology and sermons, we can surmise some of the missionaries' general understanding of the gospel as truth for the individual and spiritual salvation through Jesus Christ by faith in the Bible. Although missionaries had to adopt cultural media to communicate the gospel, a christological focus and a high view of the Bible as the word of God created an asymmetrical relationship of Scripture/tradition and culture/context in understanding the gospel. The primary task of preaching is to interpret and explicate the Bible in terms of traditions and doctrines for the life-giving

---

16. Yi, *Chogi Nehan Sugyosadulye Sinanggw Sinhak (Early Missionaries' Faith and Theology)*, 50–58.

17. Kim and Kim, *A History of Korean Christianity*, 90.

18. Jung, "Chogi Sungyosadulyeo Sulgyoye Gwanhan Yeongu (A Study On Early Missionaries' Sermons)," 310–11.

message of spiritual salvation.[19] Thus, missionaries' theological orientations mainly determined the message of the gospel for preaching rather than the contextual needs of hearers. Furthermore, missionaries' policy of separating the church from politics made the gospel silent about sociopolitical situations in Korea. In fact, the missionaries' initial attitude toward the Japanese colonial state was very friendly, accepting the administration with loyal recognition.[20] The missionaries encouraged Korean Christians not to get involved in political activities such as the independence movement in opposition to Japanese rule. Furthermore, all publications, including the weekly church's paper, had been censored, and all church activities monitored by the Japanese colonial government since the mid-1920s.[21] To protect the church from political turbulence, the missionaries tried to depoliticize Korean Christian churches and did not preach about social and political issues and therefore lost the public aspect of the gospel and the prophetic role of preaching.

Did Koreans hear the gospel from missionaries' preaching? Yes, Koreans heard the gospel. However, the gospel Koreans heard was not identical to the gospel missionaries proclaimed. Arthur J. Brown, a missionary and General Secretary of the Presbyterian Board of Foreign Missions in the early twentieth century, described that "He [the Korean] came to Christianity out of deeper sorrows than the self-confident Chinese and the masterful Japanese . . . . The oppressed, despairing, impoverished, emotional Korean approach Christ from a different angle than the proud, ambitious, and all conquering Japanese."[22] Unlike missionaries, it was the urgent sociopolitical situation that determined Koreans' way of hearing the gospel, not doctrinal frameworks. In examining the rapid expansion of Christianity in the late nineteenth and the early twentieth centuries, Chung-shin Park points out the fact that Christianity started to rapidly grow right after the Sino-Japan War in 1895 and the Russo-Japanese War in 1904. He argues that this rapid growth of Christianity resulted from the emergence of the threat of Japanese imperialism.[23] When their country became a protectorate of Japan, despairing Koreans came to the church in search of new hope for living and a new way to rebuild a powerful

19. The missionaries' understandings of preaching in the three denominations commonly emphasize the centrality of the Bible for preaching. Although some missionaries acknowledged the significance of context for preaching, context was always secondary for the task of preaching. See Jung, 289, 296, 302. Also see S. Jung, "Han'guk Gyohye Sulgyosacho I (A History of Preaching in Korean Protestant Church I)," 179–83.

20. Kang, "Church and State Relations in the Japanese Colonial Period," 98.

21. Ibid., 106.

22. Brown, *The Mastery of the Far East the Story of Korea's Transformation and Japan's Rise to Supremacy in the Orient*, 539.

23. Park, "Protestantism in Late Confucian Korea," 152.

nation. However, crises in the late nineteenth century and the early twentieth centuries were not merely political crises, but more profoundly an identity crisis. Traditionally, China was "the significant other" in the formation of Korean national identity culturally and politically. Confucianism from China provided a religious and theoretical foundation for Korean social order and ethics in which loyalty to the king and filial piety to parents constituted the two pillars of the basic social relationship. Kinship and the social relationship determined individual identity in Confucian society. The decentering of China and the destruction of the old Korean kingdom Chosun at the hands of Japan not only destroyed a traditional "Sino-centered" political order and the sovereignty of Korea, but also dismantled the Confucian social structure in Korea that was the basis for ethics and Korean identity. This crisis of Korean identity attracted many Koreans to Christianity.[24]

Koreans approached Christianity with their own sociopolitical concerns, which determined the initial direction of dialogue between gospel and context. This is not to say that the gospel proclaimed by missionaries was a mere inspiring resource for interpretation. Rather the gospel as witnessed by the Bible and missionaries were active dialogue partners. The Bible and missionaries' preaching provided their own understandings of the gospel from their own perspectives and reoriented the initial direction of the dialogue by providing new ideas and posing new questions to context. For example, missionaries' theological understanding of the gospel as personal salvation through Jesus Christ by faith challenged the traditional notion of self in Korean society, introducing a new way of understanding self as an individual. In traditional Confucian society, the sense of self was derived from a community and individuals existed only as part of the community. A community is prior to a person and submission to social norms is the way to reach the utmost level of sacredness that is the will of heaven.[25] The missionaries' emphasis on the active role of the individual in conversion and the importance of personal responsibility for faith and moral living reversed the priority between the community and the person, offering a new sense of self derived from one's personal relationship with God. Thus, the gospel proclaimed by missionaries altered early Korean Christians' traditional understanding of human beings, which was based on Confucian philosophy and social structure, and influenced their way of seeking a solution to the crisis of Korean identity. This does not mean that the Christian gospel completely destroyed the Korean cultural identity and the traditional values of the community, which many Asian countries experienced during the Western colonial period. Rather, the

24. Kim and Kim, *A History of Korean Christianity*, 79–81.
25. Kim, *The Development of Modern South Korea*, 52.

gospel witnessed by missionaries propelled and drove Korean Christians to search for a new national identity, which contributed to the emergence of Korean nationalism under Japanese colonialism. Kenneth M. Wells examines the relationship between Christianity and Korean nationalism and defines Korean Christian nationalism as "Self-Reconstruction Nationalism." Self-reconstruction nationalists thought that the fundamental causes of Korea's colonial fate were "an absence of moral fortitude and spiritual integrity, which was manifested in factionalism, a lack of public morality and a fatal tendency to rely on larger powers in times of both peace and crisis."[26] What was needed was to reform national character through the spiritual and moral reconstruction of individuals. Korean Christians believed that personal spiritual awakening and moral renewal through the Christian faith would not only change individuals' lives but also transform national character so as to eventually lead Korea to independence from Japan. For Christian nationalists, the self-reconstruction of individuals and national character was fundamentally a spiritual task rather than a nationalist strategy.[27] Thus, the gospel heard by Korean Christians emerged through a mutual dialogue between the gospel as witnessed by missionaries and particular concerns for sociopolitical crises. In the interaction between the gospel as witnessed and Koreans' sociopolitical experience, something new arose, namely, the gospel of liberation through the spiritual and moral renewal of individuals and national character. In other words, Koreans discovered the gospel in the Korean context, recognizing God's liberating and life-giving act for Korea oppressed by the Japanese empire. While the gospel proclaimed by missionaries consisted of apolitical messages of spiritual salvation and personal transformation, the gospel discovered by Korean Christians was the glad tidings of personal salvation, social transformation and political liberation through personal moral renewal, all of which served as resources for resisting Japanese colonial rule. The gospel discovered by early Korean Christians was, therefore, both spiritual and political.

Unlike the missionaries, Korean Protestant leaders frequently preached about Korean independence. According to Qu-hwan Park, many Korean Protestant preachers' sermons in the early period of Japanese colonial rule presented a strong sense of patriotic spirit and evoked a spirit of resistance against the Japanese rule by employing biblical metaphors and motifs such as Exodus and the Babylonian Exile and identifying suffering Korea with captive Israel.[28] The liberation motif in the Bible provides a firm theological basis for

26. Wells, *New God, New Nation*, 10.

27. Ibid.

28 Park, "Iljaegangjumgi Gaesingyosulgyoeui natanan Gydokgyosinangkwa Minjokgoukgaeuisik (Christian Faith and National Consciousness in Protestant Sermons during

hope for national independence. This does not mean that Korean preachers merely used the Christian message for the political task of independence from Japan. In response to the contextual needs of that time, Korean Protestant leaders developed a national consciousness and spirit of independence, which was deeply rooted in their Christian faith, and contributed to the formation of modern Korean nationalism.[29] This means the missionaries' attempt to depoliticize Korean Christianity failed.[30] In other words, the gospel as witnessed by missionaries is not the same as the gospel discovered by Korean Christians. Even those who witnessed to the gospel could not control the power of gospel responding to the wound of the context. The gospel influenced the transformation of the context while the context also expanded the scope of the gospel, embracing sociopolitical dimensions of the good news. The gospel sown in Korean soil by the missionaries bore unexpected fruit: Korean Christian nationalism and the March First Independence Movement in 1919.

The March First Independence Movement was a peaceful protest against the Japanese colonial state. Unfortunately, the March First Independence Movement failed due to the violent suppression of the Japanese government, and the Korean Protestant church became a main target of that suppression and surveillance. As a result, the majority of Korean Protestant Christians withdrew from political involvement in the independence movement and pursued a purely religious path, separating Christian faith from politics. Turning away from sociopolitical issues, Korean sermons after the mid-1920s often emphasized individual piety, repentance, and holy living. What distinguished them from sermons in the earlier period was that preachers tended to spiritualize and individualize every matter in our lives, even social problems, and described them as sins of individuals that needed to be addressed by personal repentance rather than social transformation. In this way, preachers made hearers accept the current social order and norms and thus Korean Christianity had lost its public dimension of the gospel.[31] Furthermore, the suppression under Japan also influenced the consolidation of some features of Korean Protestant popular religiosity like "ethical-theological conservatism," "faith

---

the Japanese Occupation)," 254.

29. Christianity is not the only resource for Korean nationalism. Many nationalist groups such as socialist and communist ones existed in Korea during the Japanese colonial rule. Christianity contributed to the formation of cultural nationalism that emphasized nurturing new leaders of the younger generation, who would educate people and awaken national spirit for independence, through modern education. For Christian cultural nationalism, see Choi, "Christianity and Nationalism in East Asia," 35.

30. Park, "Iljaegangjumgi Gaesingyosulgyoeui, (Christian Faith and National Consciousness,)" 259.

31. Ibid., 262.

seeking blessings," and a premillennial eschatological orientation.[32] Although these characteristics of Korean Protestant religiosity emerged as a response to the particular sociopolitical situation of oppression, this religiosity has profoundly oriented, for good or for ill, the way of hearing the gospel for subsequent generations of Korean Protestants. What is necessary is to rediscover and rearticulate the gospel in relation to the contemporary context, expanding the narrowly articulated understanding of the gospel prevalent during the Japanese colonial period and recovering sociopolitical dimensions of the good news.

THE DEEP SCAR ON THE KOREAN PENINSULA AND THE GOSPEL OF RECONCILIATION

In search of the meaning of Korean history, Sok Hon Ham, a philosopher, historian, and social activist in Korea, contended that the basic thrust of Korean history is suffering.[33] The geopolitical location of Korea made it "the Queen of Suffering."[34] As a relatively small country in the midst of powerful ones, Korea has continuously experienced numerous foreign invasions by surrounding countries throughout its history. Korea often became the battlefield between rival countries and was occupied by the winner, Japan, for thirty-six years. Although Korea was liberated from Japan in 1945, Korea did not gain its independence. Korea was divided by two global superpowers, the United States and the Soviet Union. Bruce Cumings argues that Korea's division was the result of the ideological division associated with the Cold War.[35] A few days before Japan's surrender on August 15, 1945, two young US military officers arbitrarily decided on the thirty-eighth parallel for the dividing line of Korea in order to secure the capital city of Korea, Seoul, in the American zone, and the Soviet Union accepted the United States' proposal.[36] No Koreans were involved in this decision-making process. Thus, the decision of Korea's division was unilateral. Most Koreans viewed the United States as a liberator from Japan. However, what historically and politically happened was the United States' occupation of Korea. Cumings contends, "the United States occupied Korea . . . and set up a full military government that lasted for three years and

---

32. Kim and Kim, *A History of Korean Christianity*, 139–43.
33. Ham, *Queen of Suffering*, 19.
34. Ibid., 22–24.
35. Cumings, *Korea's Place in the Sun*, 188.
36. Ibid., 187.

deeply shaped postwar Korean history."[37] During this military occupation, the US military government actively interfered with the internal political affairs of Korea, suppressing political voices from the left wing and establishing a pro-American Korean government. During the same period, North Korea became a communist country with the support of the Soviet Union. Korea soon became another battlefield between two competing ideological parties whose war devastated the entire peninsula. Thus, the pain of suffering and sorrow, which was imposed upon Koreans by foreign countries, has been deeply engraved in the life of Koreans. According to Andrew Sung Park, these traumatic experiences of foreign invasions, wars, political oppressions, and unjust sufferings over many generations create collective unconscious *han*, the critical wound of the heart. *Han* of the past has been transmitted from generation to generation through the framework of ethnic ethos, tradition, and culture, still impacting the present lives of Koreans.[38] The Korean Demilitarized Zone (DMZ) which runs across the Korean Peninsula most vividly visualizes the collective experience of *han* and a deep scar in the heart of every Korean. No one would oppose reading the contemporary sociopolitical situation of Korea as a wound that demands a response of change. If the gospel is to be the good news, it must, in the first place, respond to the *han* of the people and heal the deepest wounds in their hearts. The first step for the positive disintegration of *han* is awakening: recognition of the reality of *han* and identification of the cause of *han*.[39] I will begin with identifying the cause of *han* in divided Korea in order to name the gospel in context as the response to *han* since I have demonstrated the reality of *han*.

On the surface, the division of Korea caused by two foreign powers, the tragic experience of the Korean war and the enduring division of Korea for seventy years are the root causes of *han*. However, the real cause of *han* is what has made this reality of the division of Korea self-perpetuating. To identify the cause of *han* in relation to the task of preaching the gospel, we need to frame the complex contemporary sociopolitical situation of Korea to make it more manageable. Mary McClintock Fulkerson provides valuable insights for this task. In framing a situation by using a postmodern theory of place, Fulkerson defines place as "a gathering of meanings that endures through practices."[40] Place has a unity, holding diverse elements together in a particular configuration that creates a kind of unified reality, and its enduring pattern is sustained

---

37. Cumings, *The Korean War*, 104.
38. Park, *The Wounded Heart of God*, 38–41.
39. Ibid.,138.
40. Fulkerson, *Places of Redemption*, 36.

by ongoing practices.[41] From this perspective, we need to consider the following: first, how various elements such as power and memory relating to North Korea have been ordered in a particular configuration, creating a kind of unified reality; and second, what practices sustain this enduring pattern of reality, namely, the division of North and South Korea. Preaching the gospel may not change the situation itself, but it can alter some core practices that sustain the persisting pattern of division.

The traumatic experience of the Korean War and the prolonged military tension between the two Koreas have profoundly shaped political discourse and practices. Although the Cold War ended long ago, the dominant political framework and the image of North Korea as the primary enemy are still entrenched in the Cold War era. In the unstable political situation of the divided Korea, national security has always been of the utmost importance and has united various sociopolitical elements in a particular configuration. Inner social and political conflicts between parties or different social groups always decrease as the tension between North and South Korea mounts. However, security and insecurity are a matter of the political imagination in response to external circumstances rather than reality itself. The North and South Korean states monopolize all aspects of security and strictly control cross-border relations. Due to the absence of face-to-face relationships among the ordinary citizens of North and South Korea, the two states construct and reproduce the particular image of the other Korea as a threat to national security, evoking old memories of the war and provoking fear toward one another. States construct a kind of unified social and political reality through national security practices. Furthermore, states' imaginative political construction of reality has profoundly shaped the Korean identity. People derive their identity from various sources such as family, religion, and ethnicity. However, the Cold War and the experience of the Korean War have made ideological identification as the prevailing factor that shapes the Korean identity over all others.[42] In other words, the dominant factor that determines the Korean identity is one's ideological identification either with communism or capitalism. In this sense, Ronal Bleiker argues, "Identity in Korea is essentially constructed in negative terms; that is, in direct opposition to the other side of the divided nation."[43] He also points out that antagonistic identity practices by states are the main source of tension between North and South Korea.[44] The North and South Korean states have not only controlled individuals' images of the sociopolitical reality,

---

41. Ibid., 28, 32.
42. Bleiker, *Divided Korea*, 10.
43. Bleiker, "Identity and Security in Korea," 126.
44. Bleiker, *Divided Korea*, 18.

but it also shaped Korean identity. This exclusive and antagonistic identity construction becomes a source of oppression and discrimination against all "others" who do not belong to the in-group. The difference is often regarded as a threat to the unity of the society. Thus, the cause of *han* perpetuating the division of Korea is rooted in the sociopolitical construction and reproduction of antagonistic identities by the states in the name of national security.

Unfortunately, except for a few progressive Protestant churches, the most conservative Korean Protestant churches internalized the antagonistic identity imposed by the state. Instead of being agents of reconciliation, Korean Protestant churches became institutions that largely reproduce the anti-communist identity, stimulating fear and hatred toward North Korea. The primary reason why Korean Protestant churches were made vulnerable to the state's manipulation is the principle of separation of church and state, keeping political affairs apart from the church and the pulpit. Due to the strong influence of missionaries on the Korean Protestant church's understanding of the church-state relationship and the Japanese suppression of the church, Korean Protestant churches separated spiritual matters from political matters. Consequently, Korean Protestant churches often unconsciously accepted an imaginative binary sociopolitical construction of reality by the states and internalized an antagonistic identity that has profoundly shaped many Korean Christians' way of hearing the gospel. Due to the internalization of such an exclusive system of identity, Korean Protestant churches have gotten "the Korean disease."[45] Korean Protestant churches have frequently developed dualistic and antagonistic ways of reasoning that lead to the division of Korean churches. Korean Protestant churches have often labeled those who have different interpretations of the Scripture as heretics or less pure churches. Dualistic and antagonistic ways of thinking hinder Korean Protestant churches from working together for the reconciliation of Korea. Another obstacle to Korean Protestant churches becoming agents of reconciliation is the prevailing influence of Korean Protestant popular religiosity that has shaped Korean Protestant Christians' way of hearing the gospel. This does not mean that Korean Protestant popular religiosity is entirely negative. Korean Protestant popular religiosity is the outcome of a sincere religious quest for the Christian faith in response to a particular cultural and sociopolitical situation of suppression and suffering under Japanese colonial rule. In short, Korean Protestant popular religiosity contributes to the formation of the conservative ethos of Korean

---

45. The Korean disease refers to some negative characteristic of Koreans society such as "extreme clannishness, stubborn regionalism, excessive loyalty to the alumni network, fanatical sectarianism, pretentious classism and deep-seated patriarchy." See Min, "The Division and Reunification of a Nation," 269.

Protestant churches seeking for *status quo*, a faith of seeking this-worldly blessing and other-worldly salvation. The gospel is often narrowly understood as the good news about personal spiritual salvation by faith or material and spiritual blessings in Korean Protestant popular religiosity. Hence, Korean Protestant churches have lost their prophetic voice for society. One theological task of preaching is critical reflection on Korean Protestant popular religiosity and its ways of understanding the gospel. Such reflection would discern its positive and negative contributions for preaching the gospel. If necessary, preaching as a theological act has to deconstruct the popular understanding of the gospel and propose a new way of understanding the gospel. In other words, an essential theological task of preaching is to articulate a provisional theology of the gospel in relation to the contemporary Korean context. What is the gospel in the contemporary sociopolitical situation of divided Korea? It is the gospel of reconciliation.

THE GOSPEL OF RECONCILIATION: SEEKING FOR AN ALTERNATIVE SOURCE AND WAY OF IDENTITY CONSTRUCTION IN THE DIVIDED KOREA

As I have delineated, one of the main causes of *han* that permeates a divided Korea is the state's imaginative construction of an antagonistic identity toward the other Korea. To be good news, in the first place, the gospel must be a response to this wound in the Korean situation. Preaching the gospel of reconciliation has both deconstructive and constructive tasks: revealing a disguised oppressive structure of contemporary binary identity politics in Korea, and offering alternative sources and ways of identity construction rooted in the Christian story that contributes to the formation of a culture of reconciliation and the peaceful unification of the Korean peninsula. This does not mean that the gospel of reconciliation always has to deal with the sociopolitical issues of the reconciliation of divided Korea. Rather the good news is that who we are is ultimately defined by how God relates to us. Although the experience and memory of the past, the way we relate to ourselves, and the way others relate to us do shape our identity, the Christian believes that his/her identity is fundamentally defined in relation to God who loves him/her, creates him/her, relates to him/her and calls him/her into communion with God, other fellow human beings and all creation. Thus, the gospel of reconciliation ultimately tells us who we truly are.

However, accepting Christian accounts of identity does not preclude the possibility of other accounts of identity, nor does it seek a monolithic

Christian identity. Diverse sociopolitical and religious accounts of identity compete with each other in Korean society and mutually influence each other. What is at stake is finding a way to reconnect Christian accounts of identity to the public sphere in order to define and redefine Korean identity in ways that enable peace and reconciliation in the Korean peninsula. Ananda Abeysekara's postcolonial understanding of the relationship between the religious and the secular, and "identity for and against self" provide a useful theoretical framework for this task. In search for a form of criticism in the study of postcolonial religion, Abeysekara challenges common assumptions in western academia about the normalization of the division between the religious and the secular and the Self-Other binary identity construction. By examining conflicts in Sri Lanka between Tamil rebels and the Buddhists, Abeysekara shows how the classical Western theoretical frameworks fail to grasp the complexity of identity negotiations between the Self and the Other in Sri Lanka. He also demonstrates how the secular state in Sri Lanka found a particular religious ally for the defense of its proposal that enhance peace among conflicting parties.[46] His argument was not that the distinctions between secular and religious should be completely erased, but "the debates and disputes about what such distinctions should embody, how and in what kinds of ways they should be drawn, take place in discursive spaces not determined by the available conceptions of the public and the private."[47] In this way, he destabilizes and pluralizes the dominant Western understanding of the relationship between religion and secularism, opening up new possibilities for redefining their relationship in discursive space. From this perspective, religions in Korea, including Christianity, can be sources of defining Korean national identity in ways that foster peace and reconciliation between the two Koreas. Crossing conventional boundaries between the public/secular and the private/religious, Korean Christianity can participate in the wider discourses and practices of Korean national identity construction from the standpoint of the Christian faith.

Abeysekara opposes binary constructions of identity in terms of the self and the other. Although identity is configured and reconfigured on the basis of a number of Otherings, Abeysekara argues that the moment of identity for and against itself is "a moment of debate and dissent in which the Sinhalas and Tamils, Muslims and Hindus, contend to disrupt and contest both between (i.e., Buddhists arguing with Tamils) and among themselves (i.e., Buddhists arguing with Buddhists) the normalized practices and discourses of exclusion

---

46. Abeysekara, "Identity for and Against Itself," 993.
47. Ibid., 986.

of "Others" by virtue of their supposed intrinsic qualities of "otherness."[48] In other words, the Self or identity of in-group is also divided in the moment of defining the Self in relation to the Other. No hegemonic identity can claim its privileged position in this public space of debate in which various claims of the Self contest and disrupt the predominant and normalized discourse of the Self. Thus, the moment of identity for and against self is a moment of the political, namely, what he calls "a moment of agonism as opposed to antagonism,"[49] a moment of destabilizing the normalized discourse of binary identity construction. In this public space of debate between diverse identity claims, an ethic of "care for the Self" is necessary, but at the same time, it must be an ethic of "care for the Other."[50] In the Korean context, a political account of Korean identity is the normalized discourse of the Korean Self and supported by the government. Korean Christianity can participate in public discourses of Korean national identity formation as an Other Self, or as an identity against the Self, which destabilize the normalized discourse of Korean identity by the state. It can contribute to reconfiguring the normalized binary construction of identity between North and South Korea in ways that enable peace and reconciliation between two Koreas. On the one hand, instead of giving ideology absolute authority to determine Korean identity, Christians can take a critical distance from the dominant discourse of identity, discern and make a judgment against evil in dominant sociopolitical identity construction by accepting the good news that we are fundamentally who we are because of God. On the other hand, we can also be aware of the diversity of Christian identities by recognizing and respecting otherness of the Self. For the task of reconciliation in the divided Korea, nurturing distinctive Christian identities is necessary.

Antagonistic Korean identity is built on painful memories of the Korean War and politically constructed narratives of North Korea as a threat to national security. However, Christian identities are on the basis of the gospel of reconciliation, which is rooted in the passion narrative of Jesus Christ, namely, the story of reconciliation between God, and gospel in context, namely, God's liberating and life-giving act in Korean context. Keenly aware of "the scandal of the cross,"[51] Miroslav Volf places the cross at the center of Christian iden-

---

48. Ibid., 977.
49. Ibid., 994–95.
50. Ibid., 996.
51. Although Volf acknowledges diverse critiques of the idea of divine self-donation on the cross, he still values the idea of God's self-giving love on the cross as a theological resource for Christian identity and social ethics in the violent world. Volf, *Exclusion and Embrace*, 26–27.

tity. He points out two dimensions of the cross: "self-giving love which overcomes human enmity and the creation of space in himself to receive estranged humanity."[52] God embraces hostile humanity into divine communion with God on the cross through self-giving love. God's will to embrace us through self-giving love is prior to our repentance. This is the good news because God already loves us before we change. Through faith, we can open ourselves to God's self-giving love that transforms us and gives us a new identity. The way God relates to us is also a model for how we ought to relate to others. "Will to give ourselves to others and 'welcome' them, to readjust our identities to make space for them, is prior to any judgment about others."[53] As the triune God relates to us with the will to embrace us, the will to embrace others is prior to any other elements in relating to others including North Korea. Instead of coercing others to be changed, we must have the will to readjust our identity to make space for them so that they can come to us as they are.

Anchoring Christian identities to a God-given identity in the Christian narrative may seem to be an effort to establish a fixed identity in terms of a particular religious essence, solidifying a boundary between Christians (the Self) and non-Christians (the Other). However, it is impossible to make any claims of identity and judgment against the practices of exclusion without boundaries or a particular center. If the Korean church does not have its distinctive identities, differentiating itself as a counter-community from the wider Korean society, it cannot resist the state's exclusive identity politics. Volf argues that the center of the self for Christian is a decentered center, namely, Jesus Christ and self-giving love represented on the cross lies at the center of the decentered center.[54] Volf locates the center of the self not in some unchangeable essence, but in self-giving love, which is radically open to others. In the same sense, Richard Lischer points out that the most distinctive feature of Christian identity is "its willingness to risk itself by embracing others."[55] Thus, Christian identities are not a self-enclosed, fixed, and exclusive identity rooted in some religious essence. Rather, Christian identities are more fluid and open to change in relation to others. In this perspective, Christian identities can effectively challenge the we-they binary in the state's identity politics and blurred politically constructed boundaries between North and South Korea without being trapped in essentialist identity politics. Christians, who have a decentered center as the center of self, cannot passively accept an antagonistic identity that is built on the will to exclude others. The gospel

52. Ibid., 127.
53. Ibid., 29.
54. Ibid., 70–71.
55. Lischer, *The End of Words*, 134.

of reconciliation based on the passion of Jesus Christ challenges antagonistic identity practices by states. The good news calls us to repent of enmity toward others and change ourselves, inviting us to be agents of reconciliation.

Another resource for the gospel of reconciliation is based on God's liberating and life-giving act, which has already been present in Korean context. In other words, any traditional cultural and religious heritage that enhances a culture of reconciliation can be a valuable resource for articulating the gospel of reconciliation in the Korean context and Korean Christian identities. Sam-kyung Park introduces a contextual theological understanding of reunification in *Sangsaeng* Theology. *Sangsaeng* theology has incorporated the traditional cultural and religious concept of *haewon-sangsangseng* in theological reflection and articulated ethical principles that guide the process of reunification. *Haewon* refers to the resolution of all grudges and resentments and *sangsaeng* means living together.[56] The concept of *haewon* particularly relates to reconciliation and healing broken relationships. *Haewon* is composed of two Chinese words: *hae* means "to resolve" and *won* means "emotion of fury, frustration, unresolved resentment against oppression and injustices suffered, a sense of helplessness, and a feeling of total abandonment."[57] Accumulation of *won* becomes *han*, a critical wound of the heart. *Haewon* is the first step toward reconciliation and healing broken relationships between people. The gospel of reconciliation in the divided Korea must enable resolution of any accumulated resentment between North and South Korea. Korean *minjung*, the oppressed, had overcome present suffering and resolve *won/han* caused by unjust sociopolitical oppression through various cultural performances such as the mask dance and religious rituals such as *Kut*, a traditional shamanistic ritual. The primary religious purpose of *Kut* was to resolve the *won/han* of the deceased. However, like mask dance, *Kut* as a social practice and cultural performance becomes a cathartic moment for those who participate in it. The various experiences of unjust suffering and emotions of *won/han* are dramatically re-presented and religiously and artistically resolved in *Kut*. For the task of *haewon*, preaching the gospel of reconciliation should reflect the reality of suffering by the division of North and South Korea, bringing unspoken pains and suffering into view and helping people transcend them in a positive way. However, the more fundamental reason for reflecting the reality of suffering in articulating the gospel of reconciliation is theological. In his search for meanings of the cross in relation to the lynching tree, James Cone argues that the cross needs the lynching tree as much as the lynching tree needs the

---

56. Park, "The Notion of Reconciliation in Sangsaeng Theology for Korean Reunification," 97.

57. Ibid., 98.

cross. "The cross needs the lynching tree to remind Americans of the reality of suffering—to keep the cross from becoming a symbol of abstract, sentimental piety.... Yet the lynching tree also needs the cross, without which it becomes simply an abomination."[58] The cross becomes a mere religious symbol of abstract, losing its transformative power without recognizing the cross in our social reality, in the case of Korea, the division of North and South Korea. As the cross and the lynching tree interpret each other, the cross and the reality of suffering in the divided Korean context mutually interpret each other. Instead of unilaterally representing theological voices from the Christian tradition in articulating the gospel of reconciliation, like *minjung* theology, we need to embrace concrete stories of separated families' suffering and their *won/han* by the division and their experiences of God in the midst of their suffering. From perspectives of their experiences, theological understandings of the cross can be challenged, tested, and revised, and God's liberating and life-giving act in Korean context can be discovered. Through this inductive way of doing theology, the gospel of reconciliation does not lose its relevance to the context, but it also can contribute to resolving *won/han* of those who suffer from the division.

Robert Schreiter points out the significance of healing memory and of hope for social reconciliation.[59] Because memory continuously shapes our past and present identity, without healing traumatic memories of the past such as the Korean War, there can be no reconciliation between North and South Korea. Further, reconciliation is a long and even unfinished process. Therefore, we cannot continue to work for reconciliation without hope. In this sense, we need to redeem the traumatic memories of the Korean War and the narrations of the memories that continuously shape the collective identity of Koreans, and retain our hope that the reconciliation and the unification of the Korean peninsula is possible. The gospel of reconciliation can guide this process. Although the gospel of reconciliation closely relates to the passion narrative of Jesus Christ, it is essentially linked to the broad Christian story, namely, creation, redemption and final consummation. By placing our painful memories of the Korean War into this broader Christian narrative and memory, new connections between the traumatic memory of the war and the sacred memory of God are made from which new meanings of the past memories and a new vision for the future can gradually emerge.[60] Further,

---

58. Cone, *The Cross and the Lynching Tree*, 161.

59. Schreiter, "Establishing a Shared Identity," 13.

60. Schreiter and Volf propose a similar argument about the relationship of healing memory and the sacred memory of communities. See Schreiter, "Establishing a Shared Identity," 18–19. See also Volf, *The End of Memory*, 96–102.

Christian narrative provides the theological ground for hope for reconciliation. This hope is not based on blind optimism, but on the eschatological vision of the final reconciliation. The final reconciliation is God's work, not our work, so it is grace. However, the gospel of reconciliation also calls people to work for "a nonfinal reconciliation based on a vision of reconciliation that cannot be undone."[61] Preaching the gospel of reconciliation is a moment of reenactment of the sacred memories of the past, the communal memory of the Passion, and the memory of the future, that is, the vision of eschatological reconciliation. By drawing hearers from the present into this sacred moment of encountering God, preaching the gospel of reconciliation prophetically can "nurture, nourish, and evoke a consciousness and perception alternative to the consciousness and perception of the dominant culture around us,"[62] resisting states' imposition of an antagonistic identity and finding radically inclusive, fluid Christian identities rooted in the Christian story.

IMPLICATIONS FOR KOREAN PREACHING AND NORTH AMERICAN HOMILETICS

The strong influence of Western missionaries in the early period of the Korean Protestant church and the persisting effect of Korean Protestant popular religiosity have influenced and shaped basic characteristics of Korean preaching. These common features of Korean preaching are personal spiritual salvation, exclusive commitment to Christianity, and search for this-worldly blessing and other-worldly salvation. Its message is very apolitical and often acontextual. As I have delineated in this article, these features of Korean preaching, as well as dominant Korean Protestant churches' understanding of the gospel, developed as a response to particular religio-cultural and sociopolitical situations throughout history. However, the gospel named in the past is not always good news in the present. Sometimes, it makes us oblivious to evil in a new context. Therefore, the gospel named in the present context not only challenges a hidden reality of evil in the world, but also expands the scope of the gospel articulated in the past. The gospel of reconciliation is social and political by nature. It challenges Korean Protestant churches' apolitical articulation of the gospel and makes them reconsider the church's blind acceptance of the political construction of reality and identity by states. The gospel of reconciliation makes the boundary between church and state or between spiritual matters and political matters blurred and porous. In fact, both theology and politics

---

61. Volf, *Exclusion and Embrace*, 110.
62. Brueggemann, *The Prophetic Imagination*, 3.

are "disciplined imaginations of space and time"[63] in different ways. Hence, we cannot simply separate church and politics. What is necessary is to recover sociopolitical aspects of the gospel as the early Korean Christians recognized. Instead of only focusing on personal and spiritual salvation, Korean preaching needs to recover a prophetic voice and enter into the public sphere in order to contribute to the creation of a culture of reconciliation and a shared identity.

Preaching the gospel of reconciliation is postcolonial preaching in a Korean context. Sarah Travis points out that the era of colonialism/imperialism seems to have ended long ago but colonialism/imperialism as well as colonial discourse continues in different guises even today. Colonialism and imperialism as present sociopolitical realities affect Christian identity, distorting human relationships by hindering discourses of love and friendship.[64] While "colonizing discourse seeks to fix identities and social relationship into a hierarchy of categories,"[65] decolonizing preaching disrupts colonizing discourse and its binary identity construction. Based on postcolonial theories and the understanding of the social Trinity, Travis relates the perichoretic space of the Trinity with a postcolonial concept of Third Space in which our identities and others' identities are formed and reformed in relation to self, others, and God.[66] In the same sense, Kwok Pui-lan, a postcolonial feminist theologian, defines postcolonial preaching as "a locally rooted and globally conscious performance that seeks to create a Third Space so that the faith community can imagine new ways of being in the world and encountering God's salvific action for the oppressed and marginalized."[67] A Third Space is the "in-between space" where different cultures and identities meet and a new hybrid identity is forged. It transgresses clear boundaries that sustain the separation between self and other, challenging the tyranny of binary logic and exclusive identity politics. Antagonistic identity politics in divided Korea is a residue of the Cold War that ideologically colonized Korea after the liberation from Japan. The gospel of reconciliation seeks to create a Third Space where the binary and antagonistic construction of Korean identity becomes blurred and a hybrid identity, which enables us to move beyond anti-community and anti-capitalist Korean identities, can be forged. By accepting that our identity is ultimately defined by God, we can take a critical distance from where we belong and create space for others and embrace them as part of our own identity. Instead of seeking a homogeneous identity, preaching the gospel of reconciliation aims

63. Cavanaugh, *Theopolitical Imagination*, 1–3.
64. Travis, *Decolonizing Preaching*, 54.
65. Ibid., 29.
66. Ibid., 129.
67. Pui-lan, "Postcolonial Preaching in Intercultural Contexts," 10.

to destabilize hearers from the common sense of antagonistic identity by exposing the hidden reality of identity constructions by states.

By deconstructing a rigid and exclusive system of identity, the gospel of reconciliation not only aims to contribute to the reconciliation of North and South Korea, but also reveals structural evils within Korean society such as racism, sexism, and the oppression of LGBTQ communities. Due to excessive emphasis on a univocal Korean identity based on a closed partisan system of identity, those who do not fit into traditional systems of identity such as immigrants, mixed-race children, and LGBTQ persons are discriminated against and even regarded as inferior to those who belong to the dominant group. The gospel of reconciliation acknowledges that all people are children of God and regards differences and otherness as God's gift rather than as a threat. The will to embrace others is fundamental for Christian identity. In this sense, preaching the gospel of reconciliation does not seek to establish a univocal identity, but an open-ended and fluid Christian identity in the face of Others.

What does all this mean to North American preaching? The gospel of reconciliation in Korea not only challenges the identity politics of Korean states, but also questions the United States' identity politics. Similar to Korea, national security is the main rhetoric that the US government often uses for identity construction. North Korea has been labeled as "the axis of evil" by George W. Bush's administration since 2002. Following US government's official propaganda, the US news media has been reproducing the image of the North Korea as a "rogue state" and one of the most dangerous nations ruled by an atrocious dictator with weapons of mass destruction and long-range missiles that threaten the national security of the United States and international peace in the East Asia. However, is it really true that North Korea is a threat to the United States? Jung-Sun Noh, a prominent *minjung* theologian and reunification theologian, argues that the accusation of North Korea as part of the axis of evil is a form of scapegoating of the weak by the powerful.[68] The United States is the most powerful country in the world with the most advanced military technology, including hydrogen nuclear weapons and intercontinental ballistic missiles (ICBM). The United States is also the world's biggest arms exporter, selling dangerous weapons all over the world. However, in the name of international security, the United States tries to dismantle the nuclear capability of North Korea and ban North Korea's arms exports by applying economic sanctions for nearly sixty years that have caused millions of deaths in North Korea.[69] Thus, the United States has imaginatively constructed North Korea as an enemy and conducted a witch-hunt. The rhetoric of the axis

68. Noh, "Strategies for Peace and Reunification in Korea," 151.
69. Ibid., 148.7

of evil presupposes a we/good-they/evil binary identity construction. However, this kind of binary identity politics, which is combined with judgment of the other as evil, aggravates peace between North Korea and the United States because good and evil cannot coexist. The United States is a "significant other" in forming Korean national identity and the US relationship with North Korea has affected the relationship between North and South Korea.[70] In other words, the United States' international policy and exclusive identity politics are constitutive elements of the contemporary Korean situation. The interrelatedness between the three countries calls North American preachers to take this theological and ethical issue seriously. Instead of blindly accepting politically constructed identity, preachers in the United States need to reconsider who they really are in relation to God and how they should response to those who are regarded as the axis of evil.

IMPLICATIONS FOR HOMILETICAL THEOLOGIES OF THE GOSPEL

Jacobsen points out that articulating one's theology of gospel is the starting point for doing homiletical theology because a theology of gospel influences how one interprets the Scripture and context.[71] At the same time, the contextual nature of gospel requires including particular contextual concerns in understanding what gospel is in a context. In other words, contextual concerns are an integral part of reflecting on gospel. Gospel as good news in responding to bad news or wounds of particular contexts cannot be defined acontextually. In this sense, a homiletical theology of gospel needs to begin with reflecting people's concrete experiences of suffering and their struggles for liberation, peace, and reconciliation instead of starting from abstract theologies of gospel in tradition/Scripture. Alyce M. McKenzie defines homiletical theology as a sapiential hermeneutic, which refers to "an interpretation of daily life from the perspective of biblical wisdom's inductive approach."[72] Homiletical theology as a sapiential hermeneutic does not apply general principles to a particular situation but infers general principles by observing and discerning the specifics of daily situations.[73] In the same way, the gospel of reconciliation in a divided Korea is not the result of applying theological principles to Korean context. Rather, the gospel of reconciliation in the Korean context emerges through

---

70. Shin, *One Alliance, Two Lenses*, 8–11
71. Jacobsen, "Introduction," 10.
72. McKenzie, "The Company of Sages," 92.
73. Ibid., 93.

reflecting urgent sociopolitical needs of Korean context in response to the critical wound, *han*, of Koreans. Contextual and practical concerns guide the process of reflecting and articulating gospel in Korean context from the very beginning. In this sense, a homiletical theology of the gospel is practical theology in that it is concerned with practical needs and aiming at the transformation of contexts. A homiletical theology of the gospel seeks God's liberating and life-giving act in context, discerns and names it clearly through a critical dialogue with Scripture/tradition.

A homiletical theology of the gospel does not seek a universal gospel but searches for particular good news for the context in which it unfolds. In this sense, any homiletical theology of the gospel is, first of all, a local theology. In the midst of their struggles for faith in the violent world, a community of faith searches for gospel, God's liberating and life-giving act in their context, in order to sustain their faith and transform the context in ways that cohere with a life-giving message of God. Thus, a concrete experience of local community is the starting point for a homiletical theology of the gospel. However, a local community of faith and context synchronically and diachronically interrelate to other communities of faith and contexts and therefore a local understanding of gospel must be in dialogue with diverse understandings of gospels in other contexts. Travis's postcolonial insights on gospel are particularly significant today for the task of defining gospel in the postcolonial and globalized world. Due to uneven power relationships among communities and the continuing negative effects of colonialism/imperialism, good news for one community can be bad news for another community. A preacher must acknowledge a transcontextual dimension of a local context and take ethical responsibility for others in preaching the gospel message. Both critical self-reflectivity and empathy with others are necessary. Without critical self-reflection, we often become blind prisoners of our own assumptions and set the gospel in service of our own benefits. Without empathy with others, we would never be able to understand how good news for us can be a curse to others and how the mystery of God's liberating and life-giving act often paradoxically unfolds in context and subverts our conventional understanding of good and bad. The gospel of reconciliation challenges Korean preachers' blind assumption of anti-communism as a part of the Christian gospel and calls Korean preachers to reconsider their conventional understanding of gospel, peace, and reconciliation in relation to the threatening other, North Korea. The gospel of reconciliation in the Korean context is a local theology in many aspects, but the interrelatedness of context of Korea and that of the United States calls North American preachers to reflect on their understandings of gospel in relation to the gospel of reconciliation in Korean context. In this perspective, a homiletical theology of the gospel is both a contextual and transcontextual theology of the gospel.[74] Any articulation of gospel must be rooted in a context but should also be globally relevant.

A homiletical theology of the gospel is political because the gospel by nature seeks to transform unjust and oppressive structures of context. In fact, all claims of the gospel are political. Separating the gospel from political affairs and spiritualizing gospel causes hearers to accept a current social order and maintain the *status quo*, which perpetuates the hegemonic power of the dominant group. Thus, any claim of an apolitical gospel itself is a political act. However, God's liberating and life-giving act is concretely manifested in the midst of human struggles for liberation, peace, and reconciliation. The gospel of reconciliation in the Korean context aims at political and social reunification of the Korean peninsula. This means that the gospel of reconciliation transgresses the conventional boundary between the religious and the political and reclaims its political and public dimensions. Instead of blindly accepting the available conceptions of the religious and the political, a homiletical theology of the gospel reconsiders and redraws the distinction between them for the task of preaching.

---

74. Kim's *Preaching in an Age of Globalization* is an example of a transcontextual approach to preaching and gospel.

5

When Our Words Fail Us

Preaching Gospel to Trauma Survivors

—*Joni S. Sancken*

Russian poet Anna Akhmatova's poem "Requiem" begins with a description of women who had witnessed and experienced trauma waiting outside a prison where their loved ones were suffering.

> During the terrible years of Yezhovshchina I spent
> seventeen months in the prison queues in Leningrad.
> One day someone recognized me. Then a woman with
> lips blue with cold who was standing behind me, and of
> course had never heard of my name, came out of the
> numbness which affected us all and whispered in my
> ear—(we all spoke in whispers there):
> "Can you describe this?"
> I said, "I can!"
> Then something resembling a smile slipped over what
> had once been her face.[1]

This chapter will address preaching the gospel in a context marked by the presence of trauma survivors. People who have experienced trauma often share a set of assumptions caused by their experience of powerlessness, imminent death, and the ineffectiveness of language. Survivors struggle to feel

---

1. Akhmatova, "Requiem," 90. See also *The Diane Rehm Show*, May 4, 2015, guest: Richard Flanagan "The Narrow Road to the Deep North."

safe, to trust others, and to find meaning in life. Survivors also may struggle with experiencing time in a natural way. The past may be frozen in the moment in which the traumatic event occurred as the survivor experiences it again and again unbidden, while the future is completely closed. While some preaching contexts, such as worship at a Veterans Affairs hospital, may have more awareness of trauma and the presence of survivors of trauma, most if not all congregations have participants who have been touched by trauma in some way and trauma has social ramifications for the community that surrounds a survivor. Two concerns lie at the heart of this chapter.

1) Often preachers turn to therapeutic language to minister to trauma survivors. I want to encourage robust theological engagement that restores the power of language and creates connections between the experiences of survivors and claims that lie at the heart of the gospel. As we too consider the question on the blue lips of the woman in line with Akhmatova, by the power of the Spirit, preachers can harness language to validate the experiences of survivors and raise awareness and hope within the context.

2) Because many trauma survivors may experience shame and isolation, I want to explore how theologically anchored sermons might draw trauma survivors into a congregation and participate in healing.

In light of these concerns, the paper will include definitions and descriptions of gospel and context as well as a discussion of trauma and the effects of trauma—in part through the lens of Post-Traumatic Stress Disorder (PTSD). I will explore how preaching that draws from the full experience of Jesus as attested to in narrative shorthand of the creed (and its undergirding doctrines) might allow for a deeper theological range in opening up opportunities for survivors of trauma to experience hope in the midst of a complex healing process. Finally, I will offer some reflection on broader implications for homiletical theologies of the gospel.

GOSPEL FOR TRAUMA SURVIVORS

For the purposes of this essay, the gospel is God's good news for our world situated most powerfully in the Christ event but also extended as promise to us through Christ. For trauma survivors, the experiences of powerlessness, hopelessness, and isolation that can follow a traumatic event or set of prolonged traumatic circumstances mean that particular aspects of gospel or good news may feel most relevant: for example, the presence of Christ and the

Christian community as the body of Christ so that the survivor is not alone, a sense of reliance on or trust in Christ when one's own power is insufficient, and a sense of empowerment in Christ to live towards the promises of God. Most significant is Christ's move from cross to resurrection, which serves as a promise of our own move from death to life and can be experienced fragmentarily in our world today in experiences of healing or finding new purpose in the wake of trauma.

A later section of this essay argues that preaching the life of Christ as expressed in the shorthand of the creed might foster a typological identification with Christ that can lead towards healing and an experience of gospel. Shelly Rambo's work concerning the Holy Saturday and the role of the Spirit in bearing witness to the space between death and resurrection is also instructive to preachers who are called to proclaim the gospel in contexts marked by the space between death and new life where God's promises are experienced only partially and where the good news inaugurated by Christ is unfinished.

UNDERSTANDING TRAUMA'S ROLE IN SITUATIONS AND CONTEXT

In his April 30, 1944 letter to Eberhard Bethge, Dietrich Bonhoeffer wrote about his concern for engaging with Jesus Christ in the present tense. He wrote, "What is bothering me incessantly is the question, what Christianity really is or who Christ really is, for us today?"[2] Jesus Christ is living so we must constantly ask who is Jesus Christ for us today? While God and the gospel itself are not dependent upon recipients, the Bible, Christian tradition, and experience all testify that God's radical good news moves toward us, toward the world. This means that our contexts in all their complexity and diversity deeply affect how we receive and bear witness to the good news or gospel in both our words and our choices and behaviors. For us as embodied and enmeshed people, gospel and context are inseparable. For preachers, charged with bearing witness to the good news through the sermon, David Jacobsen and Robert Kelly helpfully draw a distinction between "context" and "situation" as two distinct arenas in which we experience the gospel "for us."[3] Jacobsen and Kelly describe context as "those enduring realities of culture, society, and language that shape our understanding and orient for good or for ill, the way in which we hear the gospel."[4] Jacobsen and Kelly delineate *situation*

---

2. Bonhoeffer, *Letters and Papers from Prison*, 279.
3. Jacobsen and Kelly, *Kairos Preaching*, 29.
4. Ibid., 9, 29.

from *context*, so that the situation is "a moment or crisis that evokes a sense of limit or finitude that calls forth a decision."[5] For example, using Jacobsen and Kelly's definitions, the context might be viewed as the container or the interpretive lens by which we hold or view a specific event that constitutes a situation. Jacobsen and Kelly draw from David Buttrick's categorization of situations most ripe for gospel proclamation as being situations of "limit" or "decision."[6] Situations of limit put human finitude in conversation with God's transcendence, while situations of decision describe circumstances where we are in the midst of discerning God's will for our lives and future.[7] Other situations that call for gospel proclamation may include events that call into question the nature of being—how we understand ourselves in light of history, or events that necessitate moral discernment that necessitates that the church speak from its particular standpoint of both "being saved" and "being in the world."[8] While most events that are used in trauma studies would not become situations for preaching, using Jacobsen, Kelly, and Buttrick's definitions and qualifications, some traumatic events may create discrete situations for preaching the gospel. Such events may be individual such as the violent death of a loved one or communal such as a natural disaster or fire that destroys a church.

The conversation around trauma, particularly as experienced through PTSD, and preaching primarily sits at the level of context. In the aftermath of the September 11 attacks and recent wars in Afghanistan and Iraq, Journalist David J. Morris describes our PTSD as a "cultural meme" noting that it is "everywhere now, an inescapable part of our historical moment . . . an expression of deeper anxieties, it defines our era in a way not unlike female hysteria defined late nineteenth-century Europe."[9] PTSD was first included in The Diagnostic and Statistical Manual of Mental Disorders (DSM) in 1980 and has clear symptoms and treatment strategies, however in tracing its history through a study of trauma Morris also views PTSD as "a product of culture as much as a hardwired biological fact."[10] While also naming that this view of

---

5. Ibid., 9, 29–30. Edward Farley offers a somewhat different definition of "situation." His definition, "A situation is the way various items, powers, and events in the environment gather together to evoke responses from participants," encompasses aspects of context into the interpretation of a situation. Farley's definition and broader thrust of his essay places the act preaching to a situation or context of trauma within the realm of doing practical theology. See Farley, "Interpreting Situations," in his *Practicing Gospel*, 38.

6. Ibid., 38–39. See also Buttrick, *Homiletic*, 408–11.

7. Ibid.

8. Ibid., See also Buttrick, *Homiletic*, 525.

9. Morris, *The Evil Hours*, 14.

10. Ibid., 62.

PTSD is controversial and is "upsetting to many veterans," he cites the work of Allan Young, medical anthropologist at McGill University, who writes, "the disorder is not timeless, nor does it possess an intrinsic unity. Rather it is glued together by the practices, technologies, and narratives with which it is diagnosed, studied, treated, and represented by the various interests, institutions, and moral arguments that mobilized those efforts and resources."[11] It is beyond the scope of this essay to speak to whether the response to trauma is mainly timeless and biological or mediated by cultural elements, but study and literature points to the presence of both elements in the experience of those who experience trauma. Once trauma has occurred, relationship with survivors, particularly those who may have PTSD, means that their experiences contribute to the broader cultural context. One of the challenges of engaging with those who suffer from PTSD is that they tend to withdraw from relationships—this absence too becomes a part of a context in which preaching may take place.

Shelly Rambo's work engaging trauma in New Orleans following Hurricane Katrina offers a kind of "case study" into particularities that might help preachers engage trauma through both situational and contextual lenses.[12] Rambo's article, "Saturday in New Orleans: Rethinking the Holy Spirit in the Aftermath of Trauma," was written after a meeting with pastors over two years after Hurricane Katrina devastated some parts of the city. Rambo particularly explores the ongoing and more chronic contextual trauma of "after the storm."[13] The horrific situation of the storm itself unveiled and triggered "a deeper and more widespread storm of economic injustice, racism, and poverty."[14] Rambo notes the increased "post-Katrina death and morbidity rates," that the group is meeting on "funeral day," and that many pastors may lead or attend three funerals on a Saturday like this.[15] The congregations served by the pastors with whom Rambo met anticipate that they will hear the gospel on Sunday mornings, but the presence of death continues in their communities and often occludes a clear vision of new life.

In light of this encounter, Rambo turns to the period of Holy Saturday—the often-overlooked space between Good Friday and Easter—as a resource for people living in the wake of trauma.[16] While the liturgical year marks this middle ground between death and resurrection with just one day, for trauma

11. Ibid., 62, 288 (note 60). See also Young, *The Harmony of Illusions*.
12. Rambo, "Saturday in New Orleans."
13. Ibid., 230.
14. Ibid.
15. Ibid.
16. Ibid.

survivors the experience of Holy Saturday defies tidy boundaries. The space of Holy Saturday also serves as a bridge or transitional space between understanding trauma through the lenses of situation and context. Rambo emphasizes the power of trauma to disrupt a linear experience of time.[17] "Boundaries between death and life are broken down by the force of a traumatic event; temporal boundaries between past, present, and future no longer hold."[18] When the realities of "after the storm" persist, survivors find themselves living in the midst of Holy Saturday.[19]

Rambo's understanding of Saturday as a theological space set apart for "after the storm" also acknowledges that traumatic responses often move from temporary coping mechanism to involuntary habitual behavior. In the case of Hurricane Katrina, simmering contextual trauma in the form of racism and socioeconomic challenges may have intensified the situational trauma of the storm and its immediate horrific aftermath. Because of the compounding effects of these experiences of trauma, the time "after the storm" becomes a new context for the preachers where racism, poverty, and lack of opportunity merge horrifically with devastating destruction of property, loss of identity, and death associated with the storm. The space of Holy Saturday validates present suffering without rushing too quickly to Easter. Among others, Rambo turns to Alan Lewis, whose work sets apart Saturday as a time for prayer begun in silent cries to God who is finally able to bring about new life.[20] Lewis writes, "Prayer then, the sound of silence upon Easter Saturday and every day which reenacts it, is the last breath of our self-relinquishment, the freedom we give God at last to *be* God, gracious, holy, and creative, precisely in those crises where our bodies, intellects, and souls cry out in tears of anger and bewilderment that God is dead."[21]

Rambo's focus on the Gospel of John's discussion of the Spirit/Advocate (*paraclete*) in chapter 14, as one who remains with the disciples is fertile territory for the preachers of New Orleans and others who must proclaim gospel in the midst of the time "after the storm." For Rambo, this Advocate witnesses both to divine presence and absence, to what is known and remains unknown.[22] Preachers who work collaboratively with this Spirit that remains in the context of trauma "after the storm" are empowered to stand in the midst of Holy Saturday and bear witness to all who live in this space between death

---

17. Ibid., 231.
18. Ibid.
19. Ibid.
20. Ibid., 234. See also Lewis, *Between Cross and Resurrection*, 464.
21. Lewis, *Between Cross and Resurrection*, 464.
22. Rambo, "Saturday in New Orleans," 239.

and resurrection. In the context of trauma, proclamation of the gospel must begin with the work of the Spirit in this space.[23]

UNDERSTANDING TRAUMA

In the wake of the attacks of September 11 and the wars in Iraq and Afghanistan, war correspondent and former Marine David J. Morris describes the field of trauma studies as a kind of fair with various disciplines calling out like carnies from their posts, with expert perspectives ranging from clinical awareness brought by psychiatrists and neuroscientists to experiential knowledge from poets, memoirists, and anthropologists.[24] What these varied approaches have in common is confirming the thoroughly penetrating impacts of trauma on survivors and their communities. The effects of trauma are physical, emotional, cognitive, relational, sociological, and spiritual.[25] Those who have experienced a traumatic event are often not able to do "whole-brain" cohesive processing, instead more primitive "fight/flight/freeze" instincts take over.[26] Violence and trauma are often reciprocally related in that a violent act or event often causes trauma and unaddressed and unhealed trauma can lead to more violence. While Post-Traumatic Stress Disorder (PTSD) is not synonymous with the experience of trauma, Morris views PTSD as a kind of buzzword that speaks to our time.[27] As such trauma and its effects, particularly PTSD, have become part of our present cultural context. Much of the literature around trauma engages with PTSD, which emerged as an official psychiatric diagnosis in the late 1970s following the experience of combat veterans who served in Vietnam. The symptoms of PTSD obviously existed long before the specific label, with some documenting examples from early literature and the Bible.[28]

Because the term is so often used imprecisely, it is difficult to pin down a specific definition of trauma. Director of Strategies for Trauma Awareness and Resistance (STAR) Carolyn Yoder delineates between situations of extreme stress and trauma. Traumatic events "involve threats to lives or bodies, produce terror and feelings of helplessness, overwhelm an individual's or group's ability to cope or respond to the threat, lead to a sense of loss of control, and challenge a person's or group's sense that life is meaningful and

---

23. Ibid., 241.
24. Morris, *The Evil Hours*, 13.
25. Yoder, *The Little Book of Trauma Healing*, 6.
26. Ibid., 5. See also Morris, *The Evil Hours*, 51.
27. Morris, *The Evil Hours*, 14.
28. Kinghorn, "Medicating the Eschatological Body," 207.

orderly."[29] Further, events that may be merely stressful to one person may be traumatic for someone else depending on "age, previous history, degree of preparation, the meaning given to the event, how long it lasts, the quality of social support, knowledge about how to deal with trauma, genetic makeup and spiritual centeredness."[30] Trauma can be caused by single events such as losing a family member in the September 11 attacks as well as long-term living in abusive or dangerous settings.[31] These longer-term situations are known as "cumulative trauma; continuous trauma; chronic trauma; sequential trauma; multiple or plural traumas."[32] Often trauma has multiple layers. For example Hurricane Katrina survivors experienced the original trauma of the hurricane with loss of property and life along with the "structural-induced" trauma of racist systems and lack of resources for the poor in New Orleans that were present as lower-grade chronic trauma before but escalated due to the hurricane.[33] These compounding events can intensify the response and widen the circle of those affected. Broader communities and groups can experience trauma even if they are at a distance from the event.[34] Additionally, trauma can be transferred from one generation to another through time. For example, the experience of enslaved Africans brought to the United States, cultural and physical genocide of Native populations, and colonialism.[35] Another more recent field of trauma studies also includes trauma caused to those who participate or perpetrate violent or abusive acts.[36] Because of the wide variability in reactions and triggering experiences, it is important for pastors to validate a traumatic reaction regardless of how the precipitating event or events may appear to others.[37] David Morris's study focuses on a small group of widely recognized events that are known to trigger traumatic responses, for example, the experience of a devastating natural disaster such as the 2004 Indian Ocean tsunami, Hurricane Katrina in 2005, the 2010 Haitian earthquake, and the Nepal earthquake of April 2015; rape; and the experience of war, which involves both being attacked and attacking others. Until relatively recently, much literature tracing the effects of trauma has an androcentric bias

29. Yoder, *The Little Book of Trauma Healing*, 10.
30. Ibid., 11.
31. Ibid., 11–12.
32. Ibid., 12.
33. Ibid.
34. Ibid., 12–13.
35. Ibid., 13–14.
36. Ibid., 14. Some have documented a PTSD-type response called Perpetration Induced Traumatic Stress or PITS.
37. Ibid., 11.

and has focused on male soldiers in a context of war rather than on the act of rape, which is most commonly an atrocity experienced by women or girls. However, many other events and chronic conditions can cause trauma, from the murder of a colleague or a car accident to childbirth, serious illnesses or pandemics, human-caused natural disasters such as an oil spill, homelessness, being a refugee, or loss of identity.[38] Further, because trauma impacts not only individuals but also groups, communities, and societies, we can see how trauma—both named and unnamed— is likely present in many congregations and other ministry contexts.[39]

Yoder's work tracks responses to trauma. The first series of responses are organized into a "survivor victim cycle," which includes whole-person responses with far-reaching impact.[40] Early responses include physiological changes such as shutting down the cerebral cortex (or thinking brain) and operating primarily from the limbic system and amygdala that register fear and the brain stem that has no sense of time other than an ongoing sense of "now" controls the "fight-flight-freeze" response as well as other instinctual actions.[41] What this feels like is a state of "hyper arousal," as heart rate and breathing increase, blood rushes to muscles, and senses are heightened. Less crucial body functions such as digestion shut down.[42] After the moment of danger, traumatized people may shake or cry uncontrollably or sweat profusely.[43] Because these reactions may appear unseemly, often people will suppress them, although allowing the body to release traumatic energy can actually be beneficial for long-term recovery.[44] Mentally, these responses to trauma can cause dissociation to keep us from being emotionally overwhelmed in the moment and memories are not created or retained in the usual way and later produce both extreme detail coupled with difficulty in recalling events.[45] Traumatic memories may return involuntarily with sensory details and a sense of collapsed time when the survivor encounters a trigger such as smell, sight, sound, or some other kind of dynamic—when a traumatized person experiences an "intrusive memory" it is as if the event is happening again in real time and the body responded accordingly.[46] Fear of triggers and a sense

38. Ibid., 15.
39. Ibid., 7.
40. Ibid., 18.
41. Ibid., 18–19.
42. Ibid., 19.
43. Ibid., 21–22.
44. Ibid., 22.
45. Ibid., 20.
46. Ibid., 21.

that they should be "over it" can cause trauma survivors to grow isolated as they withdraw from regular activities and engagement.[47] Trauma may also over time so affect brain functioning that survivors frequently operate using mainly lower-brain functions rather than the "thinking brain."[48] This means that survivors may not be capable of thinking through consequences, may speak or act without a filter, and may respond to relatively minor annoyances with extreme actions—akin to going after a mosquito with a gun.[49] When the frontal cortex re-engages, the person may feel shame, emotionally numb, or may even deny what just happened.[50]

In addition to physical, mental, emotional, and relational responses, trauma also deeply affects a survivor's sense of self and spiritual grounding. Because trauma destroys meaning and harms a person's sense of identity and ability to make meaning from her or his life, a survivor may question God and may need access to different theology and different language to make sense of life.[51] Particularly chronic or ongoing trauma leads some of the physiological and emotional responses to become regular adaptive behavior that can help people to survive in dangerous settings, yet the effects can be corrosive. Judith Herman observes that those who experience a single traumatic event may feel that they are "losing their minds" while those who experience chronic trauma feel that they have "lost themselves."[52] While large-scale natural disasters can certainly cause trauma, the most damaging trauma is caused by deliberate harmful action by a person or people.[53]

Unhealed and unattended trauma does not just "go away." Rather, the pain is often transferred and the survivor may "get stuck" in a cycle of suffering and fear marked by a lack of power and lack of hope.[54] PTSD is given as a diagnosis when severe responses to trauma persist for longer than one month.[55] Specific symptoms of PTSD often overlap with the immediate symptoms of trauma such as "flashbacks" to the event, symptoms of increased arousal such as inability to sleep, and finding patterns where none actually exist.[56] Some research shows that flashbacks are more than just "vivid memo-

47. Ibid.
48. Ibid., 22–23.
49. Ibid.
50. Ibid., 23.
51. Ibid., 24–25.
52. Ibid., 27. See also Herman, *Trauma and Recovery*, 158.
53. Yoder, *The Little Book of Trauma Healing*, 29.
54. Ibid., 30.
55. Ibid., 31.
56. Ibid. See also Morris, *The Evil Hour*, 111.

ries" and are likely stored differently in the brain than typical memories.[57] Memories can usually be verbalized but flashback memories exist beyond the scope of language, leading to frustration in explaining the experience to loved ones and professionals seeking to help.[58] PTSD is the most widely recognized response to trauma in our broader cultural vernacular but reducing all trauma to PTSD risks minimizing other responses to trauma that fall short of a specific diagnosis.[59] Focusing on PTSD is also less helpful in looking at trauma in non-Western contexts as well as trauma experienced by large groups. Finally, a PTSD diagnosis, while helpful for some, risks "pathologizing" and medicating a natural response to traumatic experiences.[60]

The horror of trauma is well documented and must never be minimized. Engaging with those who have experienced trauma is not for the faint of heart and preachers and other caregivers should not enter into relationships with naiveté or optimism built on well-meaning platitudes. PTSD is a serious diagnosis and those who have experienced trauma or who have symptoms of PTSD should be under the care of professionals who are trained and experienced in dealing specifically with trauma. However, as Christians who believe in the God who brings new life from death, the horror of trauma is not the final verdict. Those who survive trauma emerge as new people, changed by their experiences. Healing, integration, and return to meaningful relationship is possible. New gifts and potential can grow in the aftermath of trauma. In fact, while present-day practice treats those who have survived trauma as patients who need treatment to re-engage with community, Morris's historical research showed that in ancient cultures those who survived trauma often became spiritual leaders or shamans in their communities.[61] They were the ones who taught and cared for "normal people" because their experience gave them great insight into the depths of human experience.[62] In other language, this logic also resonates with the experience of Jesus' own traumatic crucifixion and death at the heart of Christianity. God's own suffering in Christ means that even the most painful aspects of being human are drawn into the life of God and can be redeemed and transformed for the glory of God. Healing from trauma may become "the turning point of a life, a sign and symbol of God's goodness and care."[63] God's own overcoming of death is good news for

57. Morris, *The Evil Hour*, 109.
58. Ibid.
59. Yoder, *The Little Book of Trauma Healing*, 31.
60. Ibid.
61. Morris, *The Little Book of Trauma Healing*, 65–66.
62. Ibid.
63. Hunsinger, *Bearing the Unbearable*. See also Cane, *Trauma Healing and*

any who have experienced overwhelming trauma, or who have loved ones who have experienced "intense fear, helplessness, loss of control, and threat of annihilation."[64]

GOSPEL AS (RE)CONSTRUCTION OF THE SELF THROUGH PREACHING THE LIFE OF JESUS

In the face of trauma, it is helpful for preachers to begin with a posture of humility, confession, and prayer. In Deborah Van Deusen Hunsinger's words, "we ourselves, with our enduring failures to love, cannot truly redeem traumatic loss, we cling in hope to the One who can and does."[65] One of the challenging tenets of trauma healing is that healing must involve empowerment of the survivor while also involving the creation of new relationships.[66] Recovery occurs in a kind of space between, not dissimilar in some ways to the space where proclamation itself occurs, a space between the active agency of preachers and listeners where control is both exercised and surrendered and the power of the Holy Spirit brings life. If given permission to accompany survivors on a journey to healing, pastors and other loved ones cannot force healing and must give over control. In addition to the forging of relationships, Judith Herman notes several other "stages of recovery" including, "safety, "remembrance and mourning," "reconnection," and "commonality."[67] Preachers in particular should rightly hold the importance of creating a safe environment for trauma survivors where they can worship without fear of triggers. Awareness of the needs in one's own immediate context and fostering a strong relationship with the trauma survivor and his or her family are key. Yet fear of saying the wrong thing is not a good reason for bypassing the important calling of preaching the gospel—particularly to those who need to experience its healing power. It may be that the best approach may be as a "compassionate witness" who can name God's redemptive and healing activity where appropriate—even in the wake of trauma.[68]

While the power of traumatic experience should certainly be validated, a trauma survivor is not to be reduced specifically to a horrific event or

---

Transformation, 17.

64. Hunsinger, *Bearing the Unbearable*, 11. See also Andrease, "Posttraumatic Stress Disorder," as quoted in Herman, *Trauma and Recovery*, 33.

65. Hunsinger, *Bearing the Unbearable*, 9.

66. Herman, *Trauma and Recovery*, 133.

67. Ibid., 133–236.

68. Bridgers, "The Resurrected Life."

events. Rather, this person is a brother or sister in Christ whose identity is in Christ and whose self and future are being transformed more and more into Christ's likeness. Nevertheless, Warren Anderson Kinghorn names the constructive role that psychiatric diagnosis plays not only as it relates to "Psychiatric technology" but also to the ways a person names and constructs her or his experience and identity as an "experiencing self."[69] In the context of exploring a mental disorder such as PTSD, the way that identity is formed has implications for an individual or community's chosen path of treatment or healing from trauma.[70] It is good and important for survivors of serious trauma to seek diagnosis and treatment from psychiatric professionals, but we should not shortchange the role or pastors and preachers. The ability to retell or reshape story and identity in the wake of trauma is an important part of psychological integration and healing. As Christians, we hold that through the waters of baptism, the identity of Jesus Christ is a definitive constructive act in shaping our own identities both here and now as well as eschatologically. The events that helped to form Jesus' earthly ministry are named in the christological section of the Apostles Creed.

> I believe in . . . Jesus Christ his only Son our Lord; who was conceived by the Holy Ghost, born of the Virgin Mary, suffered under Pontius Pilate, was crucified, dead, and buried; he descended into hell; the third day he rose again from the dead; he ascended into heaven, and sitteth on the right hand of God the Father Almighty; from thence he shall come to judge the quick and the dead.[71]

Preaching through the Apostles' Creed, either in a sermon series or explicitly allowing the doctrines present in the creed to come to the fore while preaching through Christian year, may offer preachers an approach to positively participating in the complex process of trauma healing as well as providing language and theology that may help to rebuild and restore the identity of trauma survivors in part through a "typological identification" with aspects of Jesus' life and ministry.[72] Lynn Bridgers discusses the healing potential of typological association with biblical themes, drawing from a tradition that allows for oppressed and marginalized people to draw strength and hope from

---

69. Kinghorn, "Medicating the Eschatological Body," 204.

70. Ibid.

71. I have chosen to use the "traditional" version rather than the ecumenical version likely used more frequently in worship because it includes the line, "he descended into hell." I see this element as being very important in light of the context of trauma and trauma survivors.

72. Bridgers, "The Resurrected Life," 39.

typological association.[73] For example, enslaved Africans drawing from the Exodus experience of Israel being freed from Egypt or Puritan colonists seeking religious freedom in North America connecting to Israel being brought into the Promised Land.[74] Use of these key biblical images helped shape identity in ways that preserved and nurtured identity and calling in these groups. Bridgers invites survivors to see themselves not as "bystanders in a scene that also involves Christ, but as Christians to see in their own lives the stages that mark the history of Christ's ministry."[75] Psychologically, another tool that the narrative of Christ may provide for trauma healing is association, since dissociation is one of the responses to trauma that is likely to lead to PTSD.[76]

It may be common practice in many traditions to move in and out of the Christian year or to emphasize some aspects of Christ's life and work and downplay or ignore other theological emphases that seem less important. However, since the journey to healing is multifaceted and different aspects of the Christ-event address different responses to trauma, the discussion that follows asserts that the entirety of Jesus' life should be preached, each event offers healing nuances.

"... Conceived by the Holy Ghost, born of the Virgin Mary ..."

God is deeply committed to creation and cares about what happens with human bodies in history. This is true throughout Scripture but is most deeply marked by God entering into creation as a human. God's choice to become human in a sense lifts up the value of humanity. Incarnation exemplifies God's desire to connect to people. The theological emphases found in Jesus' incarnation emphasize the necessity of safety, relationship, and community. Preaching about these very human aspects of Jesus works against loss of self and isolation that many may feel in the wake of trauma. In the immediate wake of trauma, the first step towards healing is the need for safety for the survivor. Safety needs to be both physical or external and internal or emotional/psychological. Safety was a concern for infant Jesus as Mary sought a safe place to give birth and in Matthew's gospel the family lived in Egypt to protect Jesus. The way that those with PTSD respond to physical stimuli and are unable to effectively employ self-soothing behaviors is in some ways reminiscent of a

---

73. Ibid., 43.
74. Ibid. See also Smith, *Conjuring Culture*, 55.
75. Bridgers, "The Resurrected Life," 43.
76. van der Kolk, "In Terror's Grip," 5.

newborn infant so that identification or association with the infant Jesus who is protected, honored, and loved may be helpful.[77]

Jesus' mother Mary's role and the fact that she was given a choice in Jesus' conception may be healing themes to lift up in Advent sermons. Judith Herman writes poignantly about the loss of self that can happen for those who experience trauma, particularly women who experience rape. She writes that "at the moment of trauma, almost by definition, the individual's point of view counts for nothing . . . . The traumatic event thus destroys the belief that one can be *oneself* in relation to others."[78] Jesus' ministry in some ways is characterized by being misunderstood in his closest relationships while also exhibiting a profound sense of understanding and compassion towards others.

In many contexts, it is common to preach about the "once-for-all-time" nature of Jesus' work. However, drawing from the strength of typological identification suggested by Bridgers, it may encourage connection to not speak about Christ's incarnation as a "one-time event that happened in the distant past, but that ended with Christ's death on the cross."[79] Rather, identification with Christ may be encouraged by taking a different approach that envisions "the incarnation as a rupture, as an eruption of God into the life of humanity whose impact is ongoing. The incarnation did not end with the cross but is continued in the lives of every believer today."[80] This might be fostered in preaching that uses present-tense verbs to talk about Jesus' incarnate presence and that consistently uses examples of believers acting as the present-day, incarnate body of Christ in our world.

". . . Suffered . . ."

Jesus' suffering may be one of the most theologically challenging elements in preaching, especially as it relates to involuntary suffering today related to the immediate experience and aftermath of trauma. Bridgers comments concerning the eternal "eruption" of the incarnation of Christ may be helpful here as well. Indeed, while God has ultimately defeated death through the cross and resurrection, our world exists in an era of "overlap" where old life and new life

---

77. Ibid., 6–7.
78. Herman, *Trauma and Recovery*, 53.
79. Bridgers, "The Resurrected Life," 43.
80. Ibid., 43–44. Bridgers comments on feminist concerns around women being able to identify with the male Jesus Christ, which has an exclusionary history of restricting women's authority. However, Bridgers sidesteps this concern by focusing on the form of Jesus' life. Along similar lines, I would argue for identification in Jesus' actions more than his specific gender identity.

exist together. It follows that Jesus may be understood to still be suffering with and in people who suffer today. However, this does not justify their suffering and preachers should be clear that it doesn't make their suffering a means to salvation or something that should be glorified in any way. Just the same, a link with Christ's own suffering does provide a way to find meaning and some sense of purpose or way forward in what would otherwise feel hopeless. This may particularly be the case when preachers are consistent in linking the cross with the resurrection. These two events invade our world simultaneously and we cannot speak of the cross without also engaging with the resurrection.[81] Jesus who suffers wherever there is suffering today is also the Risen Lord and is intimately involved in raising new life in our world.

Besides links with cross and resurrection, survivors often speak anecdotally of feeling Christ's presence with them in experiences of intense suffering. Jesus' presence and solidarity with suffering people is a powerful word in the face of the isolation and sense of separation that many survivors either experience based on other's discomfort or impose on themselves out of fear. Preaching that people are never alone in their experiences of suffering is an important word of comfort and hope.

". . . Was crucified, dead, and buried . . ."

Death is a part of trauma; the close brush with physical death itself through near loss of one's own life or the death of a loved one. Like Jesus on the cross, Judith Herman notes that in situations of terror people seek out elemental sources of "comfort and protection."[82] "Wounded soldiers and raped women cry for their mothers or for God. When this cry is not answered, the sense of basic trust is shattered. Traumatized people feel utterly abandoned utterly alone, cast out of the human and divine systems of care and protection that sustain life . . . they belong more to the dead than to the living."[83] Jesus' own cry, "My God, my God, why have you forsaken me" resonates with this experience and testifies to the gospel promise that God hears those cries and ultimately acts. Following the establishment of bodily safety and safe relationships, the second phase of recovery from trauma named by Herman is "remembrance and mourning." This is essentially the reclaiming and telling of the traumatic experience or memory so that it might be integrated into an emerging way

---

81. See also ibid., 45.
82. Ibid., 52
83. Ibid.

forward.[84] Because much of traumatic memory and experience is stored in the brain without words, speaking the story and shaping it is transformative for survivors in part because it tells the truth of what happened and it allows them to become whole people.[85] Herman writes, "In the telling the trauma story becomes testimony.... Testimony has both a private dimension, which is confessional and spiritual, and a public aspect, which is political and judicial."[86] In telling the story, the survivor moves from "shame and humiliation" to "dignity and virtue."[87] They "regain the world they have lost."[88] Creating appropriate time for testimony and allowing testimony to become part of the preaching moment may be a way for pastors to reach out to survivors. The survivor must take the lead, but the preacher will also want to be aware of the situation and the appropriateness of the testimony. Preaching that touches the complexity of atonement will want to not only build identification but also show that Jesus' actions have a vicarious power. Jesus takes on the horror for us so that we don't have to bear it alone. Jesus' death also brings a finality that can be life-giving in particular for those with PTSD who experience aspects of the traumatic event again and again without a sense of ending or finality.[89] Survivors can send their experiences to the cross with Jesus and let them end once and for all. Inviting participants to write on a paper or bring forward a symbol to place on the cross may even be a helpful worship ritual for a Good Friday service. Integrating celebration of Communion with themes from the sermon may offer a helpful way for worshippers to experience Jesus' self-giving presence physically in ways that are beneficial when pain and brokenness are beyond the words.

These means of rehearsing the death and resurrection of Jesus in a way that allows for deep identification offers potential healing paradigms for survivors of trauma. When the reliving of the traumatic experience is able to end, the memory changes and the psychological response changes as the survivor is able to more forward again in new life.[90] However, ritual action and accompanying proclamation rarely address the questions of "why" and "why me" that follow integration of the trauma experience.[91] Here Bridgers again suggests that the life of Jesus is helpful, although the perspective of Jesus' followers

---

84. Herman, *Trauma and Recovery*, 175.
85. Ibid., 175–81.
86. Ibid., 181.
87. Ibid. See also Mollica, "The Trauma Story," 312.
88. Herman, *Trauma and Recovery*, 181.
89. van der Kolk, "In Terror's Grip," 3–4.
90. Ibid., 5.
91. Herman, *Trauma and Recovery*, 178.

may be more relatable than Jesus himself. Jesus' disciples did not understand the promise of the resurrection until it happened. Our human perspective has limitations and it can be beneficial for preachers to acknowledge these unknowns, it is not a cop-out to acknowledge mystery, rather it affirms our creaturely relationship to God.

". . . He descended into hell . . ."

The "middle day" of the Easter Triduum passes quietly in many traditions, but this time between Christ's death and resurrection where Jesus "harrows hell" may serve as a theological holding space for trauma survivors who may also feel caught in the middle between the past and the future, between life and death.[92] Trauma survivors may see their own journeys as a kind of descent into hell—a place of torment where others cannot reach and from where there is no return. Part of Jesus' redeeming act is to reach into hell—to reach beyond where humans can reach and return. Jesus is not limited, even in his death. Jesus is Lord of the dead and the living.[93] While preaching the descent into hell may take the form of pure lament in the tradition of the biblical psalms directed to a God who is present and listening, James Kay brings in Jewish understandings of Sheol as a place of the dead—where they exist as "shadows" cut off both from the world of the living and "oblivious to (the praise of) God."[94] This sounds like an apt description of those who are suffering the isolation of PTSD. Early commentators on the Apostles' Creed describe Jesus' actions in hell as involving proclamation and liberation where the good news is preached and the damned are set free from the chains and prisons that have held them.[95] Thus the first taste of resurrection is offered to those who are dead and enslaved and Christ's descent into hell is the transitional move from cross to resurrection.[96]

This is profound good news for any who have been to "hell," but preaching Christ's descent into hell may be particularly helpful for ministering to a particular group of those who suffer from trauma, those who perpetrated violence against others—those who are guilty of crimes or who may have killed enemy combatants or innocent civilians in the context of war. Some congregations may have special worship services for recent parolees whose

---

92. Rambo, "Saturday in New Orleans," 231–2.
93. See also Kay, "He Descended into Hell."
94. Ibid., 20
95. Ibid., Kay cites Rufinus, *A Commentary on the Apostles' Creed*, 51–52, 61.
96. Kay, "He Descended into Hell," 23.

conditions of release do not permit them to worship in traditional church settings.[97] Some may suffer from Perpetrator Induced Traumatic Syndrome (PITS) due to the honest and justifiable guilt they may experience from past actions. When he descends to hell, Jesus takes on the punishment reserved for the worst of the worst.[98] He takes his ranks among them. In Kay's words,

> Here we stand before an incomprehensible mystery where the Father and the Son, joined by a mutual Spirit of love and freedom, take into the very dynamics of their relationship the ravages of sin in order to destroy its dominance over the human creature.... Divine power is now seen as that which comes all the way down in suffering love to the depths of depravity and estrangement to bring forth eternal life. By descending into hell, God in the person of Jesus Christ places the worst that can befall human beings within the redeeming embrace of the cross.[99]

Finally, treatment and healing from trauma take time. The journey is long. Marking Christ's descent into hell and the "middle time" of Holy Saturday acknowledges that the move from death to new life may be slow and painful. Preachers may want to mark this day as way to slow the congregation down in the "rush" to get from Good Friday to Easter.[100] For family members and friends who accompany survivors on their journey, Christ's descent into hell offers assurance that Christ's power extends beyond the earthly and heavenly realms to those who are unable to respond and seem beyond reach and beyond hope.[101]

"... He rose again from the dead ..."

Resurrection or new life in the form of a new start that brings something new from death, is a deeply embedded theme in literature related to trauma and

---

97. I am most familiar with Dismas Fellowship services that primarily serve recently released sex offenders. I volunteered with Dismas from 2007–2009. The congregation where my husband served as pastor hosted these services in Hamilton, Ontario. Dismas Fellowship or similar services may feel controversial for congregations and can raise issues particularly for some trauma survivors in the congregation. Preaching Jesus' descent into hell may be a helpful means for a pastor to work through the theological rationale for a program like this with a congregation.

98. Kay, "He Descended into Hell," 24

99. Ibid.

100. Rambo, "Saturday in New Orleans," 234, citing Brueggemann, "Readings from the Day 'In Between,'" 110–11.

101. See also Kay, "He Descended into Hell," 23–24.

trauma recovery. Survivors often use language that is reminiscent of the language the church uses to talk about death and resurrection to talk about their experiences of trauma and it is common for family members to speak similarly ("John was a different person when he returned from Iraq"). Allowing the paradigm of Jesus' resurrection to offer narrative and formative structure to impact the way a survivor talks about his or her experience may be healing.[102] Theologically framing resurrection as not only an event that happened to Jesus long ago but as an eschatological event has on-going implications for creation may offer hope to survivors who must repeatedly choose life over death as they slowly move towards healing.

This perspective takes time and it cannot be forced on a survivor, but many find healing and purpose in allowing the traumatic experience to become a "gift" to others, part of a sense of mission or calling in the world.[103] When a person successfully works through her or his experience, she or he may desire to share about it and the sermon may be a space where this can happen.

". . . He ascended into heaven and sitteth on the right hand of God the Father Almighty."

The doctrine of the ascension is not often addressed or engaged in preaching, but when held together with the fullness of Christ's identity and work it offers nuances that may be helpful for preaching in the context of trauma. Part of the healing process for some trauma survivors is finding a sense of containment for the traumatic experience.[104] A way to leave it behind so that it doesn't leak in and contaminate all parts of life. When Jesus ascends to heaven, he does so as the Crucified and Risen Lord, the experience of the cross has been integrated into his identity but he is not bound by it—the cross remains contained while Jesus is free and sovereign. Worship itself can also become an isolation-defeating communal act and a holding space where participants can name the grief and loss associated with trauma and move liturgically towards praise and acknowledgment of the life-preserving power of God made manifest in Jesus.[105] As Jesus is lifted up, so too our lives, experiences, and concerns are lifted up to God.

---

102. Bridgers, "The Resurrected Life," 42–43.
103. Ibid., 47.
104. Hunsinger, "Bearing the Unbearable," 17.
105. Ibid., 24; Bridgers, "The Resurrected Body," 51.

Jesus' ascension also marks his promise and gift of the Holy Spirit who serves as both comforter and advocate in the midst of both trauma and the long, slow process of healing. Indeed, the Spirit is the one that empowers our own advocacy on behalf of those who may be suffering in on-going situations of chronic abusive trauma. In the glory of Jesus' heavenly reign, we also have a glimpse of our own eschatological destiny. In Hunsinger's words, "We find comfort in the midst of affliction when we are reminded that the One who descends into every human hell we create and unwittingly or maliciously perpetuate is the very one who sits at the right hand of the Father in glory."[106]

"From thence he shall come to judge the quick and the dead."

Many preachers struggle to preach about Jesus' second coming and the final judgment. However, for survivors who long for retribution and revenge, preaching Jesus' return may offer a release as revenge and retribution are given over to God. The roots of much violence, both interpersonally and on a larger scale may originate in unresolved pain and trauma. Director of the Center for the Study of Violence at the Harvard Medical School James Gilligan writes, "All violence is an effort to do justice or to undo injustice."[107] Unresolved trauma may cause survivors to "act-out" on others or "act-in," harming themselves. For those who have unanswered questions and who have experienced the profound injustice of trauma (particularly chronic trauma caused by abuse over time) we can proclaim that Jesus will return and set things right. For those who have afflicted trauma on others, who suffer trauma from honest and earned guilt, Christ's coming judgment may be framed "cosmically" so that Jesus judges all that represents death and destruction.[108] All actions and experiences are subjected to the "universal victory of life over death."[109]

While many survivors may experience at least some measure of healing this side of the Eschaton, Jesus' return signals the final consummation of God's promises for the healing for all of creation and ultimate restoration. When Jesus returns, every tear shall be dried and the world will be made right.

---

106. Hunsinger, "Bearing the Unbearable," 25.
107. Gilligan, *Violence*, as quoted in Zehr, " Doing Justice, Healing Trauma," 15.
108. Kay, "He Descended into Hell," 25.
109. Ibid.

CONCLUSIONS AND IMPLICATIONS FOR HOMILETICAL THEOLOGIES OF THE GOSPEL

Christian ethicists and preachers have long called upon the faithful to live "in the way of Jesus."[110] The "way of Jesus" encompasses both the Living Christ as the means to life as well as living the "way" Jesus lived. Thus "the way of Jesus" is also the way to healing and hope and like all discipleship mysteriously involves both the grace-filled love and power of our God that comes as miraculous gift along with "an active decision to forgive" the one or ones who caused the trauma—even if that includes oneself.[111] Trauma must be attended to seriously and by psychiatric professionals and preachers should not be naïve about the effects of trauma and the challenges of ministering to survivors of trauma; however this essay has proposed that preachers and congregations can be channels for Christ's healing and has described the experience of trauma and the presence of trauma survivors as a context for preaching, exploring "the way of Jesus" as professed in preaching the narrative and theological emphases of the Apostles' Creed as a means of fostering association with Jesus and positively supporting healing for trauma survivors.

As in other contexts, in the midst of a context of trauma, many challenges emerge for preachers who seek to bear witness to the gospel. One challenge concerns the unfinished nature of how we experience God's good news this side of Christ's return. We experience the in-breaking of God's realm and signs of resurrection life only in fragments. Our preaching rests on the promises of God. In light of the incomplete nature of how we experience gospel, the practice of testimony or bearing witness holds promise for the circumstances of trauma survivors and broader discussions surrounding homiletical theologies of gospel. One of Judith Herman's pivotal stages of healing involves the trauma survivor telling her or his story to a witness.[112] Shelly Rambo elaborates upon the importance of this act, "Bearing witness is a practice that brings to light what has receded; it involves acknowledging the distortions of time, body, and speech that deter a survivor from *living on* in meaningful relationships with others."[113] Indeed, Rambo's work describing the middle space of Holy Saturday and the Spirit/Advocate who remains to testify to life and death, to what is known and unknown resonates with the challenges faced by preachers. Here we may also find a meaningful connection with the biblical concept of bearing

---

110. Yoder, "The Radical Revolution in Theological Perspective," 111 as cited in Hess, "Traumatic Violence and Christian Peacemaking," 203.

111. Hunsinger, "Bearing the Unbearable," 20.

112. Herman, *Trauma and Recovery*, 175.

113. Rambo, "Trauma and Faith," 242.

witness and the task of preachers to bear witness to the gospel—even in its unfinished and fragmentary nature.

A second challenge concerns what Rambo refers to as the Spirit/Advocate's witness to divine presence and absence.[114] Revelation has two sides: that which is revealed or shown to us, and that which God hides from us. Both the revealed and hidden aspects of revelation are grace for us in that our finitude and humanity limit what we can understand about God. The hidden sense of revelation is not unlike God's tender sheltering of Moses in the cleft of the rock in Exodus 33:21–23. Without God's gracious veiling, Moses would not survive an encounter with the full glory of God.

The late Lutheran theologian Gerhard Forde writes about proclamation and the dialectic of God's presence and "active absence" drawing from Martin Luther's understanding of "God preached" and "God not preached."[115] Forde emphasizes that properly done theology "fosters, advocates, and drives to proclamation."[116] Through the lens of proclamation, Forde situates our "talk about God" within the positive experience of revelation.[117] Forde begins with the positive side of Luther's dialectic—God speaking to us through proclamation of the gospel—God preached, while outside of proclamation, we experience separation from God—God not revealing God's self to us—God not preached.[118] Outside of positive proclamation, people can experience God as strange, wrathful, or absent. We are torn between our experience of God as "eternal," "anchor," "truth," and "beauty" and as "threat to us."[119] He writes, "We are caught between seeking and fleeing God's presence."[120] Obviously, preachers mainly deal in what is revealed to us, primarily in the person of Jesus Christ. However, in order for revelation to be meaningful, there must be a counter side—things that are not revealed, that which is hidden or actively veiled from humans. Like Rambo, Forde highlights that the absence of God is part of God's presence.[121] Often theology or doctrine feels like it is of little help in how to actually live with the "active absence" of God. Forde admits that thinking about God can lead to "an awesome string of abstractions."[122] Preaching can provide a way through the abstractions surrounding God "un-

---

114. Rambo, "Saturday in New Orleans," 239.
115. Forde, *Theology is for Proclamation*, 16.
116. Ibid., 1.
117. Ibid., 14.
118. Ibid., 14.
119. Ibid., 15.
120. Ibid.
121. Ibid., 16.
122. Ibid., 15.

preached" and God "preached" as God reveals God's self as "the present-tense Word from God, spoken 'to you . . .'"[123] This turn towards personal encounter means that preachers must grapple with the complexities of human experience.

Christine Helmer's book, *Theology and the End of Doctrine*, explores the complex relationship between context, human experience, and church doctrine through exploring the work of Schleiermacher and his critics who argued against his more "interior," experience-driven understanding of Christian belief with more of a focus on the Word of God as external and "other" in relationship to humanity.[124] Navigating this terrain, she names her theological assumptions: "Theology is a discipline that is at once oriented to the transcendent and thoroughly located in a particular time and place. It arises out of personal needs and social crises but looks beyond them to truth. The theologians' study is always and necessarily open to the surrounding world, heaven, and earth."[125]

Critics of Schleiermacher have tended to hold that his theology gives too much weight to "subjective" human experiences and human agency and too little weight to the biblical text.[126] However, one of his strengths is emphasizing the "living tradition" of Christianity so that God's presence in Christ in our world, expressed for Schleiermacher particularly through proclamation, opens up possibilities to experience Christ now and in the future.[127] Schleiermacher's theology is particularly interesting for preachers through the lens of Helmer's study concerning the relationship between language and doctrine, which in part seeks to address the question of "how . . . language change[s] under the . . . pressure of experience."[128] Schleiermacher uses the term *mystical* to help explain the relationship of Jesus Christ's redemptive power and the proclamation of the church.[129] Significant to the experience of trauma survivors, Schleiermacher's view of the mystical role of Christ in relationship to human language holds that in Helmer's words, ". . . experience transcends language. A mystical encounter with Christ cannot be captured in the third-person objective discourse of theology."[130] Edward Farley too ac-

---

123. Ibid., 17.

124. Helmer, *Theology and the End of Doctrine*, 26.

125. Ibid., 2–3.

126. Ibid., 50–51. Schleiermacher would argue that experiences with Christ are foundational to the New Testament (115). Issues with agency concern salvific redemption and the need to distinguish between the individual believer, the role of the church communicating Christ, and Christ himself (121).

127. Ibid., 113. Interestingly, Schleiermacher shares this almost sacramental view of preaching with critics such as Barth.

128. Ibid., 114.

129. Ibid., 121.

130. Ibid., 122.

knowledged the necessity of a theology of preaching that allows it to move nimbly as the "mysteries" of redemption that help comprise the "world of the gospel" engage both with Scripture as well as "new situations" that emerge in our world.[131] While language may have its limits, an experience certainly echoed in trauma survivors for whom language proved ineffective in limiting a traumatic experience or experiences, Schleiermacher positively holds that an experience of encounter with Christ, which may happen through proclamation, may completely transform a person so that her or his ground of self is completely shifted and the person becomes, in the Apostle Paul's language, "a new creation."[132] This transformation through an experience of Christ offers profound hope for trauma survivors as well as preachers and communities of faith who walk alongside survivors.

Amidst the reflection and questions of systematic theology, "the move to proclamation is itself the necessary and indispensable final move in the argument."[133] Theology cannot exist apart from human experience and the contexts of our world but people also cannot ultimately accomplish theology's end aims—only Christ can do it. What Forde calls the "naked" God of abstraction and transcendence, can only be borne by the "clothed" God of presence—of immanence, Jesus Christ, God incarnate.[134] In fact, Forde calls faith "The ever-renewed flight from God to God: from God naked and hidden to God clothed and revealed."[135] It is Jesus Christ who is revealed by the gospel. He is God preached, the Lord of proclamation.

The promised truth is that trauma is "not the last word."[136] Jesus Christ has ultimately overcome death and the forces of death that drain life and meaning. Upon Christ's final return, the rupture between the Realm of God and our world will finally be healed. God will make God's home among people—wiping away tears and bringing peace and abundance. It can be challenging for pastors or chaplains to continue to bear witness to this promised truth when they preach in the presence of death, yet part of our calling as witnesses is to watch for even fragmentary and incomplete signs of God's healing presence in the wake of trauma, to acknowledge the complexity, and begin to testify to that which may lie beyond words.

---

131. Farley, *Practicing Gospel*, 91–92.
132. Helmer, *Theology and the End of Doctrine*, 124–25.
133. Forde, *Theology is for Proclamation*, 5
134. Ibid., 22.
135. Ibid., 22.
136. Serene Jones's phrasing, in Rambo et al., "Theologians Engaging Trauma Transcript," 227.

— 6 —

Gospel as Transfiguring Promise
The Unfinished Task of Homiletical Theology in a Context of Disestablishment, Empire, and White Supremacy

—David Schnasa Jacobsen

In her important work on practical theology Mary McClintock Fulkerson argues that theology begins with a wound.[1] The trouble with wounds, however, is that left long enough they can bring new troubles in their train. The site of a wound can become the locus of secondary infections, unforeseen complications, and even if healing starts, scar tissue. I extend McClintock Fulkerson's metaphor about theology for a specific reason. If the central task of homiletical theology, and of the practice of preaching that embodies its theological task, is the naming of the gospel, this work is done not in some once-and-for-all state, but with the complications, secondary infections, and scars as they emerge over time. Theology begins with a wound. But homiletical theology is always just getting started—it has unfinished gospel business.[2]

But the task of naming the gospel in context features a further complication: context itself. We might agree that part of the tentativeness that accompanies our work in naming gospel is tempered by the "mystery" of the gospel. Edward Farley himself notes that gospel cannot be named in some simple formula or phrase.[3] Here, however, it may become important to note that we

1. Fulkerson, *Places of Redemption*, 12ff.
2. Jacobsen, "Preaching as the Unfinished Task of Theology."
3. Farley, *Practicing Gospel*, 80.

bump up against mystery in context as well. A corollary of the hermeneutic of suspicion should rightly be that contexts (whether in terms of the Freudian unconscious, Marxist economic interest or the Nietzschean will-to-power) are not always readily graspable to the inquiring subject(s). In this sense, contexts are "mysterious" because they are in an age of suspicion profoundly subject to an occluding mystification. More than that, however, contexts are also the place where wounds *compound and complicate* for persons caught up in them, whether as a result of self-interest, oppression, or both. This is to say that contexts are themselves frequently mystifications that end up occluding the true mystery, the mystery that is God. In his book *Race: A Theological Account*, J. Kameron Carter points out that the wound is where the suffering is—and where the place of suffering is, there is that strange mystery of God.[4] To approach context in this way is not simply to re-inscribe the dilemma so often lamented that too much attention to "problem" leads to a an inadequate or unfaithful gospel "solution."[5] To approach context as the wound where theology begins its work is to name both the mystifications and the Mystery in *conversation* with gospel.

NAMING GOSPEL AS PROMISE IN DIALOGUE WITH CONTEXT IN LIGHT OF A SITUATION OF RACIAL VIOLENCE

For me the starting point of homiletical theology is discerning some provisional sense of gospel as promise, perhaps something like what my colleague André Resner elsewhere calls a "working gospel" that is operative whether in preaching from a biblical text or speaking to a situation.[6] For this project, however, we authors are all trying to realize how important context already is for discerning gospel in any given time and place. My initial thought in this essay was to pursue with greater depth a contextual issue surfaced by Douglas John Hall. He argues that the challenge of liberation theology for a mainline Protestantism in the process of being culturally disestablished is not to adopt

---

4. Carter, *Race*, 374.

5. Charles Campbell criticizes soteriologically focused preaching models that operate from a problem/solution orientation as christologically inadequate to a faithful rendering of the biblical narrative of Jesus in *Preaching Jesus*, 221–22. Paul Wilson tries to distinguish his vision of trouble/grace preaching from problem/solution thinking in *Preaching and Homiletical Theory*, 98.

6. For a more detailed treatment of gospel as promise, see David Schnasa Jacobsen and Robert Allen Kelly, *Kairos Preaching*, 25–28. André Resner's notion of "working gospel" came from his insightful article, "Reading the Bible for Preaching the Gospel," 223.

liberation theology consumeristically, but to truly contextualize its own theology—an anti-triumphalistic vision that Hall pursues both in *Has the Church a Future* and even more poignantly in *The Cross in Our Context*.⁷ Yet as I write these words in the summer of 2015, I find the gospel *keeps dislocating me*, and thereby calls me even deeper into context *in light of an unfolding situation*.⁸ This happened in the first stage of this essay's drafting earlier this year. I realized that I would need to acknowledge how postcolonial theology pushes even Hall's trenchant analysis to a deeper realization of the ways in which a disestablished mainline Protestantism fails to name gospel in terms of its own neo-colonial identity. Here, as Sarah Travis and Pablo Jimenez have demonstrated, we are even now coming to see how a postcolonial context impacts and complexifies the ways we relate gospel to matters of identity and power in the presence of empire.⁹ Over the course of the year, however, even this complexification had to make way for ever deeper analyses of the role of race in my white mainline Protestant context. As I wrote this essay, I found it difficult, in other words, to keep thinking about gospel apart from the appalling events of Michael Brown in Ferguson, Tamir Rice in Cleveland, Walter Scott in North Charleston, Eric Garner in New York, and Sandra Bland in Texas, among far too many other names. It has become clearer to me that to talk about gospel and context also requires understanding what any preacher and any community "notices" in such situations and is otherwise "oblivious to"—including precisely those elements of context I personally have yet to grapple with fully.¹⁰ Can the gospel name promised g(race) without cognizance of the situation of race in the context of the disestablished North American white Protestant church? Homiletical theology, a grasping together of gospel and context, is about bringing Christ to bear in the present situation so as to open a new future.¹¹ Yet in the presence of such cultural, colonial, and racial wounds, it is provisional, fragile, *unfinished* theological work.

---

7. Hall, *Thinking the Faith*, 13–14.

8. For a similar notion of dislocation, see Campbell and Cilliers, *Preaching Fools*, 102. My concern for situation here connects with Farley's reflections on situations, in all their complexity, as part of the unique task of practical theology in *Practicing Gospel*, 29–43.

9. Jiménez, "Toward a Postcolonial Homiletic," 159–67 and "The Troublemaker's Friend," 84–90, and Travis, *Decolonizing Preaching*.

10. My analysis here depends in part on the very insightful work on obliviousness in the work of Fulkerson, "A Place to Appear."

11. Farley, *Practicing Gospel*, 80.

David Schnasa Jacobsen—*Gospel as Transfiguring Promise*

TOWARD A REVISED THEOLOGY OF THE GOSPEL IN CONTEXT

This essay endeavors to show how this central task of homiletical theology is done in deep relationship to context. At the same time, because of the nature of the gospel in context in light of a situation *and* the complicating feature of wounds, homiletical theology needs to acknowledge that the gospel it names is ever mystery—that its contexts sometimes escape our ideological notice, and that situations can intrude even on the obliviousness of privilege to demand further homiletical reflection on the gospel itself. In all these respects, the task of homiletical theology is indeed unfinished—even as it seeks to name gospel clearly. In particular, this paper will carry forward the argument from my article in *Theology Today*, "Preaching as the Unfinished Task of Theology: Grief, Trauma, and Early Christian Texts in Homiletical Interpretation." While in that article the focus is on the unfinished theological work of the Scriptures, here in this essay the focus will shift more explicitly to context and situation: the dynamics of each as they shape the homiletical-theological task—even in the presence of wounds, complications, and scars. And yet the task is opened profoundly in faith—the risen One *is* the crucified One, as even Hall would confess. Such a path toward naming gospel is troubled, but it is nonetheless profoundly gracious.

In what follows I intend to show that the context for naming gospel in the white mainline church is sufficiently situationally complicated to revisit key elements of a theology of the gospel. It begins with the struggle of coming to terms with identity in relationship to the gospel/culture dynamic. It turns ultimately to this struggle's unique relation to promise, both in the sense of the promise's presence of Christology, and promise's eschatological invitation to communion. Throughout I will draw in particular on the work of postcolonial theorists as well as theologians of race like J. Kameron Carter and Willie Jennings. As we do so, we will retrace a wound deep within the memorial tradition as it was formed under empire and re-opened in terms of race. In this way we who are mainliners will be taking up the unfinished theological task of the largely white Protestant church in North America in order to name gospel in its midst.

A DIPTYCH OF THE WOUND: ALEXAMENOS MEETS TITUS'S ARCH FOR A GOSPEL FORUM

The task of naming a theology of the gospel was set up strikingly in Charles Campbell and Johan Cilliers's *Preaching Fools*. Using the well-known graffito of Alexamenos on Palatine Hill in Rome, Campbell and Cilliers make a powerful claim for a vision of the gospel understood as foolishness.[12] Within the scheme of Roman power and knowledge, the crucified donkey bears witness to the foolish claim that is the Christian gospel. From this second-century-CE inscription we can see the foolish core of that message. It is, to my mind, a stunning pre-Constantinian ironic mockery of the gospel that now disestablished mainline Protestants can embrace in a post-Constantinian context. In the face of Roman power, the gospel is foolishness.

If one, however, were to continue wandering from Palatine Hill through the Forum in Rome, one would come across yet another important, this time official, inscription from the Roman imperial period. To commemorate the destruction of the Jerusalem Temple during the Jewish War, Titus commissioned an arch for the event of the victory parade through Rome. On this late–first-century-CE arch you can see a picture of a menorah, a symbol of the spoils of war and the humiliation of the community it represents. It is this traumatic event, of course, that drives the production of so much of the New Testament after Paul. And the conflict that this destruction sets loose for an early Christian movement still within Judaism is profoundly formative.

Within a short historical time span, and even a shorter distance in the inscribed and monumental spaces of the city of Rome, you can see these two icons that function for Christians as contextual-theological bookends to the struggle of the early church. Whatever the message of the Christians is in all its foolish opposition to Roman power, it is also tied deeply to the Jewish context of Temple destruction and historical grief in which that gospel arose. Thus, the diptych reminds us that the early Christian message is related to an identity being formed in relation both to Rome and with respect to a Jewish community undergoing cultural redefinition. The gospel is formed, I would suggest, in relation to Rome and the trauma of the destruction of the Second Temple. The gospel is named in the presence of wounds.

REVISITING THE WOUND: GOSPEL IN IDENTITY AND CULTURE TODAY

Contemporary preaching happens in the space between preachers and hearers in the world. It is an intrinsically contextual activity. This requires preachers to be able to reflect not just theologically on the content of preaching—as important as that is—but to think theologically about the context that connects pulpit to pew and church to the world. This contextual space has generated, of

---

12. Campbell and Cilliers, *Preaching Fools*, 2ff.

course, several ways of thinking about the nature of the gospel in preaching and its relationship to culture. With the rising awareness of the cultural disestablishment of the Protestant mainline and the eclipsing of its privileged role as a kind of chaplain to power, many practitioners have begun to articulate a gospel witness that goes beyond liberal formulations to postliberal ones. That is as it should be. Yet coming to terms with the church's disestablishment with an embrace of its post-Constantinian status may be only part of the issue. We have already noted how theologian Douglas John Hall argues that the theological challenge of the mainline Protestant church in North America is its need to *contextualize itself*. I am convinced, however, that an embrace of Hall's non-triumphalist role for the mainline Protestant church may not be sufficient for a rearticulation of the gospel in its present context. To contextualize for the sake of the gospel, I would like to argue, we mainliners need to revisit the wound. We need not just to recognize that the mainline white church is being disestablished, but "decolonized," too.[13]

This may sound like a strange claim. In order to describe this phenomenon and why it might be important for today, I need to proceed in two steps. First, it is important to rehearse how "we" got here—how the disestablishment of a largely white, mainline North American Protestantism led to new ways of thinking about context, culture, and the church's role in the world. In a second step, I want to explore how postcolonial theory and theology can aid the mainline Protestant church in rediscovering its sense of gospel in light of the postcolonial context.

The Changing Shape of Gospel, Context, and Identity in the Mainline Church

Classical liberal theologies tended to occlude matters of context because of their commitment to universal individualism. On the part of preachers, this meant that the particulars of identity were left largely off the table. At the level of the hearer (and the choice of the "singular" here is significant), distinctions and differences among hearers and their positionalities were largely left out of the conversation. The frequent result was a gospel spoken to the universal individual with very little sense of context and particularity.

In response to the pretensions of liberal universalism, postliberalism sought to advance the cultural particularity of the *ecclesia* while also addressing the problem of cultural disestablishment among the North American

---

13. I try here to link the idea of "being" disestablished with "being" decolonized. These processes in the life of the mainline Protestant church have only just begun in piecemeal and fragmentary ways.

mainline churches. Early on, advocates of a postliberal view, like Stanley Hauerwas and William Willimon, sought to reconfigure the way the church thought of itself relative to culture. The church for them was a particular community with a peculiar identity. Its preaching was not a universal word for everybody, but a specific word for the community of faith. The vision was not tied to some universal vision or field of action. The program of the church, they argued, was to *be* the church as a kind of alternative *politeia* or *colonia*.[14] For many figures from this perspective, the identity of the church was not to be elided with any universal liberal views, but was instead to be established through a close relationship with the church's Scriptures. The Scriptures provided an identity, even a *culture* or *grammar*, by which a unique, countercultural Christian identity could be received.[15] In this view, the gospel would be a performance or living out of an ecclesial culture shaped profoundly by its Scriptures. While this postliberal view went a long way toward embracing the particularities of the church's identity, it did so in part by backing away from dialogue with the culture at large. The postliberal church was satisfied with being "exiles" as way of being like the pre-Constantinian church in a now post-Constantinian, disestablished North American context.

The postliberal critique was, I believe, a necessary moment in thinking about the mainline church's gospel vision in light of its culture and identity after its long, liberal enmeshment in modernity. Its embrace of particularity over liberal universality opened the door to thinking more clearly about what the gospel sounds like today. I suspect that church and world may no longer need a default, invisible culture and identity cloaked in the language of liberal universalism. However, the embrace of particularity in postliberalism, by virtue of its counter-cultural stance, sometimes makes it harder for the mainline church to engage a religiously diverse and even non-religious public square. Here there is a further need to proceed to an even deeper contextual analysis. Perhaps the problem is that the mainline Protestant church is not just being "disestablished," but thereby also being decolonized—even if in bits and pieces, fits and starts. Because of the inherent intercultural focus of postcolonial theory and theology, however, the question of disestablishment now becomes entwined with vestigial and pervasive elements of privilege in mainline ecclesial life, including matters of race and cultural power.

---

14. Hauerwas and Willimon, *Resident Aliens*.

15. This particular notion is carried forward in the work of Lindbeck, *The Nature of Doctrine*.

The Promise of a Postcolonial View of Gospel, Context, and Identity

I am convinced that a familiarity with postcolonial theory and theology can help loosen up the ways in which the mainline Protestant church can think about its understanding of the gospel in relation to its identity and relationship to culture. There is, I believe, a space beyond the acultural gospel of cloaked identity in liberal universalism and the purely counter-cultural approach of a disestablished, "circle the wagons" view of a postliberal church as *politeia* or *colonia*. This "third space" may just be a promising postcolonial way of thinking about the mainline Protestant church

Postcolonial theory can be traced back to the work of such thinkers as Homi Bhabha, Franz Fanon, Edward Said, and Gayatri Chakravorty Spivak.[16] One of the first things to recognize in terms of definitions is that the "post" in postcolonial does not mean "after." In fact what postcolonial theory tends to recognize is that any "de-colonizing" by European and North American powers has really resulted in *a neo-colonial* context—where power and control over other countries and cultures is wielded more indirectly than directly, as under colonial rule.[17] It is precisely in this awareness of the pervasiveness of oppressive power and control exercised through new means of military threat and economic influence that requires the mainline Protestant church to become more self-reflexive about its position and how that impacts its witness in disestablishment and decolonization. While disestablishment has meant that whatever is left of the church's witness under liberalism can no longer plausibly function on the basis of its prized position in the culture, the mainline Protestant church still stands in a complex relationship with the powers that be and the wider world it finds itself in. There are, I suspect, still vestigial elements of privilege that shape the life of the mainline church. We who are mainliners may fancy ourselves "exiles" in this culture, but we also still benefit from some vestigial benefits of the power. Mainliners still have some presumption of cultural authority, a degree of access to power that other cultural and religious groups don't have (privilege), and even well-established denominational pension plans! The romanticism of being "exiles," a separate *politeia* or heavenly *colonia* may sound nice, but we who are mainliners still have *relative* power—and that includes academics like me.

Such a postcolonial shift in self-reflexivity does more than simply modify anyone's identity or an understanding of the relationship of gospel to

---

16. For a helpful introductory summary that places some of the above named figures in the context of the literature, one may wish to read Loomba, *Colonialism/Postcolonialism*.

17. Thanks to my colleague, Dr. Adam Hearlson, who pointed out in personal correspondence with me on October 12, 2015, the similarity of this claim to Michelle Alexander's argument in *The New Jim Crow*.

culture. It also means that, as the disestablished church *decolonizes* it becomes aware that its identity is not some glorious self-possession—whether viewed in terms of liberal universality or a romantic counter-cultural particularity. The identity of the mainline church is, as I would call it, "given and riven." It is "given" in the sense that it is not a self-possession, something mainline Protestant churches "have" apart from others. Whether in the Enlightenment mastery of the universal individual or in the hermetically sealed counter-cultural identity of the pre-Constantinian church, we who are mainliners are accustomed to thinking of identity as something "we" possess. Identity in postcolonial theory and theology is something that is more fluid, porous, and, yes, given in interaction with others. The complexity of relationships shaped by colonial histories is such that identities are not simply "fixed" or "possessed" but received in interactions interculturally. To claim that identities are "riven" is to acknowledge that since they are not fixed, we always stand in a negotiated space that acknowledges how power divides but sees that even the powerful need to be decolonized. This "riven" identity where mainliners stand both in relation to power and *deformed by it* opens up a different mode of self-understanding beyond the old liberal/postliberal binary.

The positive implication of revising identity in a church being disestablished *and* decolonized is that it begins to see identity in a more profound relationship of openness to others. Instead of seeing identity as a form of cultural purity to be protected, whether in universalist or counter-cultural form, a "given and riven" view of identity presupposes that intercultural interaction is the nature of life itself. One Canadian cultural critic, Andrew Potter, argues that cultures are not systems to be kept romantically pure in opposition to others, but more like immune systems that *require* interaction with others to be strong, healthy, and related.[18] Imagine how a postcolonial imagination of culture and identity might affect the way mainliners think about their church's relative privilege, its use of power *in connection with others*, and the way it talks about the world.

Some colleagues in homiletics have already begun to bring such insights to bear to the church's task in preaching. Pablo Jiménez has begun to explore the relationship of preaching and postcolonial theory in ways both particular and practical.[19] Canadian Sarah Travis has tried to unpack what a decolonized pulpit might look like in deep connection with others through a powerful interactive and perichoretic vision of the social Trinity.[20] In a recent publication postcolonial theologian Kwok Pui-lan has creatively envisioned

---

18. Potter, *The Authenticity Hoax*, 203.
19. Jiménez, "Toward a Postcolonial Homiletic" and "The Troublemaker's Friend."
20. Travis, *Decolonizing Preaching*.

a performative vision of preaching that sees its work not solely as that of the preacher, but the preacher in relation to the congregation—all of whom seek in a kind of "third space" of the preaching moment to forge new identities and new ways of being in the presence of God and others beyond the univocal identities that colonialism presupposes and polices.[21] These visions for a postcolonial preaching could have a profound influence on a mainline church struggling to understand its own identity after disestablishment and the way it might relate gospel to culture, one not bound to a cloaked identity through universalism or a pure, counter-cultural identity through postliberalism.

TENDING TO THE WOUND

I contend that with postcolonial theology many of us in the mainline Protestant churches have the opportunity to take up the unfinished theological work around gospel, culture, and identity—even in these troubling times of coming to terms with our own situational struggles with race and the legacy of white supremacy. This situation is our chance to tend to the wound. In many ways the relation of the gospel to the crisis of the Temple's destruction set loose a dynamic with which Christians still live today—every time Christians speak of the Jews as identity foils and struggle in naming gospel in light of Roman colonial power.[22] The postliberals are correct in seeing the particularities of identity as a central issue. Context affects us mainliners deeply both by the context we know and think we understand (disestablishment) and in light of the situations that emerge in troubled interaction with others (postcolonialism and racism). Both may call forth grief in the mainline churches. Both call those of us who are mainliners to go deeper both into the gospel and into the wound of context by which gospel is discerned and named.

Theologians Willie Jennings and J. Kameron Carter contend that the focal point of this wound in the tradition is a supersessionist Christology. Carter in particular argues that there is a deep connection between a Christology born of a struggle with Judaism that eventually discards the oriental Jesus at the dawn of modernity and thus helps make possible an elision of Christianity's essence with whiteness:

> Christianity's central figure, Jesus Christ, came to be racialized ultimately as a figure of the Occident, though as regards his bodily status he was deemed to be not of the West. As regards his flesh he was of the Orient, an oriental Jew. Reconceived as an occidental

21. Pui-lan, "Postcolonial Preaching in Intercultural Contexts," 8–21.
22. Crossan and Reed, *In Search of Paul*.

(rational) religion, Christianity was transformed into the cultural property of the West. Christian civilization became Western civilization, and vice versa. Thus, embedded within the social imaginary of the civilizations of the West is the theological problem of the *Rassenfrage* . . . . Modernity/coloniality *is* quintessentially the product of an ideological usage of Jesus.[23] (emphasis author)

In an interview with Adam McInturf, Carter goes on to summarize the issue—and in relation to the crisis of a now disestablished Christianity with the crisis of whiteness and colonial hegemony. Carter argues that what the theological world witnesses in the kind of turn to tradition and *resourcement* seen in postliberalism and radical orthodoxy is actually characterized by a malaise he calls "post-colonial melancholy."[24]

Carter then offers a different tradition for reading Christology that undoes the de-linking of Jesus with his Jewishness in the name of subsequent colonial and racial claims—and in a way that helps us white mainline Protestants to live with the wound toward healing:

> To account oneself a Christian who is, in theological terms, a Gentile, that is, a non-Jew, but nevertheless accounts their salvation as coming from the Jew who is Jesus, who himself is the culmination of the story of Israel's relationships with their God, and therefore is the Messiah of Israel, is, in many ways, an *interracial claim*. What this means in effect is that as a Gentile, I am in the position of Ruth in the Bible, where my family of commitment is in a people who are not my people but who received me, and that is my salvation. What is a Gentile Christian? A Gentile Christian is one who echoes the promises of Yahweh to the people of Israel, which have redounded to the whole world. Now, in the racial terms of modernity, that sounds like *mulatto* existence.[25]

A nonsupersessionist Christology that works through the wounds of the gospel's first articulation in context is important not just for dealing with the tradition, but for the accompanying complications brought about through colonial and racist overlays. It does not purify or absolve the tradition, but allows contemporary Christians to live in "differentiated proximity" with that tradition and with others, too.[26]

---

23. Carter, *Race*, 372.
24. McInturf, "Race," 83.
25. Ibid., 84.
26. Jacobsen, "Preaching as the Unfinished Task of Theology," 415.

This way of living critically with the tradition in the name of the gospel to which the tradition witnesses in all of its contextual pain and struggle requires another theological move, one owing a great debt to Willie Jennings. In his book *The Christian Imagination: Theology and the Origins of Race*, Jennings envisions a telos of *communion*, one that is capable of holding memories of not just race, but space, a common life not built on pure racial identities and economies of sameness built on white supremacy and ordered by colonial appropriations of space. Jennings writes:

> For some, my account of Jesus-space and of communion will seem idealistic, a denial of Christian failure.... If my account of space looks like an idealist account, it is precisely because it is an account held in contrast to the utter inversion of the Israel/Gentile relation. If my account of communion looks like an ideologically naïve ideation, it is because the very fragments of memory of Gentile existence have been altered and reconfigured to make room for other identity-facilitating realities. In the remade world born of the colonialist moment, Christian possibilities of communion and cultural intimacy have been subverted to draw all people toward an existence marked by a reversal of its telos.[27]

The reorientation is one away from the dividing up of space and the use of the categorizing power of race to organize the world through whiteness to a communion which in Jesus-space, marked by his body. Jennings's vision focuses on the relationship of Jews and Gentiles and the problem of racism as intertwined around issues of place/identity and in light of the new belonging that Jesus offers in a communion in his body to the God of Israel.

TRANSFIGURING THE WOUND

The goal here is not the repristinating healing of the (now closed and mystified or forgotten) wound that so troubles the Christian tradition and the texture of the common life of mainline Protestant churches in relation to other cultural-theological traditions.[28] We have been laying hold of the idea

---

27. Jennings, *The Christian Imagination*, 288.

28. This concern seems in part to drive the research into the "refiguring" of wounds into scars in my colleague Shelly Rambo's important contribution "Refiguring Wounds in the Afterlife (of Trauma)" in *Carnal Hermeneutics*. While Rambo also uses the notion of transfiguring wounds, she does so with a view to seeing them transformed or "refigured" into a scar or otherwise "faint" trace. I intend to use the term here differently in that I want to get at the unresolved struggle that in the tradition and though later complications continues to haunt the naming of the gospel and thus *remains* wound—even in resurrection

that even a theology of the gospel begins with a wound, both in McClintock Fulkerson's sense and in the surprising notion of J. Kameron Carter's linking of mysterious divine presence to suffering. Reconciliation, healing, closure, are all beautiful but fail to correspond to the complications of the wound and the provisional nature of the homiletical-theological moment. Here we might build on the work of the philosopher Richard Kearney, whose reflections on transfiguration and its relation to Aristotelian notions of tragic catharsis lead us not just to wound at the beginning, but promise at the end.

In his article on the place of wounds and trauma in Father/Son relations in the narrative works of Homer, Shakespeare, and Joyce, Kearney notes two features about catharsis that help us understand its power. First, in the cathartic moment pity and fear are *transfigured* into pleasure. What happens with the wound recognized (e.g., Ulysses) in narrative is not a detoxification or getting rid of. Indeed, Kearney writes of narrative as

> "impossible story: storytelling which forever fails to *cure* trauma but never fails to try to *heal* it. And in this very effort itself there is pleasure: the pleasurable purgation of pity and fear."[29]

As I like to point out, in the eschatological vision of Revelation 21:4 tears are not absent, but they are wiped away. The sea may be "no more," but salty tears may just be the wounded locus of the kind of cathartic transfiguration of "rewriting" that Kearney imagines. Second, narrative is not simply about closure, but openness. The tragic, wounded overlay that runs from Homer (by means of Shakespeare's tragedies) through Joyce is a process of rewriting and creative failure. Kearney points out, "we need to think about the genuinely cathartic role of trauma stories as requiring open narratives that never end, rather than closed narratives that presume to wish away *wounds* rather than working through *scars*."[30] It is this to which we as preachers bear gospel witness in taking up the unfinished theological task of the NT Scriptures somewhere between Titus's Arch and the graffito of Alexamenos. In preaching we mainliners in particular take up our beautiful and wounded tradition in the midst of our contexts, known and even now intruding on our obliviousness, and "hand it over" yet again, and even more, bring its transfigured telos of identity and differentiated communion to gospel speech.

The nature of that gospel, for me, is eschatological promise. Here Kearney helps to move us forward as well.[31] Kearney uses the notion of transfiguration,

---

narratives where that eschatological gospel is proclaimed.

29. Kearney, "Writing Trauma."
30. Ibid.
31. What follows is a brief summary of two key notions from Richard Kearney treated

but here in the biblical-narrative sense of the burning bush of Exodus 3:14, the mountain of Mark 9, among other textual sites. For Kearney, transfiguration is a place of onto-eschatological crossing. On the one hand, it is a place where we meet the divine, traversing presence of God: not the God who *is*, nor the God who *will be*, but the God who *may be*. On the other hand, this promising God of possibility also empowers us to engage in the midst of troubled memory by prying opened closed actualities. This God who may be depends on us, but not without possibilizing the present. Again, this does not obliterate the wound, let alone "close" it. Yet the promise is the means by which the wound is being transfigured, rewritten, and taken up into the unfinished task of a theology of the gospel in context—even a context of establishment, empire, and white supremacy.

IMPLICATIONS FOR A HOMILETICAL THEOLOGY OF THE GOSPEL

Edward Farley argues that a theology of gospel is not a fixed entity, not some predetermined piece of content that can be applied to a given context, but rather a way of bringing Jesus Christ to bear in the present so as to open a new future.[32] For me, to talk about the gospel promise is of a piece with Farley's concern for untoward limitation and purpose for a gospel utterance of "opening." Promise, as understood in contemporary speech-act theory, is not just a matter for a correspondence of terms theory of reality, not some purely denotative understanding of language whose "content" refers to some external object that exists apart from the promise. Promise as a speech act is at its heart an event: an event of self-involvement of the promiser and an event in which a kind of possibilizing is opened up (Kearney). At the same time, what makes a promise go awry is not a lack of correspondence to a content, object, or reference, but an "infelicity of speech." This is to say, that a homiletical theology of promise in context hinges on the self-involvement of a divine Promiser and a pushing back on seemingly closed actualities and their accompanying epistemologies. This is all the more important when we mainliners seek to relate such a notion of promise to a context like disestablishment and a situation of entrenched racism and colonialism as it pertains to black lives in 2014–15 and beyond.

We have characterized this meeting of context and situation as a wound—a wound both complicated by the relation of white mainline Protestant

---

in much greater detail in his book, *The God Who May Be*, 20–52.

32. Farley, *Practicing Gospel*.

disestablishment to a neo-colonial context and a situation determined by racialized identities. Since a homiletical approach to any situation is not easy to square with a problem/solution vision of preaching, we charged with speaking gospel must approach the wound not so much that it be healed, but that it be a site of *healing*. As Jim Wallis puts it in his book on the same conflation of woundedness within the evangelical church, "It's time for white Christians to be more Christian than white . . . ."[33] The question is not one of setting up newly binaried identities that occlude the complicated, wounded realities of context, but whether identities in all their fluidity, in all their sense of being both "given and riven" can be named for what they really are and become a site not of cure and reconciliation, but healing and reconciling.

The result of these reflections, which trace the wound that both dialogues with gospel naming and continues to call it into question is threefold. I see three important implications for seeing a theology of the gospel in context as the starting point for doing homiletical theology.

Provisionality of Gospel and Context, Promise and Wound for Homiletical Theology

First, there is a provisionality to both gospel and wound. Farley freely acknowledges that the gospel is rearticulated anew in every time and place, in every context. For Farley, it is where the memory of Jesus is brought to bear in such a way that it opens up newness. The analysis here pushes us mainliners to acknowledge that there is also a troubling provisionality at the level of context itself. This encompasses not only the mystifications of context in the presence of power and privilege in the present, but also the way in which contemporary contexts are shaped by the unfinished and now complicated wounds of the past. In other words, the unfinished task of homiletical theology has both to do with the mystery of salvation in the gospel and the mystifications by which the wound is sometimes prematurely "closed" and not tended.

In contemporary Germany such wounded memory is recalled by the use of *Stolpersteine*, "stones of stumbling." Over the last few years, German communities have begun to erect cobblestones on sidewalks and stones on the faces of homes that bear witness to the names of Jewish families who used to live in these homes and operate these businesses prior to the Holocaust. The goal is not to perpetuate guilt, but to hold to memory in such a way that the wound is not simply lightly healed and therefore covered over or occluded. We, for whom the cross is itself a stone of stumbling, a *skandalon*, should

---

33. Wallis, *America's Original Sin*, xviii.

understand. To live under the sign of the cross is to point to both a wound and a promise. It is a link that makes even more sense in the North American history of white supremacy given the searing vision of James Cone in *The Cross and the Lynching Tree*. The cross and the lynching tree, in the contemporary context, and especially for those who benefit from privilege and power, are understood in light of each other—not because the wound is closed, but still needs tending and is still being "transfigured." The unfinished task of homiletical theology is deeply tied to the provisionality of both gospel and context where text or situation touches on "the wound."

Gospel in Context Means Homiletical Theology is Dialogical at the Site of the Transfigured Wound

Second, homiletical theology is not about possessing the "gospel in context," but a matter of opening and reopening the dialogue between gospel and context by virtue of texts and situations—and at the site of the wound being transfigured. It is far too easy to get hung up on a notion that either keeps the gospel pure in some ideal state (an eternal *kerygma* or idealized gospel practice in the present of a specific community) or to reduce all of gospel reflection to an epiphenomenon of culture (gospel is merely a function of a cultural tradition). A commitment to seeing gospel and context/culture in dialogue is a means to ensure that the gap is not merely covered over: either in the direction of a purely "downhill" homiletical theology that guards the *extra nos* of the gospel in a text/narrative/theology that somehow escapes history and culture or in the direction of a cultural reductionism that leaves all gospel reflection as a mere projection of communities, practices, and traditions. The gap must somehow be acknowledged. The gap between gospel and context, after all, is where a transforming, transfiguring dialogue can take place with reference to biblical texts and troublesome situations.

In his work *The New Measures*, homiletician Ted Smith identifies the problem of this gap in a way that acknowledges how both liberationist and postliberal ways of dealing with gospel and culture falter at the same point. Smith calls this gap, this unfinished space for dialogue, the difference between picture and caption.[34] The unfinished business of homiletical theology requires an acknowledgment of this gap between picture and caption, or in our case, between gospel and context, so a real dialogue takes place and the ever-transfiguring wound might *continue* to be healed. In this sense such healing

---

34. Smith, *The New Measures*, 16–42. Smith does this reflection on the cultural turn in theology in reference to the work of Delores Williams and Stanley Hauerwas respectively.

functions as what Smith calls an eschatological memory, a future pushback on the present that keeps the present open, and I would argue, open precisely for the dialogue between gospel and context that is homiletical theology.[35] The wound keeps the dialogue moving and honest.

Homiletical Theology Acknowledges Limits in the Presence of Mystery

Third, homiletical theology must in all honesty continue to acknowledge mystery in the presence of a promising gospel. Healthy preaching must name from time to time what it "doesn't know." Homiletical theology that takes mystery seriously can help to distinguish between what Luther called "God preached" and "God not preached." Luther, of course, was pushing back against the speculative theology of the medieval church. Homiletical theologians are, least of all, prepared to pull back the curtain of the mysteries of God, and yet preaching is also charged to say something: to acknowledge a piece of what it does know is being disclosed in God in Christ.

This reality takes on special poignancy when we white, mainline Protestants acknowledge the complications of wounds and the complexity of context. The gospel is not everything that can be said. It should be, however, enough for the day. It may not reconcile, but it can be reconciling. It may not heal, but it can still be *healing*. This sober sense of the mystery of salvation is summed up in Luther's understanding of the life of the believer the face of *Anfechtung*:

> This life, therefore, is not godliness but the process of becoming godly, not health but getting well, not being but becoming, not rest but exercise. We are not now what we shall be, but we are on the way.[36]

Again, the mystery that holds future and present in tension opens up the homiletical-theological task of naming "enough" for this particular text and/or in this particular situation.

All of this is also to say that there is an underside to envisioning the gospel as promise in relation to wound. Promise is never just the good news that stands on the other side of eschatology: a transversing presence and a reign of God whose "already" is always bounded by its "not yet." The underside of the promise points to the "not yet" in such a way that any articulation of the mystery of salvation in the gospel carries forward that which is *not yet*

---

35. I describe this in much greater detail in the way I describe the gospel culture relationship on in *Kairos Preaching*, 29–33.

36. Luther, *Luther's Works* 32:24.

redeemed. Martin Luther King Jr., in his famous "I Have a Dream" address spends the first several minutes speaking about a "promissory note" that is still unredeemed: promises in the Constitution and Declaration of Independence that black people are still waiting for as he speaks on the Washington mall. King's use of the figure of the "promissory note" is illustrative for our work, too. Part of the mystery of articulating gospel promise is the way that even its underside animates an ever deeper articulation of its "not yet" in moments of woundedness. Sometimes the mystery of the promise is articulated as the flip side of lament in practice. Part of the mystery of promise is that it opens up a contested space for homiletical theology in that it breaks open fissures of lament *and* a possibilizing of the present.

CONCLUSION

Homiletical theology begins with discerning a theology of the gospel in context. There is, says Farley, a *habitus* to theology, a practical wisdom about the gospel that starts the conversation—for me, the notion of promise. But the work of homiletical theology is a dialogical one between gospel and context. Its purview affects us every time we mainliners begin again to reflect on gospel in light of a biblical text or a situation that presents itself for preaching. At the moment, the *habitus* meets the dialectic of what Farley calls *theologia*, a critical-reflective capacity for thinking through the gospel in light of this text and this situation in context.[37] Where *habitus/scientia* meets texts and situations in the context of woundedness, there homiletical theology happens anew.

---

37. The term *habitus* is found in the work of Farley, *Practicing Gospel*, 3–13. In a review that took up Farley's earlier vision of *habitus* in *Theologia* and tried to relate it to methodological developments in practical theology, Don Browning argues that theology is always a negotiation between the *habitus* that is practical wisdom and the dialectic of theological method, "The Revival of Practical Theology."

Bibliography

Abeysekara, Ananda. "Identity for and Against Itself: Religion, Criticism, and Pluralization." *Journal of the American Academy of Religion* 72.4 (2004) 973–1001.
Akhmatova, Anna. "Requiem." In *Selected Poems,* translated by Richard McKane, 90. London: Oxford University Press, 1969.
Alexander, Michelle. *The New Jim Crow.* 2nd ed. New York: The New Press, 2012.
Andrease, N.C. "Posttraumatic Stress Disorder." In *Comprehensive Textbook of Psychiatry,* 918–24. Baltimore: Williams and Wilkins, 1985.
Angell, Stephen. "Quakers: From Slave Traders to Early Abolitionists." http://www.pbs.org/thisfarbyfaith/journey_1/p_7.html.
Bae, Yo-Han. "Lee Ju-Jeongeui sinanggobakmunaedaehan Yugyochulhakjuk boonsuk (A Confucian Analysis of Lee Su-Jeong's Confessional Essay)." *Jangsinnondan* 38 (2010) 481–504.
Barton, John. *People of the Book? The Authority of the Bible in Christianity.* Louisville: Westminster John Knox, 1988.
Beker, J. Christian. "The Authority of Scripture: Normative or Incidental?" *Theology Today* 49 (1992) 381.
———. *Paul the Apostle.* Philadelphia: Fortress, 1980.
Berger, Peter. *The Sacred Canopy: Elements of a Sociological Theory of Religion.* Garden City, NY: Doubleday, 1967.
Berger, Peter, and Thomas Luckmann. *The Social Construction of Reality: A Treatise in the Sociology of Knowledge.* New York: Penguin, 1966.
Best, Ernest. *From Text to Sermon.* Philadelphia: John Knox, 1978.
Bhabha, Homi K. *The Location of Culture.* New York: Routledge Classics, 2004.
Bleiker, Roland. "Identity and Security in Korea." *The Pacific Review* 14.1 (2001) 121–48.
———. *Divided Korea: Toward a Culture of Reconciliation.* Minneapolis: University of Minnesota Press, 2005.
Bonhoeffer, Dietrich. *Letters and Papers from Prison.* New York: Collier, 1972.
Borg, Marcus. *Conflict, Holiness, and Politics in the Teachings of Jesus.* London: Bloomsbury T & T Clark, 1998.
Bourdieu, Pierre. *The Logic of Practice.* Translated by R. Nice. Stanford, CA: Stanford University Press, 1980.
Bridgers, Lynn. "The Resurrected Life: Roman Catholic Resources in Posttraumatic Pastoral Care." *International Journal of Practical Theology* 15.1 (2011) 38–56.
Brown, Arthur Judson. *The Mastery of the Far East the Story of Korea's Transformation and Japan's Rise to Supremacy in the Orient.* New York: Charles Scribner's Sons, 1919.

Bibliography

Browning, Don. "The Revival of Practical Theology." *The Christian Century* 101.4 (February, 1988) 134–44.
Brueggemann, Walter. "Readings from the Day 'In Between.'" In *A Shadow of Glory: Reading the New Testament after the Holocaust*, 110–11. New York: Rutledge, 2002.
———. *The Prophetic Imagination*. 2nd ed. Minneapolis: Fortress, 2001.
Bultmann, Rudolf. *Jesus Christ and Mythology*. New York: Scribners, 1958.
Buttrick, David. *Homiletic: Moves and Structures*. Philadelphia: Fortress, 1987.
Campbell, Charles, and Johan Cilliers. *Preaching Fools: The Gospel as a Rhetoric of Folly*. Waco, TX: Baylor University Press, 2012.
Campbell, Charles. *Preaching Jesus: New Directions for Homiletics in Hans Frei's Postliberal Theology*. Grand Rapids: Eerdmans, 1997.
Cane, Patricia Mathes. *Trauma Healing and Transformation*. Watsonville, CA: Capacitar, 2000.
Carter, J. Kameron. *Race: A Theological Account*. Oxford: Oxford University Press, 2008.
Cavanaugh, William T. *Theopolitical Imagination*. New York: T & T Clark, 2002.
Childs, Peter, and Patrick Williams. *Introduction to Post-Colonial Theory*. London: Prentice Hall, 1997.
Choi, Youngkeun. "Christianity and Nationalism in East Asia: Focusing On Protestant Nationalism in Korea under Japanese Imperialism." *Korea Presbyterian Journal of Theology* 37 (June, 2010) 9–50.
Cone, James H. *The Cross and the Lynching Tree*. Maryknoll, NY: Orbis, 2011.
Conwell, Russell. *Acres of Diamonds*. Philadelphia: Temple University Press, 2015. http://www.temple.edu/about/history/acres-diamonds.
Crossan, John Dominic, and Jonathan Reed. *In Search of Paul: How Jesus' Apostle Opposed Rome's Empire with God's Kingdom*. New York: HarperOne, 2004.
Cumings, Bruce. *Korea's Place in the Sun: A Modern History*. New York: W. W. Norton, 1997.
———. *The Korean War*. New York: The Modern Library, 2010.
Duck, Ruth. *Worship for the Whole People of God: Vital Worship for the 21st Century*. Louisville: Westminster John Knox, 2013.
Elson, William. Henry. *Chapter VI, Colonial New England Affairs*. New York: MacMillian Company, 1904. http://www.usahistory.info/NewEngland/index.html.
Fanon, Frantz. *The Wretched of the Earth*. New York: Grove, 1965.
Farley, Edward. *Practicing Gospel*. Louisville: Westminster John Knox, 2003.
———. *Theologia: The Fragmentation and Unity of Theological Education*. Philadelphia: Fortress, 1983.
———. "Preaching the Bible and Preaching the Gospel." *Theology Today* 51.1 (April, 1994) 90–103.
"Farm Workers in Washington State History Project." Online: http://depts.washington.edu/civilr/farmwk_intro.htm.
Farris, Stephen. *Preaching That Matters: The Bible and Our Lives*. Louisville: Westminster John Knox, 1998.
Feuerbach, Ludwig. *The Essence of Christianity*. Translated by G. Eliot. New York: Harper & Row, 1957.
Fiorenza, Elisabeth Schussler. *Wisdom Ways: Introducing Feminist Biblical Criticism*. Maryknoll, NY: Orbis, 2001.
Forde, Gerhard. *Theology is for Proclamation*. Minneapolis: Augsburg Fortress, 1990.

Bibliography

Fulkerson, Mary McClintock. "A Place to Appear: Ecclesiology as if Bodies Matter." *Theology Today*, 67 (2007) 159–71.

———. *Places of Redemption*. New York: Oxford University Press, 2007.

George, Carol V. R. *God's Salesman: Norman Vincent Peale and the Power of Positive Thinking*. New York: Oxford University Press, 1993.

Gilligan, James. *Violence: Reflections on a National Epidemic*. New York: Random House, 1996.

Hagin, Kenneth E. "Healing and Miracles through United Prayer." *The Word of Faith Magazine* (1998) 4–8.

———. *New Thresholds of Faith*. Tulsa: Rhema Bible Church, 1985.

———. "Redeemed from the Curse of Poverty." In *Classic Sermons*, 173–86. Tulsa: Faith Library Publications, 1993.

Hall, Douglas John. *Thinking the Faith: Christian Theology in a North American Context*. Minneapolis: Augsburg Fortress, 1989.

———. *Waiting for Gospel*. Eugene, OR: Cascade, 2012.

Ham, Sok Hon. *Queen of Suffering: A Spiritual History of Korea*. Edited by John A. Sullivan. Translated by Sang Yu. Philadelphia: Friends World Committee for Consultation, 1985.

Hamilton, Charles V. *The Black Preacher in America*. New York: Morrow, 1972.

Harrell, David Edwin. *Oral Roberts: An American Life*. Bloomington, IN: Indiana University Press, 1985.

Harrison, Milmon F. *Righteous Riches: The Word of Faith Movement in Contemporary African American Religion*. New York: Oxford University Press, 2005.

Hauerwas, Stanley, and William Willimon. *Resident Aliens: Life in the Christian Colony*. Nashville: Abingdon, 1989.

Hearlson, Adam. "Preaching as Sabotage: Power, Practice and Proclamation." PhD diss., Princeton Theological Seminary, 2013.

Helmer, Christine. *Theology and the End of Doctrine*. Louisville: Westminster John Knox, 2014.

Henry, Carl Ferdinand Howard. *God, Revelation, and Authority*. 6 vols. Wheaton, IL: Crossway, 1999.

Herman, Judith. *Trauma and Recovery*. New York: Basic, 1992.

Hess, Cynthia. "Traumatic Violence and Christian Peacemaking." *Brethren Life and Thought* 51.4 (Fall 2006) 203.

Hessel, Dieter T. *Social Themes of the Christian Year: A Commentary on the Liturgy*. Philadelphia: Geneva, 1983.

Hiltz, Fred, et al. "Response of the Churches to the Truth and Reconciliation Commission of Canada." http://presbyterian.ca/2015/06/11/churches-response-trc/.

Hirsch, E. D. *Validity in Interpretation*. New Haven, CT: Yale University Press, 1967.

Hunsinger, Deborah Van Deusen. "Bearing the Unbearable: Trauma, Gospel, and Pastoral Care." *Theology Today* 68.1 (2011) 9.

"Introduction to Colonial African American Life: Slavery Existed in Every Colony." http://www.history.org/Almanack/people/african/aaintro.cfm.

Jacobsen, David S. "Introduction." In *Homiletical Theology: Preaching as Doing Theology*, 3–19. Eugene, OR: Cascade, 2015.

———. "Preaching as the Unfinished Task of Theology: Grief, Trauma, and Early Christian Texts in Homiletical Interpretation." *Theology Today* 70.4 (January 2014) 407–16.

Bibliography

———. "Research Question." Homiletical Theology Project Web Site. http://www.bu.edu/homiletical-theology-project/research-questions/.
———. "The Unfinished Task of Homiletical Theology." In *Homiletical Theology: Preaching as Doing Theology*, edited by David S. Jacobsen, 39–55. Eugene, OR: Cascade, 2015.
Jacobsen, David S., ed. *Homiletical Theology: Preaching as Doing Theology*. Eugene, OR: Cascade, 2015.
Jacobsen, David S., and Robert Kelly. *Kairos Preaching: Speaking Gospel to the Situation*. Minneapolis: Fortress, 2009.
Jennings, Willie. *The Christian Imagination: Theology and the Origins of Race*. New Haven, CT: Yale University Press.
Jenson, Robert W. *Canon and Creed. Interpretation: Resources for the Use of Scripture in the Church*. Louisville: Westminster John Knox, 2010.
Jiménez, Pablo. "Toward a Postcolonial Homiletic: Justo L. González's Contribution to Hispanic Preaching." In *Hispanic Christian Thought at the Dawn of the 21st Century: Apuntes in Honor of Justo L. González*, 159–67. Nashville: Abingdon, 2005.
———. "The Troublemaker's Friend: From Text to Sermon in a Postcolonial Context." *Apuntes* 34.3 (Fall 2014) 84–90.
Jordan, Merle. *Reclaiming Your Story: Family History and Spiritual Growth*. Louisville: Westminster John Knox, 1999.
Jung, Jangmyeon. "Chogi Sungyosadulyeo Sulgyoye Gwanhan Yeongu (a Study on Early Missionaries' Sermons)." *The Gospel and Praxis* 20 (2009) 287–315.
Jung, Sunggu. "Han'guk Gyohye Sulgyosacho I (A History of Preaching in Korean Protestant Church I)." *Sinhakjinam (Journal of Theology)* 192 (Fall 1981) 174–206.
Junker, Tércio Bretanha. *Prophetic Liturgy: Toward a Transforming Christian Praxis*. Cascade, OR: Pickwick, 2014.
Kang, Wi Jo. "Church and State Relations in the Japanese Colonial Period." In *Christianity in Korea*, edited by Robert E. Boswell Jr. and Timothy S. Lee, 97–115. Honolulu: University of Hawai'i Press, 2006.
Kay, James F. "He Descended into Hell." *Word & World* 31.1 (2011) 17–26.
Kearney, Richard. *The God Who May Be: A Hermeneutics of Religion*. Bloomington, IN: University of Indiana Press, 2001.
———. "Writing Trauma: Catharsis in Joyce, Shakespeare and Homer." http://www.abc.net.au/religion/articles/2012/07/19/3549000.htm.
Keck, Leander. *The Bible in the Pulpit*. Nashville: Abingdon, 1978.
Kelsey, David. *The Uses of Scripture in Recent Theology*. Philadelphia: Fortress, 1975.
Kim, Eunjoo Mary. *Preaching in an Age of Globalization*. Louisville: Westminster John Knox, 2010.
———. *Preaching the Presence of God*. Valley Forge, PA: Judson, 1999.
Kim, Insoo. *Hankuk kidokgyohyoeui yuksa (History of Christianity in Korea)*. Seoul: Qumran, 2011.
Kim, Kyong Ju. *The Development of Modern South Korea: State Formation, Capitalist Development and National Identity*. New York: Routledge, 2006.
Kim, Sebastian C. H., and Kirsteen Kim. *A History of Korean Christianity*. Cambridge: Cambridge University Press, 2015.
Kinghorn, Warren Anderson. "Medicating the Eschatological Body: Psychiatric Technology for Christian Wayfarers." PhD diss., Duke University, 2011.
Koester, Anne Y., ed. *Liturgy and Justice: To Worship God in Spirit and Truth*. Collegeville, MN: Liturgical, 2002.

Bibliography

Kuruvilla, Abraham. *Privilege the Text! A Theological Hermeneutic for Preaching.* Chicago: Moody, 2013.

———. *Text and Praxis: Hermeneutics and Homiletics in Dialogue.* London: Bloomsbury T & T Clark, 2009.

Lee, Duk-Joo. *Han'guk Gyohye Yiyagi (A Narrative of Korean Church).* Seoul: Sinanggoa jisungsa, 2009.

Lee, Jung. *Korean Preaching: An Interpretation.* Nashville: Abingdon, 1997.

Lewis, Alan. *Between Cross and Resurrection: A Theology of Holy Saturday.* Grand Rapids: Eerdmans, 2001.

Lindbeck, George. *The Nature of Doctrine: Religion and Theology in a Postliberal Age.* Louisville: Westminster John Knox, 1984.

Lischer, Richard. *The End of Words: The Language of Reconciliation in a Culture of Violence.* Grand Rapids: Eerdmans, 2005.

Little, David. *Religion, Order, and Law: A Study in Pre-Revolutionary England.* Chicago: University of Chicago Press, 1969.

Living Word Christian Center. "History." http://www.livingwd.org/lwcc-history/.

Long, Thomas G. *Preaching and the Literary Forms of the Bible.* Minneapolis: Fortress, 1988.

———. *The Witness of Preaching.* Louisville: Westminster John Knox, 1989.

Loomba, Ania. *Colonialism/Postcolonialism.* 2nd ed. London: Routledge, 2005.

Luther, Martin. *Luther's Works 32: Career of the Reformer II.* Edited by Jaroslav Pelikan et al. Saint Louis: Concordia, 1955.

Manegold, C. S. "New England's Scarlet 'S' For Slavery." *The Boston Globe,* 2010. http://www.boston.com/bostonglobe/editorial_opinion/oped/articles/2010/01/18/new_englands_scarlet_s_for_slavery/.

Mather, Cotton. *The Negro Christianized: An Essay to Excite and Assist That Good Work, the Instruction of Negro-Servants in Christianity (1706).* Lincoln, NE: University of Nebraska-Lincoln, 1706. http://digitalcommons.unl.edu/etas/28/.

McConnell, D. R. *A Different Gospel: A Historical and Biblical Analysis of the Modern Faith Movement.* Peabody, MA: Hendrickson, 1988.

McGonegal, Julie. *Imagining Justice: The Politics of Forgiveness of Reconciliation.* Montreal: McGill-Queens University, 2009.

McGrath, Alister. *A Passion for Truth: The Intellectual Coherence of Evangelicalism.* Downers Grove, IL: InterVarsity, 1996.

McInturf, Adam. "Race: A Theological Account: An Interview with J. Kameron Carter." *Cultural Encounters* 5.2 (Summer 2009) 77–86.

McKay, Stan. "Expanding the Dialogue on Truth and Reconciliation—In a good way." http://speakingmytruth.ca/v2a/?page_id=693.

McKenzie, Alyce M. "The Company of Sages." In *Homiletical Theology: Preaching as Doing Theology,* edited by David Schnasa Jacobsen, 87–102. Eugene, OR: Cascade, 2015.

McLeod, John. *Beginning Postcolonialism.* Manchester: Manchester University Press, 2000

Melcher, Sarah J. "The Problem of Anti-Judaism in Christian Feminist Biblical Interpretation: some pragmatic suggestions." *Cross Currents* 53 (2001) 22–31.

Mentieth, Hector Robertson. *Aspects of the Rise of Economic Individualism: A Criticism of Max Weber and His School.* New York: Kelley and Millman, 1959. https://archive.org/details/aspectsofriseofeoorobe.

Miller, Donald G. *The Way to Biblical Preaching.* Nashville: Abingdon, 1957.

Miller, Patrick. *Stewards of the Mysteries of God.* Eugene, OR: Cascade, 2013.

Bibliography

Min, Anselm Kyonsuk. "The Division and Reunification of a Nation." In *Christianity in Korea*, edited by Robert E. Buswell and Timothy S. Lee, 258–79. Honolulu: University of Hawai'i Press, 2006.

Mintz, S., and S. McNeil. *The Great Migration*. Houston: Digital History, 2016. http://www.digitalhistory.uh.edu/disp_textbook.cfm?smtID=2&psid=3385.

Mollica, R. "The Trauma Story: The Psychiatric Care of Refugee Survivors of Violence and Torture." In *Post-Traumatic Therapy and Victims of Violence*, 295–314. New York: Bruner/Mazel, 1988.

Morris, David J. *The Evil Hours: A Biography of Post-Traumatic Stress Disorder*. New York: Houghton Mifflin Harcourt, 2015.

Mumford, Debra J. *Exploring Prosperity Preaching*. Valley Forge, PA: Judson, 2012.

Nieman, James. *Knowing the Context*. Minneapolis: Fortress, 2008.

Nirenburg, David. *Anti-Judaism: The Western Tradition*. New York: W. W. Norton & Company, 2013.

Noh, Jung-Sun. "Strategies for Peace and Reunification in Korea." In *Peace and Reconciliation: In Search of Shared Identity*, edited by Sebastian C.H. Kim and Greg Hoyland, 147–59. Burlington, VT: Ashgate, 2008.

O'Connell, Patrick M. "Rev. Johnnie Colemon, Chicago Megachurch Founder, Dies at 94." http://www.chicagotribune.com/news/ct-johnnie-colemon-obituary-met-20141224-story.html.

"Official Reports of the Debates of the House of Commons of the Dominion of Canada. First Session, Fifth Parliament, May 9, 1883." Pages 1107–1108. http://parl.canadiana.ca/view/oop.debates_HOC0501_02/2?r=0&s=1.

"Our Core Values." http://www.tierra-nueva.org/our-core-values/.

Park, Andrew Sung. *The Wounded Heart of God*. Nashville: Abingdon, 1993.

Park, Chung-shin. "Protestantism in Late Confucian Korea: Its Growth and Historical Meaning." *Journal of Korean Studies* 8 (1992) 139–64.

Park, Qu-Hwan. "Iljaegangjumgi Gaesingyosulgyoeui natanan Gydokgyosinangkwa Minjokgoukgaeuisik (Christian Faith and National Consciousness in Protestant Sermons During the Japanese Occupation)." *Christianity and History in Korea* 39 (September 2013) 251–79.

Park, Sam-kyung. "The Notion of Reconciliation in Sangsaeng Theology for Korean Reunification." *Madang* 18 (December, 2012) 95–113.

"Pastor Fred Price Jr." Ever Increasing Faith Ministries. http://www.crenshawchristiancenter.net/ccc-leaders.aspx.

Peale, Norman Vincent. *The Power of Positive Thinking*. New York: Simon & Schuster, 1952.

Penn, William. *The Political Writings of William Penn*. Indianapolis: Liberty Fund, 1670. http://oll.libertyfund.org/6.

———. *Pennsylvania Charter of Privileges*. Constitution Society, 1701. http://www.constitution.org/bcp/penncharpriv.htm.

Perriman, Andrew and World Evangelical Alliance. Commission on Unity and Truth among Evangelicals. *Faith, Health and Prosperity: A Report on Word of Faith and Positive Confession Theologies by ACUTE (Evangelical Alliance Commission on Unite and Truth among Evangelicals)*. Carlisle, UK: Paternoster, 2003.

Potter, Andrew. *The Authenticity Hoax: How We Get Lost Finding Ourselves*. Toronto: McClelland and Stewart, 2010.

Bibliography

Powell, Mark Allan. "Gospel." In *The HarperCollins Bible Dictionary*, 3rd ed., 337. New York: HarperCollins, 2011.
Pui-lan, Kwok. "Postcolonial Preaching in Intercultural Contexts." *Homiletic* 40.1 (2015) 8–21.
Rambo, Shelly. "Refiguring Wounds in the Afterlife (of Trauma)." In *Carnal Hermeneutics*, 263–78. New York: Fordham University Press, 2015.
———. "Saturday in New Orleans: Rethinking the Holy Spirit in the Aftermath of Trauma." *Review and Expositor* 105.2 (2008) 229–44.
———. "Trauma and Faith: Reading the Narrative of the Hemorrhaging Woman." *International Journal of Practical Theology* 13.2 (2009) 242.
Rambo, Shelly, et al. "Theologians Engaging Trauma Transcript." *Theology Today* 68.3 (2011) 224–37.
Resner, André. "No Preacher Left Behind: A New Prerequisite for the Introductory Preaching Course." *Teaching Theology and Religion* 13.4 (2010) 339–49.
———. "Preacher as God's Mystery Steward: Preaching Healing in an Apocalyptic Frame." In *Slow of Speech and Unclean Lips: Contemporary Images of Preaching Identity*, 61–66. Eugene, OR: Cascade, 2010.
———."Reading the Bible for Preaching the Gospel." *Collected Papers of the 2008 Annual Meeting of the Academy of Homiletics*, 204–15.
Reuther, Rosemary Radford. *Faith and Fratricide: The Theological Roots of Christian Anti-Semitism*. New York: Seabury, 1974.
Roberts, Oral. *The Miracle of Seed-Faith*. Tulsa: Oral Roberts Ministries, 1970.
Royal Canadian Mounted Police. "Missing and Murdered Aboriginal Women: A National Operational Overview." http://www.rcmp-grc.gc.ca/pubs/mmaw-faapd-eng.htm.
Rufinus. *A Commentary on the Apostles' Creed*. Translated by J. N. D. Kelly. New York: Newman, 1978.
"Russell H. Conwell." Temple University Press. http://www.temple.edu/about/history/russell-conwell.
Sanders, E. P. *Paul and Palestinian Judaism*. Philadelphia: Fortress, 1977.
Schreiter, Robert. "Establishing a Shared Identity: The Role of the Healing of Memories and of Narrative." In *Peace and Reconciliation: In Search of Shared Identity*, edited by Sebastian Kim, Pauline Kollontai, and Greg Hoyland, 7–20. Burlington, VT: Ashgate, 2008.
Segovia, F. F. "Biblical Criticism and Postcolonial Studies: Toward a Postcolonial Optic." In *The Postcolonial Bible*, edited by R. S. Sugirtharajah, 49–65. Sheffield: Sheffield Academic, 1998.
Shin, Gi-Wook. *One Alliance, Two Lenses: U.S.-Korea Relations in a New Era*. Stanford, CA: Stanford University Press, 2010.
Simpson, George Eaton. *Black Religions in the New World*. New York: Columbia University Press, 1978.
Smith, Ted. *The New Measures: A Theological History of Democratic Practice*. Cambridge: Cambridge University Press, 2007.
Smith, Theophus H. *Conjuring Culture: Biblical Foundations of Black America*. New York: Oxford University Press, 1994.
Smolinski, Reiner. *Biography: Cotton Mather*. Atlanta, GA: Georgia State University, 2011. http://matherproject.org/node/22.
Soards, Marion. *1 Corinthians*. New International Biblical Commentary. Peabody, MA: Hendrickson, 1999.

Bibliography

Stendahl, Krister. *Paul Among Jews and Gentiles*. Philadelphia: Fortress, 1976.

Thirteen/WNET. "Slavery and the Making of America." http://www.pbs.org/wnet/slavery/timeline/1619.html.

Tisdale, Leonora Tubbs. *Preaching as Local Theology and Folk Art*. Minneapolis: Fortress, 1997.

Travis, Sarah. *Decolonizing Preaching: The Pulpit as Postcolonial Space*. Eugene, OR: Cascade, 2013.

Trible, Phyllis. *Rhetorical Criticism: Context, Method, and the Book of Jonah*. Minneapolis: Fortress, 1994.

Truth and Reconciliation Commission of Canada. "Honouring the Truth, Reconciling for the Future: Summary of the Final Report of the Truth and Reconciliation Commission." http://nctr.ca/assets/reports/Final%20Reports/Executive_Summary_English_Web.pdf.

———. "The Mandate for the Truth and Reconciliation Commission." http://www.trc.ca/websites/trcinstitution/File/pdfs/SCHEDULE_N_EN.pdf.

van der Kolk, Bessel A. "In Terror's Grip: Healing the Ravages of Trauma." http://www.traumacenter.org/products/pdf_files/terrors_grip.pdf.

Volf, Miroslav. *The End of Memory*. Grand Rapids: Eerdmans, 2006.

———. *Exclusion and Embrace*. Nashville: Abingdon, 1996.

Wallis, Jim. *America's Original Sin: Racism, White Privilege, and the Bridge to a New America*. Grand Rapids: Brazos, 2016.

Walton, Janet R. *Feminist Liturgy: A Matter of Justice*. Collegeville, MN: Liturgical, 2000.

Watson, Philip S. *Let God be God! An Interpretation of the Theology of Martin Luther*. London: Epworth, 1947.

Weber, Max. *The Protestant Ethic and the Spirit of Capitalism*. New York: Charles Scribner's Sons, 1958.

Wells, Kenneth M. *New God, New Nation: Protestants and Self-Reconstruction Nationalism in Korea 1896–1937*. Honolulu: University of Hawai'i Press, 1990.

West, Cornel. *Race Matters*. Vancouver: Vintage, 1994.

Westermeyer, Paul. *Let Justice Sing: Hymnody and Justice*. Collegeville, MN: Liturgical, 1998.

Wilson, Paul Scott. *The Four Pages of the Sermon: A Guide to Biblical Preaching*. Nashville: Abingdon, 1999.

———. *Preaching and Homiletical Theory*. St. Louis: Chalice, 2004.

Wolterstorff, Nicholas. *Hearing the Call: Liturgy, Justice, Church, and World*. Grand Rapids: Eerdmans, 2011.

Wood, Charles. *Vision and Discernment: An Orientation in Theological Study*. Atlanta: Scholars, 1985.

Word of Life Christian Center. "Apostle Leroy Thompson, Sr. Darrow." http://my.eiwm.org/About-Us.

Worthington, Linda, and Jacob Lee. "A Dream for Peace On the Korean Peninsula." http://www.umc.org/news-and-media/a-dream-for-peace-on-the-korean-peninsula.

Yi, Dukju. "Chogi Nehan Sugyosadulye Sinanggw Sinhak(Early Missionaries' Faith and Theology)." *gidokgy uksayunguso (The Institute of the History of Christianity in Korea)* 30.64 (1997.2) 30–64.

Yoder, Carolyn. *The Little Book of Trauma Healing*. Intercourse, PA: Good Books, 2005.

Yoder, John Howard. "The Racial Revolution in Theological Perspective." In *For the Nations*, 97–124. Grand Rapids: Eerdmans, 1997.

Bibliography

Young, Allan. *The Harmony of Illusions: Inventing Post-Traumatic Stress Disorder.* Princeton, NJ: Princeton University Press, 1995.
Young, Robert J. C. *Postcolonialism: A Very Short Introduction.* Oxford: Oxford University Press, 2003.
Zehr, Howard. "Doing Justice, Healing Trauma: The Role of Restorative Justice in Peacebuilding." *South Asian Journal of Peacebuilding* 1.1 (Spring 2008) 2–16.